D1084335

HOMO *A*ESTHETICUS

HOMO

Aesthetiaus

THE INVENTION OF
TASTE IN THE
DEMOCRATIC AGE

LUC FERRY

TRANSLATED BY ROBERT DE LOAIZA

THE UNIVERSITY OF CHICAGO PRESS   CHICAGO & LONDON

Luc Ferry is professor of philosophy at the Sorbonne and the University of Caen. His many books include the three-volume *History of Philosophy* and (with Alain Renaut) *Heidegger and Modernity,* both published in English by the University of Chicago Press.

The University of Chicago Press, Chicago 60637
The University of Chicago Press, Ltd., London
© 1993 by The University of Chicago
All rights reserved. Published 1993
Printed in the United States of America
02 01 00 99 98 97 96 95 94 93   1 2 3 4 5

ISBN: 0-226-24459-8 (cloth)

Originally published in Paris as *Homo Aestheticus: L'invention du goût à l'âge démocratique,* © Editions Grasset & Fasquelle, 1990.

Library of Congress Cataloging-in-Publication Data

Ferry, Luc.
   [Homo aestheticus. English]
   Homo aestheticus : the invention of taste in the democratic age /
Luc Ferry ; translated by Robert de Loaiza.
      p. cm.
   Includes index.
   1. Aesthetics, Modern—18th century. 2. Aesthetics, Modern—19th
century. 3. Aesthetics, Modern—20th century. 4. Kant, Immanuel,
1724–1804—Aesthetics. 5. Hegel, Georg Wilhelm Friedrich,
1770–1831—Aesthetics. 6. Nietzsche, Friedrich Wilhelm, 1844–1900—
Aesthetics. 7. Subjectivity. I. Title.
BH151.F4713 1993
11'.85'0903—dc20   93-4910
                                                                        CIP

CONTENTS

PREFACE

THIS WORK AIMS AT RETRACING the great conceptual moments of a history of democratic individualism or modern subjectivity. For reasons I go into in the first chapter, the field of aesthetics is the one in which, even today, the sediments of such a history are most visible and richest in meaning. I had to hold on to both ends of a somewhat fragile chain: on the one hand I had to recapture the definitions of subjectivity where they had been most strongly formulated—that is, in philosophy—without, on the other, giving up the interpretation of certain aspects of a discipline, aesthetics, happily inseparable from art's concrete history. The problem lies in the fact that philosophy, unlike the historical sciences, does not belong to what is usually called "general culture." Art lovers, even erudite ones, are not always familiar with the works of Leibniz, Baumgarten, Kant, or Hegel. It would be pointless to believe that this obstacle has to do with the form or, as is sometimes imagined, with the "jargon" in which these paths of thinking are enmeshed. It goes deeper: reflection on culture does not belong integrally within culture. It supposes a distance always difficult to traverse and reduce.

I have tried to put forth this work's theses in a nontechnical way (chapter 1); the same with the main passages devoted to clarifying the two chief moments of modern aesthetics: the initial quarrel between heart and reason (beginning of chapter 2) and the—no doubt provisional—end of this history (chapter 6). These sections can be read relatively independently from the rest of the book. Their connection to a systematic history of the subject is the only thing that cannot be perceived without an incursion into philosophy.

INTRODUCTION

A SPECTER HAUNTS CONTEMPORARY THOUGHT: the specter of the subject.

Everyone knows or senses it today, even outside the limits of professional philosophy. "The death of man," much talked about in the 1960s but already chronicled by Nietzsche, raises questions to which no way of thinking has yet brought an answer. Following the trail of various predecessors, including the author of *Zarathustra,* psychoanalysis, no doubt this century's greatest intellectual acquisition, has brought to a brutal end the idea that we could consider ourselves as masters and possessors of ourselves. The subject was, as they say, "split" [*brisé*], and our states of consciousness, concepts or feelings, exposed to the infinite determination of the unconscious.

In a paradox characteristic of our democratic culture, the announcement of the death of man was accompanied by a demand for autonomy probably unique in the history of humanity. Generally speaking, in our liberal-social-democratic societies, the requirement of freedom—understood as the capacity to give oneself one's own laws—has never been stronger, whatever may be said here and there. Even those who lead the prosecution in the case against global consumerism have resigned themselves, sometimes grudgingly, to doing so in the name of the ideal of human beings taking their destiny into their own hands. Even though they may not always evoke great enthusiasm, the values of republican democracy seem set to be our only acceptable political horizon for quite a while.

A paradox, then, because the feeling of an irremediable loss of the self—yet thematized by contemporary philosophy as the effect of a demystification as healthy as it is subversive—is accompanied by a constantly growing will to reappropriation: on an individual level, in the attempt to recapture a lost past for oneself; on a collective level, in the concern not to fall prey to the infinite traps the world of commerce lays for us (at the same time that it provides us with various well-known services).

And yet it is an inevitable paradox, which we might roughly for-

1

mulate as follows: Can one be a democrat—that is, believe not only in the virtues of pluralism but also in humanity's capacity, limited though it may be, to make its own history (the presupposition, like it or not, of any critique of simple market laws)—and yet accept the thesis according to which the notion of will has been invalidated by the discovery of the various aspects of the unconscious?

That, it seems to me, is the philosophical-political equation of the end of the present century—an equation to which a response in the form of a compromise would offer only a mediocre satisfaction, as would be the case, if it must be repeated, with any pretention to "return" to forms of subjectivity prior to the emergence of the "split subject."

In an earlier book, *La Pensée 68* (translated as *French Philosophy of the Sixties*), Alain Renaut and I undertook to question those who were in our opinion the leading figures of "contemporary antihumanism," the most significant moments in the critique of the subject understood classically as consciousness and will. The work being polemical, it was with polemics that it was most often rebutted. Following the principle of two negations being equal to an affirmation, since we were criticizing the critiques of consciousness and will, we were accused of trying to return to Descartes and, in the name of a rationalism equaled only by its boorishness, to reaffirm the good old neo-Kantian values of consciousness, will, and control of one's self against Marx, Nietzsche, Freud, Heidegger, and their French disciples. But this was of course to miss our most explicit intention—not to return to the tradition of metaphysical humanism, but to ground, as we insist at every opportunity, a "nonmetaphysical humanism." Polemic, however, has its reasons that reason knows not of. After all, as kids say: "We started it."

The time for polemics is over, I hope, and we should be able to take up with serenity the question of man (of the subject). As we suggested in *La Pensée 68*, the critique of the ideologies of the death of man is not self-sufficient and, to become truly positive, the project of a "nonmetaphysical humanism" has to face up to two requirements:

—Confronted with readings tending to make uniform a modernity defined as the linear and univocal succession of phases in the constitution of a metaphysical subject, closed in on and transparent to itself, we need to restore in their conflictual plurality the various moments which have actually marked the history of modern conceptions of subjectivity.

—But, since right from the start we have set aside the hypothesis of a simple "return to," we also need to answer the question of which representation of self retains a meaning after the various deconstructions of subjectivity—a question the deconstructionists themselves must now consent to address.

In a recent book, *L'Ere de l'individu,* Alain Renaut undertook the task of studying these two questions following a philosophical approach to the history of philosophy. For my part, faithful to an approach I took in my first studies, I tried to tackle them from a perspective external to the history of pure philosophy: that of aesthetics.

That was not an arbitrary choice. The questions put by the thesis of the death of man refer back to the status of the Author, of the subject thought of as creator, a motif that has been developed especially in reflection about art. For reasons about to be discussed, aesthetics is the field par excellence in which the problems brought about by the subjectivization of the world characteristic of modern times can be observed in the chemically pure state.

From Tocqueville to Arendt and Heidegger, from Weber to Strauss and Dumont, the most profound analyses of modernity have pointed out what the emergence of individualism meant, *negatively,* in terms of the erosion of the universe of traditions: the disappearance of the orders and guilds of the ancien régime, the disenchantment or demagicalization of the world, the end of the politico-theological, the transition from the organic community (Gemeinschaft) to the contractual society (Gesellschaft), from the closed world to the infinite universe, the obsolescence of the great cosmologies and of hierarchical, objectivist visions of law and politics, the oblivion of Being and the advent of technicity, and so forth. Unless we sin through what Nietzsche would have considered as a singular lack of "tragic sense," we can't deny the force of those readings of modernity which, even when they ultimately adhere to it, as does Tocqueville, measure without concessions the price paid for what the *Aufklärer* read quite plainly as "the march of Progress."

These analyses converge on at least one diagnosis to which we can remain neither blind nor indifferent: modern times bring us into a circle which, understandably, still seems to some today—today more than ever—to be infernal. On the one hand, the progressive dissolution of the signposts inherited almost naturally from the past leaves us without an answer when faced with the simplest and most profound vicissitudes of daily existence. At the individual level, it is easier to accord a meaning to our successes than to our failures, to our "active" instants (as Nietzsche meant them) than to sickness and death, to which, however, traditional communities succeeded in assigning a practical and theoretical site. If one should write today, two centuries after Rousseau, that philosophy of unhappiness Alexis Philonenko sees in him, it would have to respond to an interrogation whose platitude might seem disarming: since it can't be placed within the perspective of a traditional community or of one or another eschatology, does human finitude still allow us to believe that our projects and objectives, necessarily limited, are intrinsically meaningful or, if one prefers to put it the other way, that meaning itself still has a meaning? Is the "innocence of becoming," dear to aristocrats according to Nietzsche, still accessible to us?

And if it's true that the crumbling of traditions leads us to the era of indefinite questioning, the latter in turn contributes mightily to their erosion: the more that questions come up, the less comfortable are we in answering them, bereft as we are of all preestablished criteria; the more these criteria fade away, the more numerous are the aspects of intellectual—but also daily—life which enter the field of individual questioning.

But we can't limit ourselves to confirming that today, for us moderns, the heaven of ideas is empty. And even less to mourning the fact (though nothing forbids this attitude, either, to which we owe, after all, from Kierkegaard to Cioran, a few works that are not inconsequential). If we are secular humans—as the end of theological-political thought constrains the immense majority of Christians to be, at least in the public sphere—we have to admit that in the next decades it will be in ourselves, therefore—in, by, and for humanity—that we shall have to find the answers to the questions that the progress of science and technology will certainly force us to raise. Biology, as we know, gives especial evidence of this. Before long the crucial problem of bioethics will be that of the setting of limits. How, by whom, according to which criteria will our democratic societies be led to setting limits to individual liberty? Like it or not, that is one question we shall soon not be able to avoid, if, that is, we do not accept that it be resolved by the simple play of economic and ideological powers.

There is thus an advantage to understanding that the history of modernity is not only (even if it is also) the history of the *decline* of traditions, it is above all, *positively*, that of the multiple faces of subjectivity, that is, of the constitution of the sole basis from which henceforth we must, *volens nolens*, attack, and perhaps sometimes resolve, the intimidating question of the limits that must be imposed on the power of man over man. On this path the history of cosmologies or of

4

the great religions can no longer serve as guide; nor can that of modern political philosophy, although, obviously, both must remain present in the mind as the negative of another history, that of aesthetics, in which are inscribed in a positive fashion not only the various conceptions of subjectivity that constitute modern times, but also their sharpest tension—that with the question, repressed but always underlying, of the individual's relation to the collective.

ONE

The Revolution of Taste

B EFORE TURNING HIS INTEREST to the philosophy of his own
times, the young Hegel wondered about the conditions under which
a religion could be in tune with the requirements of a free people. The
first requisite he assigned a reform of theology was to rid it of its "pos-
itivity," meaning everything which, by its dogmatic and institutional
character, could contribute to making a religion something alien to
the community, an ideology exterior to a people made up of free
individuals.

In many ways Hegel's question remains ours. We need only replace
the word religion with the word culture (which could be defended historically as well as philosophically) for it to find again an astonishing
pertinence and relevance: what could the culture of a democratic people
consist of—such is indeed the central problem of societies in which the
subjectivization of the world has as unavoidable corollary the progressive collapse of traditions, under the ceaseless demand that they be in
agreement with men's freedom. Under the imperatives of individualism,
contemporary culture has had to reject exteriority and transcendence to
such an extent that the reference to an order in the world has gradually
withdrawn from its principal productions.

ANCIENT, MODERN, CONTEMPORARY:
THE WORLD'S WITHDRAWAL

I have elsewhere analyzed (in *Political Philosophy*, vol. 1) the sense in
which modern individualism effects a rupture, in the juridical and political spheres, with antiquity's representation of a cosmic order seen as
closed, hierarchical, and purposeful, and which the art of the judge or
politician should strive to imitate. The notion of individualism seems to
have lost its "scientific" credibility, caught up as it has been in the inter-

pretative quarrels about the meaning and significance of the social movements of the 1960s and obscured by media usage. Besides, despite many precisions, those who oppose the use of the concept often misunderstand its deepest meaning and willingly or unwillingly confuse it with a form of egoism, just as they easily assimilate an interpretation that uses the notion of individualism as an apologia for the liberal universe.

Every time individualism is dealt with, therefore, it will have to be recalled that it refers above all to a descriptive concept, which does not a priori imply any value judgement; it does not blend into egoism but designates first of all a certain antitraditional relation to the law—a relation which may eventually take the form of movements of collective dissidence (here I can only refer the reader further to the argument that Renaut and I put forward in *68–86: Itinéraires de l'individu* [Paris: Gallimard, 1987]).

We hear a lot of talk today, if not of the "decline of the West" (unlike Heidegger, Spengler is still taboo) at least of a certain exhaustion of contemporary creation. And in fact, whatever one's opinion, many aspects of postmodernity can bring forth such a feeling through their rejection of the new, raised to the standing of a principle. If there is no reason to suppose that individual talent or even genius is less than that of past centuries, we have every reason to surmise that the individual's *relation to the world* is going through a profound dislocation, and that the relation to the idea of an objective universe, simultaneously transcending him and uniting him to others, has become singularly problematic.

The thesis I will for the moment simply sketch out is as follows: where among the *ancients* the work is conceived of as a microcosm—which permits them to think that outside of it, in the macrocosm, an objective or, better, substantial criterion of the Beautiful exists—it is given meaning among the *moderns* through reference to subjectivity, to become, for the *contemporaries,* the pure and simple expression of individuality: an absolutely singular style which does not see itself in any way as a mirror of the world but the creation of a world, a world in which the artist acts, a world to which we are no doubt allowed entrance, but which doesn't impose itself on us as an a priori common universe.

Even in Plato, who is in many ways the most "modern" of the ancients, the Beautiful is never defined purely and simply by the subjective pleasure it procures. The idea of the Beautiful is generally associated with the bringing into reality of an order where "measure" and "proportion" should rule (*Philebus,* passim). It's along these lines that Socrates addresses Gorgias in the dialogue bearing the celebrated sophist's name: "Take, for example, painters, architects, shipwrights, any other profession you like, and see how each of them arranges the different elements of his work in a certain order, and makes one part fit and harmonize with another until the whole thing emerges a consistent and organized whole" (503e, Walter Hamilton trans.).

The opinion according to which the artist should seek out harmony does not, no doubt, disappear—at least not immediately—in modern aesthetics. But this harmony is no longer thought of, and this is the real break with antiquity, as the reflection of an order external to man: it is no longer because the object is intrinsically beautiful that it pleases but, rather, we can go so far as to say that it is because it provides a certain type of pleasure that we call it beautiful.

The texts marking the very particular history which is that of aesthetics insist on this, as do, among many others, these lines I borrow from Crousaz and from Montesquieu:

Crousaz, *Traité du Beau* [Treatise on the Beautiful], 1715: "When we ask what is the Beautiful, we do not pretend to speak of an object existing outside of ourselves and separate from every other one, as we do when we ask what is a horse or what is a tree . . ."

Montesquieu, *Essai sur le goût* [An Essay on Taste]: "It is the various pleasures of our soul which shape the objects of taste, such as the Beautiful . . . The Ancients had not properly unraveled this. They saw as positive qualities those which are relative to our soul . . . The sources of the Beautiful, of the Good, of the Pleasant are thus in ourselves; and to look for the reason is to look for the cause of the pleasures of our soul."

The consciousness of having broken with antiquity is still perfectly clear for the founding fathers of aesthetics. Nevertheless, until a relatively recent date—in philosophy until Nietzsche, and in the history of art up to the flowering of the avant-gardes—this subjectivization did not purely and simply mean disappearance of the world, *Weltlosigkeit.* Unlike what happens in the contemporary era, the main problem of modern aesthetics from the seventeenth century to the end of the nineteenth is still that of reconciling the subjectivization of the beautiful (the fact that it's no longer an "in itself" but a "for us") with the demand for "criteria," thus with a relation to objectivity or, if preferred, to the world. This same cardinal tension constitutes the problematic of the first aesthetic systems: a tension which makes them fundamentally different from what precedes them as much as from what follows them, and which I for the moment designate, following current usage, as the contemporary. Modern aesthetics is certainly subjectivist in that it establishes the beautiful on human faculties, reason, sentiment, or imagination. It is nonetheless animated by the idea that the work of art is inseparable from a certain form of objectivity.

This is clear, of course, in Cartesian classicism from Boileau to Crousaz, where the dictum "imitate nature" suggests that the universality of good taste is explained by its rapport with an objective world unveiled in reason. The classical genius is not that which invents, but that which *discovers,* the term here being conceived on the model of scientific activity. But that is equally true of the radical subjectivism of the sensualists, however paradoxical that may seem. Hume, to mention only him, remains attached to the idea of the objectivity of the beautiful, even if he "founds" this objectivity on the hypothesis of a psycho-biological structure common to humanity. And in the *Critique of Judgment,* which some consider to be the zenith of modern subjectivism, it is explicitly in its relation to what Kant calls the "idea of world" that aesthetic activity can become concrete in the production of a work. It is because he can unconsciously invoke, by a natural gift, the "cosmological Idea" that the genius is genial—genialness (imaginative creative power) being always thus in a way limited by the demands of a conformity to a certain cosmic order. To speak as Kant does, "Taste clips genius's wings," and the baroque, though superior to classical regularity, itself has limits which are, precisely, the world's.

It seems to me that it is this very reference that is fading today: there is no longer an obvious univocal world, but rather a plurality of worlds unique to each artist; no longer one art, but an almost infinite variety of individual styles. The truism that beauty is a matter of taste has finally become reality, or more exactly: to the extent that there is a difference between a talented artist and one that Kant, in his inimitable jargon, would have called a "botcher," this difference tends today to become purely individual; it no longer depends on the capacity to create a world which would surpass the narrowly private sphere of the creator's lived experiences. It resides rather in the more or less elaborate cultivation of an idiosyncrasy (here is where, in the last instance, the old question about criteria still finds a niche).

To give an example not chosen at random: there is a romantic world; I am not at all certain there is such a thing as a "postmodern" world. I can, when considering romanticism, even if the movement is quite diverse (its periodization is the object of endless discussions, as is the question of the connections between the different national traditions it points to), discern a romantic aesthetic, a political mentality (in general counterrevolutionary), a theory of history, even a metaphysics, in short, a "representation of the world," a Weltanschauung shared by artists—painters, poets, musicians—, writers, or philosophers. There one finds something like a universe extending beyond individuals, a universe I may hate or love but whose supraindividual existence I cannot deny. About what movement (let's not even speak of "schools": this term which seems to abjure the idea of individual freedom has lost all meaning in the field of art) could we say the same thing today?

To avoid a misunderstanding: politically suspect, the idea of "decadence" or "decline" is theoretically not very convincing—be it formulated in "reactionary" fashion and animated by nostalgia for a lost past, as in Spengler but also among thinkers of the magnitude of Heidegger or Leo Strauss, or uttered in the "revolutionary" mode, which is certainly getting rare, once adopted by "left" critics of liberal consumerism. What characterizes contemporary art is certainly not that its works attest to less talent than those of the past. It may simply be that art's ambitions have changed: for many artists today (we'll return below to the avant-gardes and their crisis, which will lead us to postmodernity) the goal is no longer to discover the world, to use art as an instrument of knowledge of a reality alien to oneself. On the contrary, it seems that in many cases (we must here be wary of universal judgments, for there are notable exceptions: the postmodern atmosphere which, precisely, admits all genres, finds generalizations distasteful) the work is defined by the artist himself as an extension of self, a sort of particularly elaborate calling card.

After Nietzsche it's Schönberg who consecrated his best pages to this: the artist is a "solitary" whose vocation it is, in the formula oft repeated by Kandinsky, to turn away from the world the better to express his "pure inner life." One work would thus no longer be enough to say the essential: only in the artist's journey will he eventually be able to unveil himself, through the ruptures and hesitations of tone and style which pace his "interior life." Withdrawal from the world is inseparable from the cult of idiosyncracy, indeed of originality. We can measure here how far the contemporary is separate from the modern even though it is its continuity. Although he took humanity for his model and end,

11

Molière, who pretended, as we know, to "paint after nature," speaks to us of the essence of man. Contemporary language is that of "lived experiences."

It is possible to date the "end of the world" on a more philosophic plane. It doubtless goes back to the Nietzschean critique of the "scientific prejudice" which holds that "our little thought" is capable of capturing something like a "real world." One of the aphorisms of *The Will to Power* states without ambiguity: "There are no states of fact as such," but "only interpretations," not *a* world, but an "infinity of worlds," themselves only the perspectives of the living individual. "The question 'what is it' is a way to create a meaning . . . It is, at bottom, always the question 'what is it *for me.*' "

We will of course have to ask ourselves about the meaning of the "me" Nietzsche speaks of, and of the connections it might have with modern individualism (with the "metaphysics of subjectivity"). It remains that, shattering the idea of an objective reality, Nietzsche makes the bell toll for the culture of the Enlightenment and heralds the obsolescence of the world, the *Weltlosigkeit,* which more and more reigns over culture. For very basic reasons this reign tends today to orient itself in three directions.

In the realm of art, we live in a way that becomes constantly more visible, if not in a Nietzschean "universe"—a term which would be, strictly speaking, incorrect—at least in an intellectual atmosphere which strangely resembles Nietzsche's perspectivism. Art works are like "little perspectival worlds" which no longer represent the world, but rather the state of their creator's vital forces. Such and such an artist may, of course, still intend, as in the classics, to maintain a rapport with Truth, or to unveil in his work a relation to Being. He is still doing it after *his* fashion, and he must coexist with myriads of other artists whose intentions can be infinitely different. If regular visits to modern art museums teach us anything, it's that criteria are lacking, not, as is foolishly said, because by essence art shuns all sorts of criteria—this is far from always having been the case—but because today, cut off as it is from the world, it can only refer back to pure intersubjectivity.

We have the opposite situation with the "exact sciences." Not that these don't also provoke discussions and dissensions. An even superficial acquaintance with the debates within contemporary research should be enough to rid us of the idea that the field of science is par excellence that of consensus. The very special status of science teaching when compared with that of other disciplines is therefore all the more remarkable: where education has in general adopted more and more "liberal" principles, notably through the effect of the extraordinary development of "interactive methods" which (justly) insist on the necessity of the students' participation in the acquisition of knowledge, the inculcation of science remains the only one in which the relativism of personal opinion can be neither appreciated nor encouraged. Certainly a lot of time is given over to the students' learning activities, but this is purely for pedagogic purposes. Like it or not, the solution to a math or physics problem is not a matter of individual or majority opinion, and the relativism appropriate to other domains disappears in science for the good and simple reason that it represents the last remains of our relation to objectivity. It's in encountering science that the child comes up—perhaps for the first and last time—against a theoretical universe which resists his subjectivity, since it manifests itself to him in the shape of norms that he, at least at his level of learning, cannot contest. It may be the case that the natural sciences are the outcome of the "metaphysics of subjectivity." Then we must admit, if we don't want to stick with clichés, that they defeat individual opinion as does no other sphere of intellectual life.

Finally, the third partition of democratic culture is history. Here I mean history in a wider sense, History itself as well as those disciplines which, like sociology or psychoanalysis, imply an intrinsic relationship to historicity (the history of the present in sociology, the history of the individual in psychoanalysis). Publishing statistics give us eloquent witness: besides fiction, it's works of scientific popularization and historical essays that nearly systematically receive the (cultured or uncultured) public's votes—a fact that finds its roots deep within the new requirements of *homo democraticus*. History (but also, to repeat, sociology or psychoanalysis as well) is supposed to deliver us to ourselves through the appropriation of a past we ignore, but which makes us what we are today and thus reveals itself constitutive of our present. Far from being a mere recollection of events, it tends more and more to become a discipline of self-reflection through which we constitute ourselves as autonomous individuals. There is nothing surprising, therefore, in its seeming to be the queen of faculties in a universe in which human beings are forever intent on augmenting the sphere of their self-consciousness. Whether or not it's considered a cause for rejoicing, it is probable that the historico-political culture has gotten the upper hand over the humanities. Philosophy itself has witnessed the overturning of traditional hierarchies: it's becoming more and more historical and especially so,

13

ONE

paradoxically, when it leaves the domain of history of philosophy to become, if not philosophy of history, at least historicizing philosophy (Foucault could be an example here).

Microcosmic monads in the fields of art, scientific objectivity, and history: these are now, I believe—and no doubt for a long time to come—the three fundamental horizons of a contemporary culture whose main trait could well be this subjectivization in which aesthetics occupies a privileged place. Because the breakup of the world characteristic of postmodern art as well as the search for scientific objectivity and the aim of a reappropriation of self through historical knowledge are but three aspects of the same revolution: that in which man installs himself as principle and *telos* of the universe. As has been suggested, but we know we must sketch out its traits, this revolution is above all a revolution of taste.

THE BIRTH OF TASTE

According to a thesis developed by the historian Karl Borinski in his fine book on the work of Baltasar Gracian, the latter must be credited with the first use of the word "taste" in a metaphoric sense.[1] For Borinski, this figurative usage indicates a veritable rupture in the history of subjectivity: with the concept of taste, modern humanism makes its entry at the same time that the universe of the Renaissance becomes irremediably a part of the past.

It is always difficult, at times impossible to date the birth of a concept with certainty and Borinski's thesis was, as could be expected, criticized every time someone discovered a writer in antiquity who used the word *gustus* in an even slightly wider sense.[2] But one thing is certain: it's around the middle of the seventeenth century that, first in Italy and Spain, then in France and England and, finally, Germany,* where there was some difficulty finding in the word *Geschmack* an adequate translation—the term acquires pertinence in the designation of a new faculty, capable of distinguishing the beautiful from the ugly and of apprehending through immediate sentiment (*aisthēsis*) the rules of this separation, of this *Krisis* which was soon to become the endowment of art criticism. And it is beginning with the representation of such a faculty that we enter definitively into the universe of "modern aesthetics" (the juxta-

* The history of the propagation of the concept of taste in Europe is briefly dealt with in Croce's aesthetics and taken up again by Bäumler.

position of these two terms being, besides, practically a pleonasm). The point deserves consideration.

We are not here looking to be original: we will admit (with Hegel, Heidegger, and a few others) the thesis according to which modernity is defined by a vast process of "subjectivization" of the world whose model in philosophy is provided by the three great moments of the Cartesian method. Without going here into detail in the interpretation of Descartes, we may recall that the procedure of doubt he adopts in the *Discourse on Method* as well as in the *Meditations* provides the archetype for the subjectivization of all values that finds its most eloquent political expression in the revolutionary ideology of 1789. *At first,* the project is one of "abrogating through doubt" the received opinions and all inherited prejudices, so as to make a *blank slate* of tradition. Mutatis mutandis, Descartes carries out a divorce with antiquity (and especially with Aristotle) whose equivalent, outside philosophy, is the break with the ancien régime brought about by the Revolution. *Second phase:* a fulcrum, a support is sought to rebuild the structure of scientific and philosophical knowledge that has just been undermined. And since it is the *individual,* the subject (the distinction between these two terms is not, here, very important) who is carrying out the inquiry, he will arrive or not at his goal thanks to his own certitudes. As we know, it is in the cogito that, finally, Descartes finds the means to escape generalized doubt. It is, therefore, *third phase,* on his own subjectivity, on the absolute certainty the subject has of seizing himself through his own thought, that the complete *system* of knowledge is built (the word is not yet used but will soon be by Leibniz).

The blank slate, the subject's capture by himself as the only absolutely certain principle, radical constructivism—these are the three moments which define, in its principle, the advent of philosophical modernity. To get immediately to the heart of the problem created by the overturning of ways of thinking that Cartesianism instituted, or at least thematized, we have to perceive this: where in the world of the "ancients" (a term which may be understood here in its philosophical sense, designating antiquity, or in its political sense, designating the ancien régime) it was the cosmic order of *tradition* which established for men the validity of values and thus set up between them a possible space of *communication,* the problem, beginning with Descartes, becomes one of knowing how it is possible to establish, starting out *exclusively from oneself,* values equally valuable for the others (God's intervention, though not yet excluded, itself becomes mediated by the subject's philosophical reflection and is thus, in this sense, dependent on him). In a word, the problem becomes one of knowing how it is possible to establish, within the radical *immanence* of values to subjectivity, their transcendence, for ourselves as for others.

The problem will be even clearer if, before coming back to aesthetics, to see in what ways this field is quite simply foundational, we take a small detour through politics. The counterrevolutionaries saw it even more distinctly than the revolutionaries themselves; the essence of modern politics, that which expresses itself in a particularly striking fashion in Jacobin ideology, is the onset of what one could call political humanism, meaning the (perhaps exorbitant, but it doesn't matter here) pretention to establish all our political values beginning with the legitimacy of power on man and no longer on tradition, whether the latter issues forth from divinity or from nature.

In the discourse preliminary to his treatise on *Primitive Legislation* [*La Législation primitive* (Paris: Le Clère, 1802)], Bonald introduces, as is his wont, the French Revolution as a "catastrophe." As he asks himself about the causes of this "bloody disaster," he writes the following lines which deserve our full attention: "Until this time Christians had professed that *power comes from God,* and is therefore always to be respected, whatever be the particular goodness of the man exercising it . . . : legitimate power, not in the sense that the man exercising it be named by an order visibly issued from the Divinity, but because it is constituted following the natural and fundamental laws of social order, of which God is the author." But beginning in the fifteenth century, and anticipating Luther and Calvin, according to Bonald,

Wiclef saw in power only man, he maintained that power, even political power, is good only when the man exercising it is good himself, and that any little woman in the state of grace has more right to govern than a debauched prince . . . From there on followed, like forced consequences, the doctrines of conventional and conditional power of Thomas Hobbes and of Locke, the *Social Contract* of Jean-Jacques Rousseau, Jurieu's popular sovereignty, etc. Power came only from man: to be legitimate, it had to be constituted and exercised following certain conditions imposed by human beings or certain conventions made among men, to which power could be returned, in case of violation, through men's force.

One could hardly better describe the essence of political modernity and more concisely highlight the parallelism that establishes itself at the dawn of the modern era between pure thought, which in the seventeenth century is incarnated by Cartesian metaphysics, and the political thinking that was educated at the school of natural law, and which was to be illustrated by the Revolution.

The "conventionalism" which, Bonald is right, makes of man the cornerstone of the social edifice presents to us, in its principle, the same ternary structure as does Cartesianism:

1. To the blank slate made out of the prejudices of the past, which Descartes obtains thanks to the method of "hyperbolic" doubt, corresponds what the "jus naturae" theorists name the "state of nature," a veritable degree zero of politics through whose invention the idea of a transmission of power (by which is first of all meant the notion of tradition) is, so to speak, shattered. The state of nature, an essentially prepolitical notion, is invented by philosophers with an exclusively *critical* aim which forebodes the revolutionary gesture. It is above all, not some kind of phantasmagoric historical reconstruction (as most sociologists, beginning with Durkheim, believed), but a fictional hypothesis without which the question of the legitimacy of power, obscured as it is by the reign of tradition which declares it as always already settled, could not even be raised. Under what conditions can a political power be considered legitimate? That is the question which only the presupposition of a stage of humanity prior to the appearance of a policed society permits us to formulate in all its radicalness.

2. In Descartes it is the recourse to the individual, to the cogito, that allows the moment of doubt and of the tabula rasa to be overcome. Likewise with Hobbes or Rousseau, it is the invention of the people as an entity capable of free self-determination which, through the invention of a *political subject,* allows the problem of the legitimacy of power to be positively solved. Political philosophy from then on, in the seventeenth and eighteenth centuries, essentially takes the form of a philosophy of law. There are of course certain exceptions (we may think of Montesquieu), but it isn't too much to say that they confirm the rule. The near totality of the great political thinkers of the Age of Reason set out to elaborate "doctrines of law," in which the concepts of state of nature and of social contract are constantly discussed. The principal theme of these doctrines is that of putting an end to the traditional representations of political legitimacy, as most commentators have correctly seen. Beyond the various modalities in which they may have been apprehended, the concepts of state of nature and of social contract fundamentally mean that, contrary to what was the case with the ancients, and more generally with all the traditional theories of power, legitimate

political authority is not that which imitates a natural or divine order, but that based on the will of individuals or, to use the fitting philosophical term, on subjectivity. Together with the idea of a possible self-determination of the people, it's the democratic principle which thus bursts into political philosophy.

3. After the invention of the state of nature and of the people as the subject of law, the third phase of this modern vision of the world consists in the project of reconstructing the totality of the social edifice on these atoms called individuals. Whether it be in Hobbes, where the fear of death which haunts everyone in the state of nature leads each one to associate himself with every other in the quest for security, or in Rousseau, for whom the goal of civic association is not the quest for happiness but for liberty, political society appears to be through and through the realization of individual wills, at least with respect to its legitimacy. The Cartesian idea of a reconstruction of all values on what the subject can accept as such finds here its most perfected expression, its greatest extension, since the individualist model reaches without apparent difficulty into the collective sphere. In eliminating from the Declaration of the Rights of Man the idea that individuals have duties toward society, in affirming that they have nothing but rights and that the duties they may have toward others are but the symmetrical inverse of the rights others possess with the same justification as themselves, the French revolutionaries closed the circle and gave the final touch to the political logic born of the invention of man.

As has already been pointed out by Tocqueville with his usual penetration, although Descartes did not himself enlarge his radical procedure outside of pure philosophy, although he "declared that one must judge by oneself the matters of philosophy and not of politics," the credit nevertheless goes entirely to him for having abolished "received formulas," destroyed "the empire of traditions," and overthrown the "authority of the master" in such a way that his method must in the end, with the evolution of the social state, "come out of the schools to penetrate into society and become the common norm of intelligence," the latter not only French but more generally "democratic."[3]

The emergence of aesthetics must be placed in this context. Notwithstanding a certain received opinion, there is nothing timeless about the aesthetic problematic: it is, on the contrary, the surest sign of the onset of modern times. The term itself occurs initially in the title of a philosophy book in 1750. It was at this time that a disciple of Leibniz and Wolff, Alexander Gottlieb Baumgarten, produced in Latin the six hundred pages of his *Aesthetica*.

The birth of aesthetics as a philosophical discipline is permanently linked to the radical mutation the representation of the beautiful undergoes when the latter is thought of in terms of *taste* and, therefore, using as starting point that which in the human being soon comes to seem the very essence of subjectivity, the most subjective within the subject. With the concept of taste the beautiful is placed in a relation to human subjectivity so intimate that it may even be defined by the pleasure it provides, by the *sensations* or sentiments it provokes in us.

One of the central problems of the philosophy of art is of course that of the criteria which permit us to assert or not that a thing is beautiful. How is one to come up with an "objective" answer to this matter once the foundations of the beautiful have been situated within the most intimate subjectivity, that of taste? But how, then, give up this objectivity as a goal now that the beautiful, like all other modern values, is supposed to address itself to all and please the greatest number? A formidable problem, and one in which aesthetics inevitably—but a priori and in their most essential form—comes up against the comparable questions asked of individualism in the fields of theory of knowledge (how to ground objectivity using the representations of the subject as starting point?) and of politics (how to ground the collective on individual volition?). I say a priori and in their most essential form because the history of aesthetics is the place par excellence where the subjectivization of the world occurs or, to put it better, where the *withdrawal of the world* that characterizes, at the end of a long evolution, contemporary culture takes place.

THE THREE FUNDAMENTAL PROBLEMS OF AESTHETICS

With the birth of taste, the philosophy of art of antiquity gives way to a theory of sensibility. This mutation raises three questions that are decisive for the understanding of modern culture: that of the *irrationality of the beautiful* which, by way of the search for an autonomy of the sensible in relation to the intelligible, engages in its very essence the new bond between man and God that is increasingly characteristic of modernity. Then comes the birth of *criticism* which, beginning with the quarrel of the ancients and the moderns (therefore well before Diderot), brings about a questioning attitude toward tradition and simultaneously renders possible a history of art, which in turn establishes a radically new conception of the originality of the author. Finally, the apparently classical, in reality typically modern, motif of the criteria of the beautiful raises the question of communication, of the *sensus communis,* a question that appears within an individualist culture for which the problem of *mediation* between humans has become central.

1. The Irrationality of the Beautiful: The Autonomy of the Sensible as Rupture between Man and God

The beautiful, following a Platonistic tradition whose influence on French classicism is still quite visible (although it already fully belongs, as we shall soon see, to modern times), has long been defined as a "sensible presentation" (that is, an illustration) of the true, as the transposition into the sphere of material (visible or acoustic) sensibility of a moral or intellectual truth. Under such conditions the position of art can naturally only be secondary in relation to philosophy. It is hard to see in what way the apprehension of the true mediated by the sensible could be preferable to a clear and distinct knowledge of the truth in itself and for itself (except on a strictly pedagogical level, but even that isn't sure).

Besides, whether in Platonism, Christian theology, or Cartesianism, the intelligible world is always superior to the sensible world. To adopt the formulation that matters here: God's point of view is characterized by the fact that, intelligible through and through (God is omniscient, everything is transparent for him, as far as these anthropomorphic formulas even have a meaning), he is not affected by the mark of imperfection and human finitude that is expressed by sensibility.

It is therefore easy to understand to what point the project of consecrating to the study of sensibility an autonomous science, that of aesthetics, represents a decisive rupture with the classical point of view not only of theology but also of all philosophy of Platonic inspiration. We have to size it up correctly: the object of aesthetics, the sensible world, *has no existence except for man;* it is, in the strictest sense, man's own. The birth of aesthetics, implying as a specific discipline a decision taken about the autonomy of its object, expresses thus in concentrated form the upheaval the eighteenth century inaugurates in all domains. It symbolizes better than metaphysics or religion the project of providing the human point of view with a legitimacy which the development of the finite knowledge of the positive sciences is beginning to require.

We shall see in the pages that follow the way that the conquest of this autonomy of the sensible, as invention of a world in which the divine gives way ceaselessly to the human, takes place in three phases. With the *Aesthetica* of Baumgarten and the *Phenomenology* of Johann Heinrich Lambert (1766, the first of a long line of "phenomenologies") the project of working out a logic applicable to sensible "phenomena" is already embodied. Not only does the beautiful appear as man's own, as proper to man, but human sensibility is also presented as having a specific structure that God's point of view cannot totally relativize. But the *Critique of Pure Reason* must come along before the radical autonomy of the sensible vis-à-vis the intelligible will be, for the first time in the history of thought, philosophically established, thus opening up the theoretical space of the *Critique of Judgment*. It remained for Nietzsche to eliminate the intelligible world, which for Kant still had the status of an Idea necessary to reason. Abolishing in this fashion any reference to God, even as simple idea, Nietzsche consecrates the sensible world, the purely human world, in its status of one and only world (in turn fragmented into an infinity of perspectives). Doing away with the "truth-world" (Plato's intelligible, the beyond of the Christians), Nietzsche also does away with the pretentions of metaphysics in reducing the sensible world to an appearance. And since the truth becomes a fable, the philosopher must give way to the artist: *Incipit aesthetica!*

We shall of course have to establish the degree to which these various moments of the constitution of aesthetics as prototype of modern culture can be described, as we have just done (in the manner of Leo Strauss, with all due respect), as stages in a linear process, or whether, on the contrary, these progressive insinuations of subjectivity offer up resistances and tensions that defy any description in terms of an irresistible "decline." We must above all examine what conceptions of subjectivity are involved in each of these various moments in which the withdrawal of the divine (of the intelligible world, if preferred) is indissociably accompanied by the advent of the human, thought of as subject.

What is on the other hand already clear is that, in the course of the evolution through which it becomes autonomous, the beautiful object, as sensible object, slips over to the nonrational. Declared radically nonintelligible is ipso facto becomes irrational, and under this aspect aesthetics begins to look like a veritable challenge to logic. As Bäumler correctly observed, from that point on rationalist philosophy no longer is able to ignore the question of the status of what is "outside reason." From Leibniz to Hegel (and we could even add Freud) this is the central

21

problem of Germanic thought. But a new arrangement of the subject corresponds to this "objective" irrationality of the beautiful: it no longer is able to apprehend either the manifestations of the beautiful or the rules defining the latter (as far as we even admit that such rules exist) through reason but through a different kind of faculty. The reader will have guessed that it is at this point that modern aesthetics encounters the concept of taste, here understood as the subjective correlative of the irrationality of the beautiful object as sensible object. Subjectivity is thus no longer limited to the intelligible faculties, and humanity is no longer separated from animality by the sole virtue of reason.

To this new status of the human corresponds the second problem that aesthetics encounters.

2. The Birth of Criticism: History against Tradition

The conditions of possibility for criticism and art history are already embryonic in the quarrel between the ancients and the moderns. The principle of modernity is surreptitiously mobilized in the way in which Nicolas Boileau himself takes part in the debate: the superiority of the ancients in his eyes no longer consists, as it still does for the Renaissance, in the fact that they *are* ancient and as such embody a tradition in itself respectable and worthy of admiration.*

What renders the works of antiquity so valuable is their capacity to conform themselves to a norm, and thus to a principle which is intrinsically superior to them. If we add that, for the French classicists whose aesthetics is inspired by Cartesianism, the norm is that of reason, and thus of *a faculty of the subject,* we will understand the way in which the world of tradition is already so shaken that the possibility of criticism and of history becomes a reality: *of criticism,* because there exists a norm other than those of tradition, and therefore a criterion in whose name works can be judged (a criterion de facto used by those who believe themselves to be taking the side of a threatened tradition, in a paradox beyond their ken); *of history* because, under these conditions,

---

* On the Renaissance, and on the fact that in this "intermediate" period there was at least agreement in the judgement that "the artist's purely subjective and individual appreciation could never serve as criterion for a just proportion," we must always refer back to Erwin Panofsky (see especially *Idea: Ein Beitrag zur Begriffsgeschichte der älteren Kunsttheorie* [Leipzig, Berlin: B. G. Teubner, 1924], chap. 3).

the idea of an evolution or even of a progress in the presentation of ideal norms is no longer inconceivable.

Under these conditions originality also ceases to be an exemplary non-value. It even begins to be one of the qualities we may expect of an artist worthy of that name. Consequently, the true artist stops being identical to the rhapsodist who merely translates into words, sounds, or images the community's values; he becomes, strictly speaking, an author, that is to say, an individual gifted with the capacity for a creation which is itself original.

It is at the beginning of the eighteenth century that these potentialities, of criticism and of art history, which were revealed by the classicists truly take form. But they were already present from the beginning in the enthronement of the subject as the judge of tradition. To this will be added the psychologism of the sensualists and the nationalism of Dubos (and of Montesquieu) to forge the idea of a historicity of taste: not only will Voltaire's toad * find that it is his she-toad who embodies beauty, but if he is Italian, French, or German, it will be as an Italian, French, or German toad that she will incarnate the essence of the Beautiful, the *to kalon*.

Originality itself changes meaning: the concept contains within it, analytically so to speak, that of subjectivity (the originality of the work of art is always referred back to the originality of the artist as *individual* author). But historicity is added to this originary determination: it's no longer only a matter of being original when confronted with a synchronic structure—that of a salon, for example, in which wit and invention would be of the essence—originality is now measured against the yardstick of a history of art, within which one must *innovate* to win one's artistic spurs. The condition is not yet sufficient, as it will be at the end of this history, among certain avant-garde groups of our twentieth century, but it is already quite necessary—as witnessed in the institutional sphere by the cult of chronology, which will soon preside over the organization of the museum, itself created under the sign of a temporality tied in to the French Revolution.

The cult of the new, of rupture with tradition, characteristic of the subversive pretenses of "modernism," finds its deepest roots in the

---

* "Ask a toad what is beauty, the Beautiful, *to kalon*, and he will answer that it's his she-toad." (*Dictionnaire philosophique*, article on *Beau* [the Beautiful].)

emergence of subjectivity, so that contemporary art still belongs in part to the orbit of modern aesthetics in a sense we will explain with more precision later on.

3. Common Sense and Communication: Can One Argue about the Beautiful?

If the beautiful object is conceived of as purely subjective—a paradox we barely dare state, looking as it does like a logical contradiction—if it is apprehended only by this elusive faculty called taste, how could there ever be consensus on the beauty of a work of art or of nature? And yet, those who love "beautiful landscapes," the works of Homer and of Shakespeare, and the Italian painters are *numerous* . . . decidedly, the paradox is not simple. It may at first look trivial, but it isn't.

Looked at one way, it would seem that aesthetics begins where contemporary philosophy apparently culminates, with the problem of relativism. As a consequence of the Marxian and Nietzschean critiques of metaphysics, and also because of the influence of the social sciences, we have become progressively used to the idea that there are no values in and of themselves, atemporal and eternal. We look at every norm, every intellectual, moral, or political institution as the result of a history whose reconstruction supposedly fully explains its meaning. It is an understatement to say that we live today in a "crisis of the universal."

And yet this relativism took a long time to assert itself in philosophy. For a long time it described itself as subversive (this was still the case with Michel Foucault) and therefore condemned to being marginal. Could this have been real naïveté or mere cuteness? In any case we have to accept the obvious: historicism is in fact omnipresent. Far from being a way of thinking repressed because of a revolutionary potential too strong to be accepted by our liberal societies, it constitutes their most solid, most manifest principle. Its alleged marginality has become so central, as today anyone can verify for himself, that it constitutes the new dominant ideology. The idea that a truth could be "absolute" (which means only not relative, as we are forced to recall since the term has become so pejorative) makes any high school student smile, if indeed it doesn't offend him. But in all probability it shocks his only absolute conviction, that there are no absolute truths.

To repeat: this is the result of a long history, and modern philosophy begins neither with Nietzsche nor with Marx, but with Descartes, although he firmly believed, as we can't deny, in the intangibility of eternal truths.

Aesthetics is entirely different. Establishing as it does the beautiful on a faculty much too subjective for objectivity to be easily discernible within it, its history, at least up to the end of the eighteenth century, goes instead from relativism towards the search for criteria. Paradoxically, the skeptical attitude becomes less easy to maintain in this sphere than in those of pure philosophy or politics or ethics, and this for a very simple reason: it immediately collapses under the weight of its own banality. To the same degree that Nietzsche's thesis that there is no scientific truth—or, rather, that the truth of the positivistic sciences is itself the apex of illusion—can provoke interest because of its frontal clash with certain well-established certitudes, the idea that "taste is subjective" lacks attractiveness, shocking as it does nothing and no one. We may say that, on the contrary, the opinion that would maintain that it is possible to discuss matters of taste, and even to find criteria of the beautiful, would seem untenable to the common sense.

The inquiry into the criteria of beauty (of taste) characteristic of every modern aesthetic appears therefore to be all the more essential. It is at this level that the key problem of modernity in general presents itself in its most difficult and most decisive aspect: how to ground objectivity on subjectivity, transcendence on immanence? In other words, how to think of bonds (social ones, of course, but not exclusively) in a society which pretends to begin with individuals in order to reconstruct the collective? Let us state right away the thesis we shall be defending. It is in the domain of aesthetics that this question can be read in its purest form, for it is here that the tension between individual and collective, subjective and objective, is at its highest. The beautiful is that which at the same time brings us together the most easily yet the most mysteriously. Contrary to what we might expect, the consensus about important works of art is as strong and as general as in any other domain. Parodying one of Hume's arguments, we could say there is less disagreement on Bach's or Shakespeare's greatness than on the validity of Einstein's physics (to say nothing of Newton's). And yet, we are here at the very heart of the most intense and most acknowledged subjectivity.

THE HISTORY OF AESTHETICS AS HISTORY OF SUBJECTIVITY

Whatever else may be the case, philosophy "from Descartes to Nietzsche" (or, in a more Straussian vein, "from Machiavelli to Sartre") does not consist in the linear development of a metaphysical conception of subjectivity which, imperfect at the outset, at the moment of the cogito, supposedly finds its ultimate form in the technicist concept of "will to power." The tensions and oppositions among the different conceptions of the subject—among Cartesians, empiricists, in Kant's and Fichte's transcendental philosophy, with Hegel and Nietzsche finally—are in truth so deep that it would be vain to attempt to "resolve" them in one equation. To restore to a history of modern thought the diversity of these various moments constitutes, even today, one of the principal tasks of a philosophy that has as its aim the discernment of the status of the subject *after the death of man,* after the various deconstructions of metaphysical subjectivity.

It is for this project that the history of aesthetics provides a privileged access, for the reasons already stated. I have not, however, aimed at the exhaustiveness a historical work would have required; the customary considerations on Shaftesbury and Burke, Goethe and Lessing, Solger and German romanticism, and Benjamin's or Adorno's aesthetics will not be found here. But I have aimed for a certain systematicity, the goal being to track down the various singular moments of a history of modern subjectivity in all their absolute irreducibility. Certain relatively unknown authors—Bouhours for example, but also and above all Baumgarten and Lambert—seemed to me, in the context of this inquiry, to occupy an essential role in the correct analysis of these ruptures. For reasons that will become clear in the course of the argument, I've settled on five major moments corresponding each to a definite state in the question of the subject.

1. *Between Heart and Reason: The Prehistory of Aesthetics, or the Dispute of the "Cogitos"*

Contrary to an oft received opinion (a point [I'll come back to it] on which Cassirer went wrong), it is from the seventeenth century that we encounter a hardened opposition between, on the one hand, a certain classicism which conceives art by analogy with science and assigns it as its goal "to paint after nature," and thus to represent truth, and, on the other, an aesthetics of "delicacy" or "sentiment," seeing in the beautiful work an expression of that which is ineffable in the transports of passion. Behind these two conceptions of beauty—whose conflict goes on throughout the eighteenth century—two visions of subjectivity are confronting each other: one, issued from Cartesianism, locates the essence of the cogito in reason while the other, Pascalian or even sensualist, places the essential elsewhere, in the heart or the feelings. Yet these two apparently radically antinomic positions are fighting on common ground: that of individualism. In both cases the subject is thought of as a *monad* that cannot come into communication with other monads except through the intermediation of a third term. Since these monads possess, as Leibniz put it, "neither doors nor windows," the theory of *sensus communis,* which attempts to answer the difficult question of the criteria of the beautiful, rests on what could be called a "satellite" model: in this first era of individualism, culminating with Leibnizian rationalism and Berkeley's and Hume's empiricism, the intersubjectivity brought about by the beautiful object (the fact that it produces a certain consensus among the subjects) can only be thought of as starting with the idea of a God, monad among monads, who guarantees agreement among the individuals.

It's against this very model that the first aesthetics, Baumgarten's *Aesthetica,* is conceived. The arrival of this new, resolutely modern discipline presupposes the withdrawal of the divine perspective to the advantage of the human one. It's at such a price and only at such a price that the autonomy of sensibility, and therefore of the sphere within which beauty alone finds its proper expression, can be definitively conquered.

2. The Kantian Moment: Reflection and Intersubjectivity

The *Aesthetica* is not able to fully establish the autonomy of the sensible in contrast to the intelligible, caught up as it still is in the framework of Leibnizian rationalism. Despite their extraordinary innovative potential, the first aesthetics are still touched by a certain Platonism; they never can confer, in the final analysis, the same status to beauty that is given by right to the true and the good.

The argument can be sketched out with ease although it is, as we shall see throughout this history of aesthetics, absolutely decisive: if beauty is only appearance, the manifestation in the realm of the sensible of a true idea or of a moral evidence, then it is clear that its true value is by its very essence located somewhere other than within itself—in the true or the good it illustrates. It can at best lay claim to a certain talent *in the presentation* of a content that does not belong to it, which is always described and grounded outside of it, in speculative philosophy, science, or ethics. That is, moreover, the crux of every classicism: if the painting or the poem is above all valuable for the nobility of the subject it represents, if truth must reign, as Boileau put it, even if it must "spoil the rhythmic foot," then isn't art condemned from its very origins to a subordinate position in the field of culture? And that is what is at stake in the process of winning autonomy for the realm of the sensible in relation to the two aspects, theoretical and practical, of the intelligible. It is no doubt the affirmation of such an autonomy that will permit Kant to break out of the framework of classicism and to work out the principles of an aesthetics within which, for the first time in the history of thought, beauty acquires an independent existence and ceases being the mere reflection of an essence furnishing it with its authentic meaning from without.

It has to be noticed that this unprecedented reversal of Platonism (of the primacy of the intelligible over the sensible) also upsets the heritage of the history of subjectivity. We must keep in mind the idea that the realm of sense-perception (of the sensible) is the sign par excellence of the human condition, of *limited* knowledge. It is exactly that by which man, with a material body and limited intelligence, is distinct from God with his pure spirit and omniscience. The affirmation of the autonomy of the sensible means nothing less in this context than the radical, perhaps definitive, separation of the human and the divine. Even more: it implies the existence of a sphere, that of the properly human, outside all divine legislation and yet not thereby a mere imperfection, a flaw or a lack when compared to the divinity. It is a fatal blow dealt to the ancient status of the divine, an act of pride of which it is not too much to say that it is, within the realm of the intellect, comparable to the other act of lèse-divinité constituted by the French Revolution in the realm of politics.

The birth of aesthetics thus reveals itself to be strictly inseparable from a certain withdrawal of the divine. A new figure of finite subjectivity, called by Kant *reflection,* appears in the wake of this withdrawal. We shall see how—there is, of course, no chance in all this—it is with the theory of the judgment of taste, understood as a "reflective" judgment that can come only from a *finite* subject, meaning a *sensible* one living at some remove from God, that this new representation of the subject will take shape. We shall also examine how with this new figure, the contemplator of beauty, ceases to be a mirror-individual, a monad communicating with the other monads only through the mediation of the divine satellite. God's withdrawal leaves aesthetics facing up to new questions: it now has to theorize the "common sense" brought about by the beautiful object, to think out, if we prefer, the harmony of "sensibilities" (when it takes place anyhow) and that in some manner other than the theological (monadological) one. In other words, we now have to make use of a certain representation of *intersubjectivity* to understand such a harmony. We have now fully entered the modern, secular universe.

The mutation is just as decisive on the artist and creator's side; he ceases to be he who modestly limits himself to *discovering* and *expressing* in agreeable fashion the truths created by God and becomes he who *invents*. The *genius* appears and the imagination tends to become "the queen of faculties," the one that rivals the divine in the production of radically unprecedented works.

3. The Hegelian Moment: The Absolute Subject or the Death of Art

Hegel's reinterpretation of the theory of genius sets out to stop the gap opened up within classical rationalism. No one can dispute that Hegel's aesthetics are imposing. Much more than Kant's do, they take into account, at times in a dazzling manner, the concrete history of art: the interpretation of Antigone or the revelation of some of the deepest meanings of Romantic poetry remain, whatever one thinks of them, models for a philosophical critique of art. But it remains true that, from the time of its ripening during the Jena period, Hegel's system tends to reinsert the human point of view as a simple moment within the historical unfolding of the divine: "reflection," as the essence of finite subjectivity, must be "subsumed" in what Hegel calls "the speculative proposition." Sensibility thus loses the autonomy it had acquired with Kant, so that aesthetics becomes once again, in a very *classical* way, the expression of an idea in the field of the sensible. Of course, Hegel gives this alienation of the idea in an exterior sensible matter, unlike the classicism of the seventeenth and eighteenth centuries, the form of a *history* of art. But it's far from certain that the essential feature of classicism is superseded. In Hegel's eyes art remains, in the end, a manifestation of the truth which, however attractive, is nevertheless by definition inferior to that which takes place within philosophy. That is the meaning of the famous observation according to which art belongs to the past. Reflection and genius must give way to the absolute subject which only philosophy can make accessible to us.

4. The Nietzschean Moment: The Shattered Subject and the Aesthetization of Culture

However paradoxical it may sound, Nietzsche's aesthetics—perhaps the most anti-Hegelian of all philosophies of art—link up in certain ways with the Kantian project of granting the sensible autonomy in relation to the intelligible; for similar reasons, this autonomization of the sensible leads, in a relationship which is the exact inverse of that which Hegelianism has with Kantianism, to the reaffirmation of the legitimacy of the human viewpoint over against that of the divine. In other words—the words of a history of subjectivity—the "death of God" means also that of the absolute subject, at the same time that it points to the coming of the "shattered subject," one radically open to the alterity of the unconscious and therefore forever incapable of closing in on itself in the illusion of some sort of self-transparency.

The famous thesis that "there are no facts" but "only interpretations" draws to perfection the outline of this new age of individualism that Nietzsche's thinking inaugurates in the sphere of philosophy. On the one hand, the proposition can be understood in the sense of a total subjectivism or, as it were, of an absolute relativism: there is no single truth, only truths, perfectly *singular* points of view, that is, if we understand ourselves correctly, no truth at all in the sense in which the expression has been known up to then in the philosophical tradition (identity, adequateness). Yet on the other hand it would seem we are escaping the philosophies of the subject inherited from Cartesianism and empiricism, precisely because there is no longer either a monad in closure on itself (the viewing points can no longer be reassembled in the unity of a subject/substance as if they were its attributes) or a monad of monads which would guarantee, as in Leibniz, the agreement or harmony of the multiple perspectives within a *world system*. As Heidegger very well put it, Nietzscheanism is a "monadology without God."

If truth is no longer defined as either identity (the noncontradiction of propositions) or adequacy (of the judgement to the thing), it's perhaps because, in the name of a truth deeper than that of philosophy, Nietzsche conceives the real as multiplicity, fracture—as difference that only art can adequately capture.

5. The Death of the Avant-Gardes and the Coming of Postmodernity

It is, in my eyes, the double movement of Nietzschean aesthetics—hyperrelativism (or hyperindividualism) on the one hand, according to which there exists no truth "in itself" but only an infinity of irreconcilable points of view, and on the other hand the "hyperrealism" of an art which should aim at a "fractured," deeper, more secret truth, one more real in the end than that which metaphysics and platonically inspired science arrive at—which constitutes the philosophical equation underlying, if not the totality of contemporary art, then at least those of its expressions which are most manifestly connected to "avant-gardism."

If Nietzsche is no doubt not—or anyway not only—the philosopher of the "world of the technique," as Heidegger believed, he is without a doubt the thinker of the aesthetic avant-garde in so far as it is indissolubly connected to the figure of the fractured subject. In its hyperindividualist aspect the avant-garde encounters the most extreme, the most "subjective" revolutionary ideology. It then glorifies the values of innovation, originality, rupture with tradition, the, in a word, neo-Cartesian values of the tabula rasa which Nietzsche paradoxically exalts at the very moment he thinks he is destroying them "with a hammer." But in its "hyperrealist" (the expression is not, of course, used here in the meaning it has taken in recent art history) aspect avant-gardism reveals itself to be a "hyperclassicism," the contrary of any kind of baroque. From cubism to suprematism or surrealism, the goal is to render the realest reality—therefore the fascination these avant-gardes felt for the new geometries which give an inkling of as yet unexplored plastic spaces, nonetheless "more true" than the well-known ones of Eucledian perspective. "More true," meaning, as with Nietzsche (whose fascination for the "new" biology is well known), *different, multiple, fractured.*

The avant-gardes in politics have disappeared at the end of this twentieth century, as have those in art. The diagnosis is all the less doubtful when we keep in mind that it's most often pronounced by the very protagonists of this strange history of aesthetic "elites" since the 1880s. We are resolutely, if not joyously, entering into the era of the post–avant-garde or, as the architects say, of "postmodernity." Innovation ceases to be the golden rule, and the return to lost traditions, or "revivalism," acquires a certain legitimacy. The real is at the same time no longer systematically defined as chaos, fracture, difference, disharmony, or dissonance. Literature links up again with the taste for narrative and for "real" characters, painting no longer excludes figuration, proscribed until the end of the sixties, and learned music abandons the most extreme forms of 1950s serialism. The reasons for this new shift (art history is made of paradoxes) run deep, they no doubt imply a new figure of the subject and of its relation with the world—with this

31

world whose withdrawal, as we have suggested, could well be its most important characteristic today.

At the end of such a history of subjectivity, we will inevitably be led back to the problem of the status of culture in a democratic society, in a society of individuals liberated from the world of tradition.

T W O

Between Heart and Reason

Tastes and colors are not to be argued about . . .
Yet we do nothing else but!
   —F. Nietzsche

WHEN REFLECTION UPON THE BEAUTIFUL adopts the form
of an aesthetics, as values begin to be thought about using subjectivity as a starting point, the question of what should be held to be
the principle of this judgment of taste within this subjectivity remains
to be answered. Is it a question of *reason,* as the Cartesians and the
theorists of French classicism think, or of *sentiment* or *feeling,* of "delicacy" of heart, as a school of thought that draws from both Pascal and
English empiricism will state more and more clearly throughout the
eighteenth century? * If reason is chosen, one will conceive of the judgment of taste on the model of a logico-mathematical judgment. By analogy with science, its objectivity will be guaranteed, classicism's risk
being the loss of the specificity of the aesthetic judgment, the reduction
of beauty to a mere sense representation of truth. If on the contrary we
opt for sentiment as the principle of aesthetic evaluation, if taste is more
a matter of heart than of reason, we will certainly obtain an autonomous aesthetic sphere but, apparently, at the price of so radical a subjectivization of the Beautiful that the problem of the objectivity of
criteria will see itself disqualified in favor of a complete relativism.

   The conflict which, from Boileau to Batteux, from Bouhours to Du-

---

* Cf. Ernst Cassirer, *The Philosophy of the Enlightenment,* last chapter. Although he makes certain historical errors (Cassirer is especially mistaken when
he takes Bouhours to be a man of the eighteenth century, when he was in fact a
contemporary of Boileau), Cassirer's general thesis about the difference between
a Cartesian, rationalist, and deductive seventeenth century and a Newtonian
eighteenth century which has discovered observation remains, on the whole,
correct.

bos, goes on at the very center of the reflection on the nature of the Beautiful during the French classical period, constitutes in turn the veritable prehistory of modern aesthetics. The two questions it explores—that of the autonomy of aesthetics as a new discipline, different from logic, and that of the criteria of taste—direct us in the final analysis to a sole problem: that of the communicability of aesthetic experience in so far as it is subjective experience, purely individual yet accessible to others in the mode of a "common sense," of a *sharing* which nothing, apparently, guarantees a priori.

CLASSICISM AND DELICACY: THE DIALOGUES OF EUDOXE AND PHILANTHE

This dispute has been often analyzed (by Cassirer and Bäumler, of course, but before them also, and excellently, by K. Heinrich von Stein),[1] and we don't need to recapitulate its history here. I would like, rather, to direct our attention to a little known work, particularly interesting in this context, since it has the originality of presenting the quarrel in the form of a dialogue between two characters of which one, Eudoxe, incarnates Boileau's classicism while the other, Philanthe, does so for the aesthetics of delicacy. The book, by Dominique Bouhours, is called *On the Ways of Thinking Properly in Works of the Intellect* [*Des manières de bien penser dans les ouvrages de l'esprit*]. Published in 1687, this dialogue, which followed the *Conversations of Ariste and Eugene* [*Entretiens d'Ariste et d'Eugène,* 1671], was to know a great success. No doubt for the first time in the history of what was to be known as aesthetics, the opposition of classicism to delicacy was put forth as the opposition of two ideal types, or even of two types of men. Here is how this Jesuit, professor of humanities and of rhetoric, whom Ménage castigated for being a ridiculous, affected pedant and for excessively frequenting "the ladies and the minor artists," but of whom Madame de Sévigné used to say that "wit oozes out of his every pore," introduces his two characters: they are "two men of letters, whose science has not spoiled them and who have no less politeness than they do erudition . . . Although they have had the same education and they know more or less the same things, the character of their minds is quite different." It is their psychologies—or, as we would say nowadays, their "sensibilities"—that most of all distinguish the two men. Eudoxe's tastes, as his name indicates, follow classical orthodoxy: "Nothing pleases him among works of invention that be not reasonable and natural." (*Des manières,* p. 2.) He admires the ancients. As for Philanthe, "whatever is flowery, whatever shines, charms him. To his liking, the Greeks and the Romans are not worth the Spaniards and Italians" (ibid.). He loves the baroque.

We sense in the preface to the dialogue that Bouhours has chosen his camp. The point is not, he declares, "to prescribe rules, nor to give laws which may bother someone." The author, he adds, "says what he thinks and leaves to each the liberty of judging otherwise," his work desiring to be but a "short and easy Rhetoric, instructing by examples more than by precepts, and which has no other rules than the lively and brilliant good sense the conversations of Ariste and Eugène make mention of" (p. 4). Through the character of Eudoxe, it's clearly Boileau's *Art poétique* which is being aimed at, as it is summed up in these justly famous verses:

> Rien n'est beau que le vrai, le vrai seul est aimable,
> Il doit régner partout, et même dans la fable;
> De toute fiction l'adroite fausseté
> Ne tend qu'à faire aux yeux briller la vérité.
> Sais-tu pourquoi mes vers sont lus dans les provinces
> Sont recherchés du peuple et reçus chez les princes?
> Ce n'est pas que leurs sons, agréables, nombreux
> Soient toujours à l'oreille également heureux
> Qu'en plus d'un lieu le sens n'y gêne la mesure
> Et qu'un mot quelquefois n'y brave la césure:
> Mais c'est qu'en eux le vrai du mensonge vainqueur,
> Partout se montre aux yeux et va saisir les coeurs
>
> . . . .
>
> Ma pensée au grand jour partout s'offre et s'expose
> Et mon vers, bien ou mal, dit toujours quelque chose.

Nothing is beautiful but the true, the true only is worthy of love,
It must reign everywhere, even in the fable;
Every fiction's adroit falseness
Serves only to make truth's shine apparent.
Know you why my verses are read in the provinces,
demanded by the people and welcomed by princes?
It isn't that their sounds, though pleasant and numerous,
be always to the ear of equal success;
That there is never a place where the sense upsets the meter,
or that a word never defies the caesura:

It is that in them the truth, over mendacity triumphant,
everywhere shows itself and goes right to the heart

. . . .

In broad daylight my thoughts put themselves forward,
And, good or bad, something is said by my verses.

This passage from Epistle 9 contains the principal themes of classical aesthetics which Philanthe will try—against Eudoxe—if not to refute, then at least to put into doubt:

1. The art/science equivalency indicated by the reduction of the
Beautiful to the truth and, through the same reduction, the equation of
the judgment of taste to a theoretical judgment on the perfection of a
certain work, on its adequacy to a "concept," to determined rules.

2. The rejection of "fiction" and, with it, of the imagination, the
"madwoman of the household" as Malebranche prettily put it, the limited faculty Descartes had already declared incompatible with science
in a letter to Mersenne in July 1641.*

3. The idea that the artist's activity consists not in *invention* but in
discovery, as Boileau reminds us in the important 1701 Preface to his
last new edition of the *Satires:* "What is a new, brilliant, extraordinary
thought? It is not, as the ignorant come to hold, a thought no one must
have had before; it is, on the contrary, something everyone must have
thought of and which someone decides to express for the first time."
Thus, properly speaking, dis-covery, bringing to light. For "man's mind
is naturally full of an infinite number of confused ideas of the true,
which he often sees but partially, and nothing is more pleasant to him
than to see one of these ideas offered to him well lit, as in the light of
day." The artist's task, like that of the scientist and of the scholar, lies
halfway between *imitation,* as theorized in Plato's *Republic,* and *genius,*
the unconscious creation of the *new* which will be the central concept
of the romantic movement's aesthetics.

4. If art is discovery, the bringing to light of a truth still concealed
in the depths of the human heart, the beautiful object, following the
example of the scientific object, is that which in nature reveals itself to
be fully congruent with the laws of reason. As Charles Batteux, one of

---

* Spinoza has put the Cartesian contempt for the imagination very well:
"False, counterfeit ideas . . . have their origin in the imagination, that is, in
certain fortuitous sensations . . . If one so wishes, one may understand by imagination here whatever one likes, provided it be something different from the
understanding." (*Treatise on the Reform of the Understanding,* § 45.)

Boileau's main disciples in the eighteenth century, put it: "The arts do not create their own laws: these are independent of the former's whim and are invariably patterned after the example of nature."[2] But the point is not to indifferently "imitate" everything "natural." It is rather to unveil that which in a luxuriantly variegated nature is essential, congruent with reason, thus "nature not as it is in itself, but as it can be, and as it can be conceived by the mind" or, as Batteux also puts it, the veri-similar [*vrai-semblable*] rather than the true [*vrai*] (p. 24).

Batteux uses *The Misanthrope* as an example: "When Moliere set out to depict misanthropy, he did not look around Paris for an original of which the play could have been the exact copy: he would have made but a history, a portrait, he would have given half a lesson. Instead he gathered the traces of bile he had observed among men; he added all his genius could provide in the same genre; and out of all these compared and selected traits he molded a unique character, the representation not of the true but of the verisimilar" (p. 25).

5. The true artist will thus reject anything that may evoke the Spanish or Italian baroque. The word's etymology is well known, appearing in the first edition of the French Academy's dictionary in 1694: "Baroque, adj. Said only of pearls of a very imperfect roundness. A baroque pearl necklace." The figurative meaning will be accepted by the 1740 edition of the same dictionary: "Baroque is said also in a figurative sense for what is irregular, bizarre, uneven. A baroque spirit, a baroque expression, a baroque figure." The baroque is then the *shapeless*, that which, when compared to the circle, the perfect symbol of the principle of reason, can only look like an excess, like an *inelegance*—in the sense in which a mathematical proof is said to be inelegant when instead of taking the simplest approach it loses itself in useless detours, even if it obtains the right answer. From the standpoint of the standards of classicism the Italian baroque looks, strictly speaking, *monstrous,* as in Boileau's formulation:

> La plupart emportés d'une fougue insensée
> Toujours loin du droit sens vont chercher leur pensée.
> Ils croiraient s'abaisser dans leurs vers monstrueux
> S'ils pensaient ce qu'un autre a pu penser comme eux.
> Évitons ces excès: laissons à l'Italie
> De tous ses faux brillants l'éclatante folie.[3]

> Carried away by nonsensical ardour
> They go search their thoughts far from clear sense.

They would think it beneath their monstrous verses
To think what someone else has thought.
Let us avoid such excess: let us leave to the Italians
Of all these false gems, the mad radiance.

6. Since art is, like science, moved by a will toward parousia [presencing], toward a bringing to light of that which remains hidden even though shared by an eternal, because rational, human nature, it must avoid any obscurity in expression. Not only does the ineffable have no place in poetry,* the figures of rhetoric must be ceaselessly tracked down when they lead to the "equivocation" stigmatized by Boileau in verses of admirable clarity:

Du langage Français bizarre hemaphrodite
De quel genre te faire équivoque maudite?
Ou maudit: car sans peine aux rimeurs hasardeux
L'usage encor, je crois, laisse le choix des deux.
Tu ne me répons rien. Sors d'ici fourbe indigne,
Mâle aussi dangereux que femelle maligne
Qui croit rendre innocents des discours imposteurs;
Tourment des Écrivains, juste effroi des Lecteurs;
Par qui de mots confus sans cesse embarrassée
Ma plume en écrivant cherche en vain ma pensée.[4]

Bizarre hermaphrodite of the French tongue
What gender should I make you, cursed (*Fem*) equivocation?

---

* Il est certains esprits dont les sombres pensées
Sont d'un nuage épais toujours embarrassées
Le jour de la raison ne le saurait percer
Avant donc que d'écrire apprenez à penser.
Selon que notre idée est plus ou moins obscure
L'expression la suit, ou moins nette ou plus pure.
Ce que l'on conçoit bien s'énonce clairement
Et les mots pour le dire arrivent aisément. (Ibid.)

Certain spirits exist whose dark thoughts
Are forever embarrassed by a thick cloud
Reason's light cannot penetrate it:
Learn to think, then, before you write.
As your idea is or more or less obscure,
The expression does follow, or more or less pure.
What is well thought out can be uttered with clarity
The words to say it come with facility.

Or cursed (*Masc*): for to adventurous rhymers
Usage still, I believe, of either one leaves the choice.
You answer nothing. Leave this place, rogue,
Dangerous male and treacherous female
Who thinks to render false discourse innocent;
Torture of Writers, just fear of Readers;
Thanks to whom, embarrassed by confusing words
My pen in its course vainly seeks out my thoughts.

7. Although the essential goal remains that of "pleasing the people as much as the Prince"* and of "capturing the hearts," it has to be made clear that the heart, here, has nothing Pascalian about it, it fuses rather into the Cartesian concept of mind, and the pleasure brought about in it by the poem should come more from the meaning it contains than from its "richness of sonorities." Thus when Boileau borrows the vocabulary of the aesthetics of delicacy, he twists its authentic meaning and immediately gives it a rationalist connotation: "If you were to ask me in what consists this pleasure and this piquancy [*cet agrément et ce sel*], I would answer it is a *je-ne-sais-quoi* easier to feel than to put into words: *it is my opinion, nevertheless, that it consists in never offering the reader anything other than true thoughts and exact expressions.*"**

That is the very position Bouhours is trying to refute, point by point, by way of Philanthe's discourses. Against Eudoxe's rationalism, against his praise of the poetic virtues of the clear and distinct idea,

* Cf. *Art póetique, canto 1*: "*N'offrez rien au lecteur que ce qui peut lui plaire*" [*Offer the reader but that which may please him*].

** Cf. also:

Quelque sujet qu'on traite, ou plaisant, ou sublime,
Que toujours le bon sens s'accorde avec la rime:
L'un l'autre vainement ils semblent se hair;
La rime est une esclave et ne doit qu'obeir.

. . . .

Aimez donc la raison: que toujours vos ecrits
Empruntent d'elle seule et leur lustre et leur prix. (Ibid.)

Whatever is dealt with, pleasant or sublime,
Clear good sense must ever agree with the rhyme:
Vainly do they seem to hate each other;
Rhyme is a slave and must but obey.

. . . .

Therefore love reason: may from it alone
Your writings borrow their brilliance and worth.

Philanthe tries to demonstrate the part *irrationality* plays in any artistic expression of Beauty. In any poem, if it's any good, there is "a content of obscurity nothing can clear up."[5] Contrary to the tenets of classical doctrine, the *ineffable* character of the Beautiful must be affirmed: "When you ask me what a delicate thought is, I do not know where to borrow the terms to explain myself: these are things difficult to see at once and which, through their subtlety, escape you the moment you think you grasp them" (ibid., p. 194). And yet this unsayable is not illegitimate, simple indication of a weakness in the artist's capacities for expression; it is rather the most intimate essence of "delicate thinking": "The sense it contains is neither as visible nor as much in relief" as Eudoxe thinks, and "the little mystery is like the soul of the delicacy of thoughts, such that those which have nothing mysterious about them, neither at bottom nor all around and which show themselves all together at first glance, are not properly speaking delicate, however spiritual they may otherwise be" (p. 195).[6]

We perceive here all that separates the aesthetics of sentiment from those of classicism: if the judgment of taste's principle is not reason, if, as Philanthe puts it in a very Pascalian formula, "the heart is more ingenious* than the mind" (p. 81), then we must exalt the irrational and sensitive element of subjectivity. Bouhours's aesthetics rehabilitate, in opposition to the *Art poétique*, the rhetorical procedures which allow for the irrational in man, beginning with the use of *equivocal* metaphors which are "like those transparent veils which show what they cover, or like masks under which we recognize the disguised person" (p. 20). The pleasant thing about equivocation is precisely that in it there is a "remainder," forever ungraspable by the understanding (pp. 20ff.). And if "thoughts, through being true, are betimes trivial," then we must push the logic of sentiment to its conclusion and praise falseness. In fact, and Boileau is still the target here, isn't it "fiction, or something somewhat poetic, which renders ideas very pleasant in prose"? (Pp. 225–26). Thus, "a princess we once knew, of an infinitely delicate spirit, used to say that the sun brings happy days only to the common people . . . The proposition seems false, and only because of that does it have beauty" (ibid.). In a word, Philanthe might be tempted to say: Nothing beautiful like the false, only the false is praiseworthy!

In *The Philosophy of the Enlightenment*, Ernst Cassirer correctly

---

*Note, in passing, that with the notion of ingenuity the idea of genius is already evoked.

perceived, at least in principle, that which separates the aesthetics of the eighteenth from that of the seventeenth century: "The inner transition by which the domination of classical theory in the realm of aesthetics is broken corresponds exactly from the point of view of method with the change which takes place in the theory of natural science between Descartes and Newton . . . The purpose of both transitions is to free the mind from the absolute predominance of deduction; it is to make way for the facts, for the phenomena, for direct observation"[7] and to thus make more room for sensibility. The diagnosis, generally correct, has some traits of caricature about it. In truth, the conflict opposing classical to sentimental aesthetics is entirely rooted in the seventeenth century. Although it goes on in the eighteenth century in a somewhat different form—and here Cassirer is right, the eighteenth century favors observation over deduction—it is not modified in its essentials, witness the work of Boileau's disciple, Charles Batteux, *Les Beaux-Arts réduits à un même principe* [*The Fine Arts Reduced to a Single Principle,* 1746]. It proposes to bring into the reflection on the Beautiful the observation of concrete experience, rather than trust the sole virtues of Cartesian deduction: "Let us imitate the true physicists, who accumulate observations and found upon them a system which then reduces them to a principle" (p. 2). The model is of course provided by Newton's physics. Just as the latter reduces the multiplicity of celestial phenomena to a single principle, universal gravitation, aesthetics must seek to reduce the diversity of rules at play within art works to a single, unique rule, for "all rules are branches from the same trunk" (ibid.). But although the method is no longer Cartesian, the results of Batteux's research conform to Boileau's teaching; the rule of rules is still the imitation of nature or, more precisely, the imitation of that which reason unveils as the essence of nature. And if the principle of taste is reason, then it's clear that the true genius does not *invent,* he *discovers:* "The human mind can only create incorrectly: all of its productions bear the mark of a model . . . The genius who works to please should not, and cannot, leave the limits of nature itself. His function consists not in imagining what may be, but in finding what is. Invention in the arts is not a matter of conferring being to an object, it is one of recognizing it as it is where it is" (p. 11). The artist's only originality lies in the choice of a subject, and in its composition (p. 89), not in his creative faculties. His essential work consists in presenting the natural idea he wishes to express in a perceptible form—marble, colors, sounds, etc.:

What could this genius do, bound by his fecundity and his outlook, which he cannot take beyond nature? . . . All his efforts had to limit themselves perforce to making a selection out of the most beautiful parts of nature, to make of them an exquisite whole which should be more perfect than nature itself without however ceasing to be natural. This is the principle on which the fundamental plan of the arts had to be erected, and which the great artists have followed in every century . . .

What is the function of the arts? It is to transpose the traits of nature and present them in objects in which they are not natural. Thus it is that the sculptor's chisel shows us a hero in a block of marble. The painter, with his colors, makes every visible object come out of the canvas. The musician, with his artificial sounds, makes the storm grumble whilst everything is calm, and, finally, the poet, with his invention and the harmony of his verses, fills our mind with make-believe images and our heart with factitious sentiments, often more charming than if they were real and natural. (Ibid., pp. 13–14)

The difference with the seventeenth century's classical outlook is thus smaller than Cassirer thinks.

On the other side of the conflict, the abbé Dubos, the greatest eighteenth century theoretician of the aesthetics of feeling, aligns himself without hesitation in continuity with Bouhours. His *Critical Reflections on Poetry and Painting* (1719)—of which Voltaire said it was "the most useful book anyone had ever written on these subjects in any country in Europe"—is resolutely situated on the side of a critique of classicism in its affirmation of the incontestable primacy of emotion over intelligence. If the purpose of the work of art is to please—something the classicists also admit—it still has to be remarked that "of all the talents that give dominion over other men, the most powerful is not superiority of intellect or of enlightenment, it is the talent of swaying these to one's will."[8] Dubos's *Reflections* thus present themselves as a theory of the effects of art on the human heart; they leave the domain of law or rules and find themselves placed within the sphere of fact, of psychology and anthropology. Here is the book's project as formulated in its Introduction: "A book which could, as it were, display the human heart at the very instant it is rendered soft by a poem or is touched by a picture, would provide our artisans with very enlarged views and exact insights on the general effect of their works, an effect most of them seem to have so much trouble foreseeing."

It is thus clear that, within aesthetic reflection itself, more importance should be given to observation than to deduction—what Dubos, in order to display his loyalty to his own method, illustrates with examples such as this one, particularly representative of his style of argumentation: "Monsieur de Leibniz would never attempt to travel in his carriage through a spot which his driver assured him could not be gone through without the carriage keeling over, even if they had both eaten nothing, and this even if it were demonstrated to this learned man, in a geometrical analysis of the road's inclination and of the carriage's height and weight, that it should not keel over. We believe the man before we do the philosopher because the philosopher is mistaken even more easily than the man" (ibid., p. 361). Empiricism has of course come to the aid of this anti-Cartesian Pascalianism, already noticeable in Bouhours, but, essentially, the aesthetics of feeling only develops and enriches the aesthetics of delicacy: "If there is any realm in which reasoning should be quiet when confronted with experience, then surely it is in the questions one may raise concerning the merits of a poem" (ibid., p. 367).

Thus the principal aspects of the conflict remain in place throughout the eighteenth century, until the emergence of the first attempts at synthesis, of which the *Critique of Judgment* will be the ultimate achievement within speculative philosophy. The staying power of the conflict is attested by the fact that the antinomy's central problem—that of the discussibility of taste—is evaded by both Batteux and Dubos. The former does so in the name of a rationalist dogmatism, since "there can in general be but one good taste, that which approves of the beautiful nature: those who do not approve it necessarily have bad taste;"[9] the latter for precisely the opposite reason: in matters of taste, "the path of argument is not as proper for knowing the merits of verses and pictures as is that of sentiment." According to Dubos, "feeling instructs us better if the work touches us and if it makes the impression on us it should make than all the dissertations critics compose to explain merit and to calculate imperfections and flaws. The path of discussion and analysis . . . is, in truth, fitting when we must find the causes why a work pleases or does not; but it is not as proper as feeling when it comes to deciding the question: does the work please or does it not please? Is the work, in general, good or bad? It comes down to the same thing."

If the "path of argument" is rejected by the aesthetics of feeling, it's for a double reason, very explicitly stated in the *Reflections*. On the one hand, since all references to concepts or rules have disappeared—the consequence of a radical critique that incorporates nothing from classical rationalism—there remain no criteria around which discussion

43

could begin: "If the most important virtue of poems and pictures were to conform to written rules, we could say that the best way of judging of their excellence as of their ranking in the esteem of men should be that of discussion and analysis. But the most important virtue of poems and pictures is that of pleasing us," at which point we must rely on feelings to judge. On the other hand, it is because Dubos does not envision, as Kant will, the possibility of a critique of dogmatic rationalism which does not prohibit all reference to indeterminate criteria—to "Ideas," if not to rules—that he is led to compare the impossibility of aesthetic discussion to that of culinary discussion: "Would one ever set out, having posited the geometrical principles of taste and defined the qualities of every ingredient that enters into the composition of the dish, to *discuss* the proportions maintained in their admixture to decide if the stew is good? One does nothing of the kind . . . one tastes the stew and, without even knowing these rules, one knows if it's good. It is, in a way, the same thing with works of the mind and with pictures made for pleasing us by affecting us." [10] Discussion is therefore useless, "tiresome for the writer and disgusting for the reader" (ibid., p. 369).

THE END OF TRADITIONS: A DISPUTE
WITHIN MODERN INDIVIDUALISM

Between the various instances of the conflict opposing the aesthetics of feeling and dogmatic classicism there is not only opposition but also, as with any truly antinomic structure, connection. If both aesthetics lead to a shared rejection of intersubjectivity following inverse arguments, it is because they are both rooted in a monadic conception of subjectivity: the quarrel does not touch on the question of whether it is fitting to establish the beautiful on the judgment of the individual or on tradition, the way a quarrel between the ancients and the moderns would, but only on the notion of individuality to which each side would refer. To the aesthetics of feeling, the Reason of the classicists appears, no doubt, as a dogmatic authority, as that which is the least subjective within the subject. But we should not misinterpret this: even Boileau's aesthetics are truly modern in that they in no way question the grounding of the Beautiful on subjectivity, Reason being conceived of here as a faculty of the subject.

Of course, in the quarrel of the ancients and the moderns, Boileau took the side of the ancients, but we need to understand the exact nature of this choice. If, in his eyes, the ancients are preferable to the moderns, it isn't because they are ancient, as was commonly admitted up to the Renaissance, following a traditional pattern of thought which situated archetypes in the past;[11] it is because they incarnate an ideal defined by reference to Reason, understood as one of the faculties of the cogito. The ancients are thus no longer archetypes but illustrations, mere examples of a model residing in the subject and which, remaining above them, permits criticism to function. The emergence of criticism, inseparably tied to that of aesthetics, puts an end to the ancient, objective representation of the beautiful. Even though imitation remains a central concept in the *Art of Poetry,* we have seen that it should be understood as an activity of discovery comparable to that of science. The subjectivization of taste is thus found again in the sphere of artistic creation, where the individual has a certain room for action, a possibility of distinguishing himself from others in his capacity to bring to light or express the laws of nature. This bit of liberty is already manifest among the French classicists, the least modern of the moderns, through their expectation of originality, as witness this portrait which Boileau draws of himself, in all modesty:

> Au joug de la raison asservissant la rime
> Et même en imitant toujours original
> J'ai su dans mes écrits, docte, enjoué, sublime
> Rassembler en moi Perse, Horace et Juvénal.

> In the yoke of reason I have rhyme subjected
> And, though imitating, always original
> I have in my books, sublime, gay, elevated
> Gathered in me Persius, Horace, and Juvenal.

If we situate ourselves at the point of view of a traditional, nonsubjectivist, way of thinking about art, we see clearly that there is more agreement than opposition between classical aesthetics and those of sentiment. In their displacement of the principle of judgment of taste from reason to feeling the latter merely fulfill the movement toward a subjectivization of the Beautiful begun by the classicists in the wake of Cartesianism—the reason why, strictly speaking, only the aesthetics of feeling deserve the name of *aesthetics;* also the reason why they will explore the central problem of originality by criticizing imitation and denouncing the practice of plagiarism to which Dubos, significantly, consecrates an entire section of the *Reflections.* Cannot an artisan, Dubos asks, "supplement the paltry elevation and the sterility of his genius by transplanting into his works the beauties found in the works of the great masters? . . . I respond . . . that it always was permissible to help oneself through the wit of others provided it is not done as a plagiarist. Plagiarism consists in presenting someone else's work as one's own." The supreme fault but also the supreme weakness in a world dominated by individualism, in which subjectivity has imposed itself as the foundation of all values and the originality that engenders the *author* as the real sign of geniality.

If opposition there is between the reason of the classicists and the aesthetics of feeling, it is, after all, set on the basis of a shared rejection of traditional visions of art, as we can observe in the transition from the classicist to the sentimentalist conception of the public.

The beautiful is of course defined by Boileau, in the modern fashion, as that which pleases the taste of a public, such that the 1701 Preface can declare that a "work which is not at all to the taste of the public is a very bad [méchant] work." Yet this public remains in some sense atemporal, since its taste consists in the capacity—by right common to all human beings—to perceive the one and eternal truth. "A thought is only as beautiful as it is true," and "the infallible effect of the true, when it is well put, is to seem striking to men," such is the deep conviction animating the classicist conception of art's relation to a public whose errors of judgment can, at that point, only be considered as transitory. "The majority may, for a while, take the false for the true and admire bad things, but it is impossible that in the long run a good thing will not be pleasant to it." Within such a perspective a history of art cannot truly exist, variations in taste being but transitory, accidental deviations from a norm which always finds its predominance once again and imposes itself on all.

It is by complicating the idea that the goal of the work is to please that Dubos arrives at a conception of the public that is opposed, in the end, to that of the classicists, one that introduces both the historicism and the nationalism that will dominate the nineteenth century. Whereas for Boileau the public is a de jure, ideal one, incarnating the rules of reason from which it could not for long deviate, with Dubos the public becomes concrete, historically and nationally determined; the parterre does not incarnate rules for the judgment of taste existing outside and independently of itself.[12] It *is* those rules, which is why the variations it is subject to derive from a radical historicity. Psychologism here gives way to historicism, and the second part of the *Reflections* purports to seek "the cause which could have rendered some centuries so fertile and some others so sterile in celebrated artisans." Presaging Montesquieu, Dubos applies this type of analysis to the "character of nations," whose deepest origins he thinks he sees in "the power of air on the human body . . . From everything I have just expostulated I conclude," he writes after a long inquiry on the historical and geographical variations of taste, "that just as we attribute the difference in the characters of nations to the different lands, so must we attribute to the changes that take place in the qualities of the air of a certain country the variations that take place in the mores and in the genius of its inhabitants. Just as we impute the observable difference between Frenchmen and Italians to the difference between the air of France and the air of Italy, so must we attribute to the alterations in the quality of the air in France the sensible difference we observe between the mores and the genius of Frenchmen of a given century and Frenchmen of some other century" (§ 19).

The interest we may find in such an "explanation"—at times quite precise, as in this passage, typical of the *Reflections,* "And that is why, for example, Italians will always be more apt to succeed in painting and poetry than the people surrounding the Baltic"—quite obviously does not line in its "scientific" content. What matters is the legitimation it gives to the connection it establishes between an historical and a geographical relativism, in the end situating the principle of taste within a sentiment no longer merely individual but also national. This relativism is a direct consequence of the subjectivization of the judgment of taste: where the reason of the classicists still represented a universal and invariable criterion, feeling is of its essence given to change. *Variations in art are from that point on no longer thinkable as the diverse possible aspects of the illustration of a principle which is, in truth, unique, nor even as deviations from a norm: they become the norm.* Dubos thus opens the way for art history, which will soon come into being with Winckelmann and Diderot. Furthermore, the subjectivization of the Beautiful—evidenced in his *Reflections*—contains, in embryo, and notably through the critique of plagiarism it calls forth, the typically modern and antitraditional imperative of originality at any price; originality moreover which no longer refers exclusively to eternal rules as Boileau does, but whose magnitude is to be looked for in a history of the beautiful. *What here commences is nothing less than the requirement put on the artist to innovate for the sake of innovation, which will find its eventual fulfillment in the avant-gardes of the twentieth century.*

However irreducible, the conflict between classicism and the aesthetics of feeling plays itself out against a certain shared antitradition-

47

alist background. Therefore the need, for he who would seek a synthesis within modernity—in a framework, that is, in which subjectivity, however defined, must be the principle of the judgment of taste—to ask himself about the conditions under which aesthetics could differentiate itself from logic (unlike what happened with the classicists) without thereby slipping into nationalist and historicist relativism (as was finally the case with Dubos). That is the main question in the *Critique of Judgment*.

THE ANTINOMY OF TASTE

In his third *Critique,* Kant raised the quarrel which, for over a century, opposed classicism and the aesthetics of delicacy to the status of an antinomy. Behind the manifest problems—is Beauty the imitation of a truth uncovered by reason or the subjective manifestation of the ineffable movements of the heart?—he discerned, within the representations of subjectivity underlying the two moments of the antinomy, the deeper reasons why the emerging aesthetics should in the end supersede the two terms of the "dispute" and try to solve the problem of the common sense, of the objectivity of criteria, without reducing the taste judgment to a scientific judgment and thus negating its specificity. Kant's analysis is so fundamental that we should have it in mind even this early into the subject.

Following a for him familiar approach, Kant reveals the antinomy by beginning with a "topic," with an analysis of three common sayings concerning the judgment of taste. The first, "to each his own taste," presents us with no particular difficulty, it simply means that the Beautiful blends into the pleasant, that the judgment of taste is a strictly subjective matter, that it could not therefore claim someone else's necessary adhesion. The second common saying, "taste should not be argued about" [*Über den Geschmack läßt sich nicht disputieren*], is more subtle, it supposes that the judgment of taste, even though it may contain a pretension to universality, cannot be demonstrated with proofs, with arguments relying on determinate scientific concepts.

To grasp the antinomy of classicism and sensualism, to these two common sayings we must add a maxim every one can find within himself through simple reflection: "taste can be discussed" [*Über den Geschmack läßt sich streiten*]. Contrary to appearances this maxim does not contradict the second common saying since there is a difference between a *disputatio*—a scientific argument which proceeds through *conceptual demonstration*—and a *discussion* [*Streit*] aiming only at a hypothetical and very fragile agreement regarding the beautiful object. But the idea of discussion is opposed to the first common saying: "taste can be discussed (although it cannot be argued about) . . . This proposition contains the opposite of the above proposition ("to each his own taste"). For about that which it is permissible to discuss, there must be hope of coming to an agreement,[13] and therefore of transcending the monadic sphere of the cogito, of individual subjectivity.

The method of setting forth the antinomy is thus a phenomenological one, it consists in describing the contradictions actually experienced by the aesthetics consciousness in order to encourage reflection. As long as we agree to reflect, we will discover in ourselves—such is Kant's profound conviction—the intimate sentiment that it is at the same time impossible to demonstrate the validity of our aesthetic judgments and yet, in a way, legitimate to discuss them, in the hope, however often rebuffed, of sharing an experience about which we spontaneously believe that, however individual it may be, it cannot be alien to another in so far as the other is another human being. Kant invites us to the idea that the taste judgment by itself indicates an intersubjective communicational aim, an "enlarged relation of the notion of object (as of subject)" (ibid., § 57); if we set out to discuss taste, and if disagreement in this instance—unlike what happens within the culinary domain, wrongly subsumed under art when it is in fact a skill—brings about a real dialogue, then these are certainly indications of the fact that we judge aesthetic experience to be communicable even though it could not be grounded on scientific concepts, even though the communication it leads to can never be empirically guaranteed.

And that is exactly what the thesis and the antithesis making up the antinomy of taste tend to negate, each in its own way:

1. Thesis. The judgment of taste is not founded on concepts; otherwise it could be argued about (decided through proofs).

2. Antithesis. The judgment of taste is founded on concepts; otherwise it could not, despite its different aspects, even be discussed (a claim could not be made to the necessary accord of others with this judgment). (Ibid., § 56)

The antinomy pivots on the question of the communicability of the aesthetic judgment, of its capacity to transcend or not the cogito's particular subjectivity. Only from this angle is the problem of the rationality or irrationality (conceptuality or nonconceptuality) of taste approached.

In a sense, the thesis and antithesis, correctly understood, both contain some sort of truth, so that we may admit—the principle of the Kantian solution—that they are opposed only in appearance. It is true (thesis) that the judgment of taste is not based on scientific concepts and that it cannot be demonstrated, as classical rationalism believes; it is no less true that this judgment refers nonetheless to "indeterminate concepts," that is, to *Ideas of reason* which establish the possibility, if not of a *disputatio*, at least of a *discussion* which may lead to a "common sense." The opposition is thus merely apparent—"dialectical"—since the term "concept" "is not taken in the same sense in both maxims of the faculty of aesthetic judgment" (ibid.). Either, in the thesis, by "concept" is understood a scientific rule of the understanding; or, in the antithesis, only an indeterminate *Idea of reason* is aimed at. To resolve the antinomy, then, "the thesis should say: the judgment of taste is not founded on determinate concepts; the antithesis, on the other hand: the judgment of taste is founded on a concept although an indeterminate one (namely, the suprasensible substratum of phenomena); then there would be no opposition between them" (ibid., § 57).

The concrete meaning of the Kantian solution begins to emerge. Though the object of a private and intimate *feeling,* beauty awakens the *Ideas of reason* present in every man—which is why it can transcend private subjectivity and bring forth a common sense (the Ideas "awakened" by the beautiful object being in principle common to humanity). The beautiful object is simultaneously purely sensible yet intellectual; it is a reconciliation of nature and of the mind but a *contingent* reconciliation, the fruit of nature itself (of man's nature in the case of the genius) and not of a conscious will following determinate rules, as the classicists would have it.

Beyond their truth content, thesis and antithesis in the antinomy can also be interpreted dogmatically:

—The thesis then comes to mean that taste, being in the domain of feelings, is a purely subjective affair; that it is thus, at least de jure, incommunicable, ineffable. Empiricism leads to solipsism in aesthetics much as it did in speculative philosophy: "to each his own taste," * the

---

* Cf. Alexis Philonenko: "Empiricism de facto denies the possibility of communication (for otherwise we could argue about it). Actual man cannot communicate with others. The simplest words, like "I love this thing," are devoid of *sense.* We are taught that every man dies alone. Leaning on the old maxim of scholastic metaphysics—*Individuum est inefabile*—empiricism also teaches us

subject is nothing but a monad-individual, incapable of coming out of itself—whereby empiricism will prove incapable of solving the problem of intersubjectivity except, as with every monadology, through recourse to the—in the last instance theological—idea of a preestablished harmony. And if it happens that the judgment of taste, despite its subjective character, occasions a common sense, then it is only for de facto reasons which, being such, require no discussion. The ultimate consequence of empiricism is thus that "a taste judgment merits to be taken as correct only in so far *as it happens that* many come to agree with each other about it, and even this in fact not because one supposes an a priori principle behind this accord, but because (as in the palate's taste) the subjects are *by chance* organized uniformly."[14] The Beautiful is reduced to the pleasant and art to the kitchen. And, besides, the variety of tastes deserves no more discussion than their agreement: it is merely a fact to be established, and the common sense cannot be either the object nor the effect of an intersubjective dialogue. The thesis thus indicates the arrival of a psychologism soon relayed by a historicism, and later by a sociologism which will also reduce taste to some sort of material receptacle.

—If taken dogmatically, the antithesis certainly establishes the common sense but at the cost of a double error: it reduces the taste judgment to a logical judgment and art to a science. The central concept of classical rationalist aesthetics thus becomes that of *perfection*. The beautiful work is that which, in conformity to rules (to concepts) determined by a "poetic art" perfectly realizes an end itself also conceptually determined. Art's essence lies in the concept: it's thanks to it that one can determine an edifying end, thanks to it again that one can bring it to reality using the methods of technique (of which perspective in painting is one of the models). But dogmatic classicism contains a second error (in Kant's eyes, no doubt, a failing): in reducing the beautiful to a mere technical representation of an end posited by reason and taste to this very reason, it ends up losing the very subjectivity that the aesthetics of sentiment, although conceiving it incorrectly, quite rightly claimed for itself. Classicism grounds the common sense in such a way that it no longer brings together private subjects animated by feelings, but monad-individuals communicating with each other only indirectly, only

---

that one lives alone. Freedom is denied by empiricism, men being but monads." (*L'Oeuvre de Kant*, vol. 2 [1972], p. 204.)

through the concept, therefore through that in themselves which is least subjective. For classical rationalism, "the taste judgment is a hidden judgment of reason on the unveiled perfection of a thing and the relation of the diversity within it to a goal (ibid.). The important thing is whether or not the work of art is "well made," whether it conforms or not to the "rules of art" (to perspective, to three unities, etc.), sensibility being but the confused way in which the finite beings that are men perceive a reality in itself completely intelligible.

Despite their opposition, the dogmatic thesis and antithesis agree on the essential: the cogito; the individual is a monad (whether sensitive or rational mattering little in the final analysis) that can enter into communication with the other monads only indirectly, not through discussion but by the intermediary of a preestablished harmony (harmony of sensory organs in empiricism, harmony of the individual reasons within rationalism). In each case the subject is reduced to the individual and deprived of its essential dimension—intersubjectivity. In both cases discussion seems devoid of sense, among the empiricists because everything is brought down to questions of fact, with the rationalists because the concept and the rules soon put an end to all possible discussion by peremptorily decreeing where good and bad taste are to be found.

The Kantian presentation of the antinomy is no doubt abstract concerning the history of art. Racine's or Poussin's work cannot be reduced to being the effect of a flatly rationalist classicism—no more so than Picasso's or Malevitch's could be to treatises of four-dimensional geometry. But it is not without connection to concrete history if we put back into place the intermediate link aesthetics consists of as a specific discipline, halfway between speculative philosophy and artistic creation. In the conflict which, in the seventeenth century, opposes the theoreticians of classicism to the partisans of an aesthetics of "delicacy," it is most certainly the question of the common sense, of intersubjectivity, which is at the same time at the center of and seems inseparable from a well-determined philosophical representation of subjectivity.

Although it is obviously perfectly abstract (in the sense I've just indicated), the way in which Kant puts together what seems to him to be the antinomy inscribed in the very heart of taste is perhaps suggestive in clarifying the positions historically in place at the time of the emergence of modern aesthetics. What the Kantian antinomy illuminates particularly well is the way in which, in fact, the aesthetic theories prior to his own critical philosophy, beyond what opposes them to each other, sometimes come to reciprocally borrow certain of their arguments. As in every veritable antinomy, the positions in place—and this is Kant's irreplaceable contribution—are in fact less opposed than they seem or, more exactly, each one transposes itself with ease into the other, so much does each position reveal itself to be intrinsically untenable. A Kantian lesson illustrated in a particularly demonstrative way by Hume's essays on aesthetics, in their attempt to fully expound—even unto its most formidable aporias—a conception of the beautiful which seeks to plant its roots exclusively in an empiricist philosophy.

THE PARADOXES OF HUME'S AESTHETICS:
FROM (SKEPTICAL) RELATIVISM
TO CLASSICAL UNIVERSALISM

What is interesting about Hume's essays on aesthetics is the tension that animates and runs through them: beginning from a radical empiricist position—thus from a principled relativism—he tries to arrive at the idea of universal norms of taste.[15] These norms he accords a sensualist substructure, a substructure which, in the area of method, manifests itself through an explicit rejection of deduction in favor of observation. The former, "where a general abstract principle is first established, and is afterwards branched out into a variety of inferences and conclusions, may be more perfect in itself, but suits less the imperfection of human nature, and is a common source of illusion and mistake in this as well as in other subjects."[16] There where, because of this substructure, we should expect them to establish an aesthetics of feeling, these writings attempt rather to legitimate the most rigorous of classicisms, thus seeming to be one of the first attempts to solve what Kant had anticipatorily named "the antinomy of taste." The whole problem, as we shall see, comes from the fact that the Humean solution uses one of the moments that compose this antinomy, the relativist/sensualist one, as its point of departure.

This tension deserves our notice. Negatively, through the aporias it ineluctably leads Hume into, it sketches the outline of the philosophical requirements an attempt to go beyond the antinomy imposes. More profoundly, the dead ends Hume's aesthetics arrive at are highly symptomatic of the difficulties modern reflection on the beautiful encounters when, giving in to the most radical sort of immanentism and subjectivism, it cannot satisfactorily take into account the requirement of transcendence that the idea of a norm of taste, the idea of a common sense realized around the work of art, contains.

"The great variety of Taste, as well as of opinion, which prevails in the world, is too obvious not to have fallen under every one's observation."[17] This remark constitutes the minimal starting point for Hume's reflections regarding the standard of taste. Hume is not thinking of denying this de facto relativism. On the contrary, his entire theoretical philosophy permits it to be grounded without the least difficulty. With Hume, Cassirer writes apropos, "Feeling no longer needs to justify itself before the tribunal of reason; on the contrary, reason is summoned before the forum of sensation, of pure 'impression,' and questioned regarding its claims"[18]—claims to speak of the one and only Beauty or, more generally, to speak *sub specie aeternitatis* on value, both of which ideas are thus referred back to their ultimate truth: the sense impressions at the source of all ideas.

The result of this genealogical procedure is clear. In an essay titled "The Sceptic," Hume calmly asserts that a Scot could not appreciate Italian music (a no doubt reciprocal proposition) because "beauty and worth are merely of a relative nature, and consist in an agreeable sentiment, produced by an object in a particular mind, according to the peculiar structure and constitution of that mind"[19]—a structure and constitution about which we know, since Dubos and Montesquieu, the extent to which they are shaped by national traditions. "Each mind perceives a different beauty . . . To seek the real beauty, or real deformity, is as fruitless an enquiry, as to pretend to ascertain the real sweet or real bitter."[20]

The relativity of the aesthetic judgment thus reveals itself to be twofold: it is simultaneously dependent on the *particularity of the object* (the notion of Beauty is but a "word" overlying impressions that are different according to the object that brings them about) and on the *particularity of the subject* (the notion of Beauty being, from this aspect, but a convenient term to designate a psychic, then a sociological reality differentiated according to the different judging minds).

Hume's nominalism and psychologism are well known; it is still important to point out that they are not a simple matter of opinion but the expression of a fundamental philosophical choice. They are the direct effect of the reduction of Being to presence within representation through which Hume joins Berkeley's philosophy. *Esse est percipi aut percipere,* Being is to perceive or be perceived. If transcendence—the idea of a norm external to the individual—retains a psychological meaning, it has lost all transcendental truth; it exists only as a belief, Hume's entire effort then consisting in analyzing the process of formation of this type of belief, setting out from representations immanent to the empirical consciousness. (The model of this analysis remains, of course, the Humean genealogy of the concept of causality.)

We can begin to understand how the perspective adopted by empiricism within theoretical philosophy clears the way, when it becomes a question of values, and especially aesthetic values, for a veritable "culture of authenticity." If Being is reduced to mere presence within my representations, if truth resides in the final analysis in what I experience within my consciousness, then sentiment is the most authentic state of the subject, since it does not refer or send us back to anything other than itself, and points towards no exteriority. "All sentiment is right; because sentiment has a reference to nothing beyond itself, and is always real, wherever a man is conscious of it. But all determinations of the understanding are not right; because they have a reference to something beyond themselves" (ibid., p. 268), such as the idea of causality which makes us expect the appearance of the effect when we see the cause, thus inciting us to go beyond the order of pure presence.

But, paradoxically,—and it's at this point that Hume's line of argument reverses itself—it is this very immanentism that will establish art's superiority over science, the possibility the beautiful work has to escape relativism to achieve, if not absolute universality, then at least a much more general and more durable consensus than that to which the highest manifestations of scientific or philosophical thought can pretend. For art belongs entirely to the sphere of sentiment, of presence. It does not pretend to supersede the states of consciousness that representations are in order to tell truths about the reality external to its representations. It only aims at the expression of passions common to humanity, and its cardinal virtue is none other than dramaturgical authenticity.

Skeptical irony here upsets the opinion best received by common sense, which willingly accepts scientific objectivity as established but spontaneously concedes the idea that beauty cannot have the dignity of a universal reference. And yet, "Theories of abstract philosophy, systems of profound theology, have prevailed during one age: In a successive period, these have been universally exploded . . . And nothing has been experienced more liable to the revolutions of chance and fashion that these pretended decisions of science. The case is not the same with the beauties of eloquence and poetry. Just expressions of passion and nature are sure, after a little time, to gain public applause, which they maintain for ever." In a word, Descartes's physics may well replace Aristotle's: their victory remains fragile and temporary, "but Terence and Virgil maintain an universal, undisputed empire over the minds of men" (ibid., pp. 279–80).

Where one would have expected that radical immanentism, the reduction of beauty to pure sentiment, led to an absolute relativism, the inverse happens: it is because the expression of sentiment, if it be authentic, cannot mislead, that the Beautiful can be the object of a common sense to which science can not reasonably lay claim. (Cf. Dubos: "That the reputation of a system of philosophy may be destroyed; that of a poem cannot be.")[21] The sensualist relativism that Hume, quite logically, seemed to choose as the starting point for his aesthetic reflections here gives way to a universalism seeking to rejoin—setting out from sentiment and not reason—the major theses of French classicism, the problem being, of course, arriving at whatever will permit, in the last instance, establishing the quasi-universality of the Beautiful.

Though it is true that there exist great variations in taste, since "Beauty is no quality in things themselves: It exists merely in the mind which contemplates them . . . ,"[22] we cannot thereby conclude that "all tastes are equivalent": "Whoever would assert an equality of genius and elegance between Ogilby and Milton, or Bunyan and Addison, would be thought to defend no less an extravagance, than if he had maintained a mole-hill to be as high as Teneriffe, or a pond as extensive as the ocean" (ibid., p. 269). Strangely, then, the idea of a transcendence of the standard of taste over against the individual consciousness reclaims its rights: ". . . the taste of all individuals is not upon an equal footing, and . . . some men in general, however difficult to be particularly pitched upon, will be acknowledged by universal sentiment to have a preference above others" (ibid., p. 279). Besides, it seems clear to Hume—and here he takes up again the idea of a poetic art dear to the classicists—that rules of art exist, and that those rules translate an agreement "concerning what has been universally found to please in all countries and in all ages" (ibid., p. 269). We are here very far from the "each mind perceives a different beauty" of which Hume spoke as if it were obvious.

At the same time as the idea of a transcendence of the criteria of beauty returns, universalism becomes more peremptory: "The same Homer, who pleased at Athens and Rome two thousand years ago, is still admired at Paris and at London. All the changes of climate, government, religion, and language, have not been able to obscure his glory" (ibid., p. 271). How then to reconcile the two instances of such a theory of taste: its rootedness in feeling, which is by essence given to change, and the reemergence of a universalism that concedes nothing to the most rigorous classicism?

The answer can be stated very simply at its most general level: the standard of taste is nothing other than human nature. Human nature being, if we may put it this way, relatively invariable, it will provide the foundation, if not for an absolute universality of taste, at least for its empirical generality within space and time. "It appears then, that, amidst all the variety and caprice of taste, there are certain general principles of approbation or blame, whose influence a careful eye may trace in all operations of the mind. Some particular forms or qualities, from the original structure of the internal fabric, are calculated to please, and others to displease" (ibid., p. 271). If one postulates, with Hume, that men's nature, their "internal fabric," is fundamentally homogeneous— therefore that the container for sense impressions is in principle identical for all men—then variations in taste can only emerge from the fact that this container may be more or less *pure*. (Cf. Dubos: "The sentiment of which I speak is found among all men, but just as they have not all equally good ears and eyes, so have they not all an equally perfect sentiment. Some have it better than others, either because their organs are naturally better made up, or because they have better perfected them through the frequent use they make of them, and through experience.")[23] It's in the criteria that permit evaluation of the greater or lesser purity of human nature that we will have to look not only for the reason for differences of taste but also—the same question seen from a different angle—for the factors which permit us to judge that tastes are not equivalent.* Hume cites five:

1. Aesthetic objectivity requires first of all that the nature in question be sane, the most general principle of variations being the fact that the instruments of judgment, that is the senses, can be more or less well calibrated, or even disorganized, by illness. If the spirit is not serene, if illness makes us incapable of fixing our attention on the object or "confounds the operation of the whole machine" that the sensory organs are, then "our experiment will be fallacious, and we shall be unable to judge of the catholic and universal beauty . . . A man in a fever would not insist on his palate as able to decide concerning flavours; nor would

---

* "But though all the general rules of art are founded only on experience, and on the observation of the common sentiment of human nature, we must not imagine, that on every occasion, the feelings of men will be conformable to these rules." (Hume, "Standard of Taste," p. 270.)

one, affected with the jaundice, pretend to give a verdict with regard to colours."[24]

2. Besides healthy organs, guaranteeing a relative identity of the instruments the aesthetic judgment is based on, delicate and refined organs are called for. To support his thesis, Hume cites a famous anecdote from *Don Quixote* which is worth quoting in full here, since in metaphoric form it contains the ultimate principle of his aesthetic essays:

> It is with good reason, says SANCHO to the squire with the great nose, that I pretend to have a judgment in wine: This is a quality hereditary in our family. Two of my kinsmen were once called to give their opinion of a hogshead, which was supposed to be excellent, being old and of a good vintage. One of them tastes it; considers it; and after mature reflection pronounces the wine to be good, were it not for a small taste of leather, which he perceived in it. The other, after using the same precautions, gives also his verdict in favour of the wine; but with the reserve of a taste of iron, which he could easily distinguish. You cannot imagine how much they were both ridiculed for their judgment. But who laughed in the end? On emptying the hogshead, there was found at the bottom, an old key with a leathern thong tied to it. (Ibid., p. 272)

The anecdote's meaning is twofold: it indicates first of all that Hume's aesthetic model is found, in conformity with the original meaning of the word "taste," in the culinary arts, and that the Beautiful is here reduced to the pleasant. But on the other hand, if the Beautiful is only that which pleases, that which suits the internal, quasi-biological structure of men, its criterion will be provided by the most essentially human constitution, that is by that of the best experts, which will possess, de jure anyway, a certain universality (in the sense that, in so far as it is essential, it should be that of all men).

3. Hence the third criterion, found in the reference to the experts' culture. Besides a talented nature, he who pretends to judge what is beautiful and what is ugly must have cultivated it through the frequentation of works of art, for "though there be naturally a wide difference in point of delicacy between one person and another, nothing tends further to encrease and improve this talent, then *practice* in a particular art, and the frequent survey or contemplation of a particular species of beauty" (ibid., p. 274). Here, the idea that the principle that permits us to theorize the universality of taste at the same time as its relativity is one and the same principle becomes more precise: if there is a universality of taste—as attested by the permanence of Homer's, Terence's, or Virgil's works—it is because the container of impressions that human

nature is is basically the same in all men in all the historical periods. Yet it's undeniable that the human machine, like any machine, is from the beginning more or less perfect, more or less well calibrated and, with the passage of time, it refines, perfects, and adjusts itself, or on the contrary it deteriorates: "Thus, though the principles of taste be universal, and, nearly if not entirely the same in all men; yet few are qualified to give judgment on any work of art, or establish their own sentiment as the standard of beauty" (ibid., p. 278).

4. Thus, to avoid any misunderstanding, a fourth criterion will be added. Though the ultimate foundation of the judgment of taste is human nature, and though this nature and therefore this judgment can be refined and cultivated, we should not thereby confuse culture and prejudice. If it aspires to objectivity, the aesthetic judgment must stay true to its ultimate principle and remain a natural judgment, cultivated of course, but not affected or mannered: "It is well known, that in all questions, submitted to the understanding, prejudice is destructive of sound judgment . . . It is no less contrary to good taste; nor has it less influence to corrupt our sentiment of beauty. It belongs to *good sense* to check its influence in both cases" (ibid., p. 277). To good sense or, as they said in Hume's time, to "common understanding," meaning the capacity to judge as a cultured but nevertheless natural man, substituting for any other human being, outside of the prejudices attendant to such and such specific individual.

5. Consequently, a "sound understanding" (ibid., p. 278) is called for—and with this last criterion Hume once again confirms his attachment to classicism—that is an intelligence acute enough to perceive the sense of the work of art, for "every work of art has also a certain end or purpose, for which it is calculated; and is to be deemed more or less perfect, as it is more or less fitted to attain this end" (ibid., p. 277). Thus is the most classic of aesthetics, the aesthetics of *perfection*, legitimized.

Hume's reflection, far from falling into relativism, leads him to posit, within the realm of law (de jure), the universal value of a "good taste" which in the final analysis tends to be concentrated within an aesthetic aristocracy. We of course still have to examine the problems opened up by this strange conversion by the most skeptical of empiricisms to values—universality, the normative distinction between fact and law—we had expected to see more solidly grounded within a framework of a rationalist philosophy.

In truth, the difficulties come from the fact that the standards of taste are not properly speaking in the mind of the elite made up of the men of taste, but that they are, *strictu sensu,* the men of taste themselves. The experts *are* the standard, they don't *possess* it. Outside of these experts' concrete empirical existence—and the five criteria that distinguish them from ordinary mortals—standards have no reality and nothing permits establishing them by right. Meaning that in aesthetics as in theory Hume's philosophy, in Kant's formula, "rests entirely on purposiveness." Why should there be *one* human nature (represented in its pure form by experts yet still further cultivated by them) and not a *variety* of natures (which would of course permit the granting of an entirely different status to variations in taste)? For Hume's answer to the problem of standards to have any sort of relevance, we have, in fact, to admit that a happy purposiveness has organized human nature following a unifying principle, so that we may think that beyond essentially inessential dissensions, a natural consensus is by right possible. We have therefore to postulate that, through a mysterious preestablished harmony, sense impressions come to agreement within the realm of taste. And even supposing such a harmony to be philosophically admissible—although it remains an entirely gratuitous postulate there where aesthetics is located, that is, at the level of sentiment—we would still have to account for the fact that, after all, Hume doesn't grant the same importance or the same significance to culinary disagreements as he does to artistic ones. But if it's all a matter of sense impressions and more or less well-calibrated containers, why should there be two sets of standards?

An even bigger difficulty adds itself to this first line of questioning. If the standard of taste, and we have seen why, is literally confused with the experts' physical existence in so far as they have a happily suited nature, then it becomes clear that it in fact has no transcendence, or, if you will: the standard's transcendence is purely and simply reduced to the de facto difference existing between the experts and hoi polloi. The de jure question, the question of criteria, thus has a tendency to be integrally reduced to a question of fact, such that in the end the very question about norms or standards disappears. Within Hume's perspective, we should limit ourselves to observing that, the vulgarian having—let's admit it for the sake of argument—a coarse nature and unrefined sensory organs, he has such and such tastes, and the elite, possessing a more elaborate internal constitution, has on the other hand such other tastes. But by what right can we, from what is (at best) a simple observation, strictly empirical and factual, deduce the least embryo of normativity, the most tentative idea of a criterion of taste?

Moreover, in carrying on this way, does not Hume risk—precisely because he can't truly posit the question of right and has to stick to the sphere of fact—constantly mixing up his supposed "human nature" with the rather banal reality of an eighteenth-century bourgeois Scotsman? Unfortunately, Hume rather obviously cannot always avoid this criticism: not only does he denounce Homer and the Greek tragedians for their "want of humanity and of decency" (ibid., p. 282), and two of the most beautiful French tragedies for the "bigotry" which "has disfigured" *Polyeucte* and *Athalie* (ibid.), but he really takes the cake when, out of hatred for the barbarians by the Thames, he does not hesitate to greatly downgrade Shakespeare in favor of the Scottish John Home, an obscure dramatic author whose principal merit seems to have been, besides that of not being English, that of being Hume's friend and cousin, and for that reason to "possess the true theatric genius of ShakeSpear and Otway, refined from the unhappy barbarism of the one, and licentiousness of the other." [25]

Is this a regrettable symptom of Hume's fanatical patriotism? No doubt, but a symptom particularly troublesome for the solution he tries to apply to the problem of the standard of taste: since if this standard simply *is* the men of taste, and if it happens that these men of taste disagree (for example, Hume may think Home great and Shakespeare and Racine rather lousy, but there are doubtlessly "men of taste" who do not share this view), then who is to decide on the discord, and in the name of what? Since within a Humean perspective there is no term external to the experts' judgment, we can't even make out by what right someone could decide that this or that judgment is or is not tainted by prejudice. With every question of right disappearing, the discussability of the beautiful reveals itself to be impossible or at least devoid of meaning and significance in its very principle, *every one being in the end reinstituted in the untransgressable particularism of his monadic individuality.*

Paradoxically, empiricism proves to be no better than the most dogmatic of rationalisms at avoiding the narrow frames of philosophical individualism. The idea of true aesthetic communication, suggested, all the same, by the fact of discussion, can't seem to be able to obtain a legitimate status from world visions within which, in the final analysis, it's up to God—or to a secret "harmony" among beings, anyway, to some term external to humanity—to secure the "common sense."

TURNING POINT: THE FIRST "AESTHETICS"
AND THE FIRST "PHENOMENOLOGY"

Philosophy's history teaches us that the appearance of new terminology is most often, not to say always, the sign of a mutation in the realm of thought. From 1750 to 1764: only fourteen years separate the emergence of two notions whose importance has not stopped being confirmed since. About Baumgarten's *Aesthetics* and Lambert's *Phenomenology* it could be said that, in so far as they both represent specific theories of sensibility—of the sensible or phenomenal world—they are the surest sign of the arrival within philosophy of Enlightenment humanism. No doubt for the first time, the point of view of finite knowledge—strictly human, therefore sense-based—is taken into account for its own sake. It is in this direction that Lambert assigns a twofold task to the discipline for which he has created a new name. Like optics, whose intentions it must generalize, phenomenology must "save the appearances," that is, it must search for the truth behind the often misleading phenomena our senses reveal to us. For example, we must, thanks to astronomy, learn to deduce the real movement of planets from their apparent movement, or to not be taken in by the refraction of rays of sunlight in a liquid. But when the distance from the sense-bound to the true, from the phenomenon to the reality, has been traveled, phenomenology can also go in reverse. Like perspective, it can allow us to go from truth to appearance and create, especially in art, the illusion of reality.

The *Phenomenology* invites its reader to understand these ambiguous relationships between the sensible phenomenon and its truth. Strangely enough, like the *Aesthetics*, it draws its inspiration essentially from Leibniz's philosophy. How could the first two autonomous theories of sensibility have issued out of a form of thought which apparently reduced the sensible world to a form of non-being? It's a question worth going over, otherwise the profound significance of these projects risks going right by us.

LEIBNIZ AND WOLFF: THE EXHAUSTION
OF THE SENSIBLE WORLD

The paradox can be described briefly: Leibniz's and Wolff's metaphysics, to which the *Aesthetics* explicitly adheres, is without a doubt that which takes the Platonic devaluation of the sensible as against the intelligible world the farthest. The sensible, defined as the mere "phenomenal" manifestation of what are in fact entirely intelligible relations between immaterial beings, does not at first sight seem capable of providing the object for a new discipline. Strictly speaking, it has in Leibniz's universe no existence outside the human imagination: The body has no real unity. Its unity proceeds from our perception; it is a being of reason, or rather imagination, a phenomenon.

The meaning of the formula according to which the sensible is but a "confused intelligible"—thus nothing is truly real outside the limited point of view which is man's—can only be correctly interpreted in relation to the Leibnizian theory of objectivity. For reasons we don't need to go into here, Leibniz refused to define a representation's objectivity by way of the link it might have with a material external thing-in-itself. As it will later for Kant, his problem consists in finding within the subject's representations a criterion permitting him to distinguish scientific objectivity from purely subjective fugitive perceptions. As often within the Cartesian tradition, the old problem of the distinction between dream and reality will provide the very example of the general question.

Now, what does Leibniz say about this? His position has the merit of being at the same time quite clear and invariable in the various passages of his works where it is the most strongly expressed: the sensible world—the material world perceived by the senses, within space and time, as being, apparently, exterior to men—has a veritable reality in so far as and only in so far as it translates, though confusedly, a systematic order which can, though at another level, that of the intelligible, be grasped by reason. The truth of sensible things thus resides exclusively in their rational connection—the only type of connection, moreover, perceptible from the viewpoint of the rational being that is God. "The true *criterion* in the matter of the objects of the sciences is the liaison of phenomena, that is to say the connection of what takes place in different places and times." [26]

Under such conditions, it's understandable that the principal task of reason be fundamentally opposed to that of aesthetic creation. If art creates a sensible world and plays upon illusion, science, on the contrary, seeks to unveil the intelligible, that is rational, relations the objects of the senses manifest in confused fashion. Only this way can we attain objectivity since, to cite Leibniz again, "the liaison of phenomena which guarantees the truths of fact about sensible things outside of us is verified by means of the truths of reason, as the appearances of optics become clear through geometry" (ibid.). The meaning of this text, which contains in embryo the project of Lambert's *Phenomenology*, is clear: if appearance is not grounded on reason, if, in other words, it turns out that the objects of the senses are not "well linked," it's because we are dealing with a pure illusion, as is for example the case with dreams. If on the other hand we can find a rational law for the linking of sensible representations, then the latter are "well grounded," they are not pure illusions but "phenomena," that is, etymologically speaking, manifestations of a reality which, though confusedly perceived as sensible, is nonetheless, in itself or from God's viewpoint, intelligible through and through.

Here lies the criterion of distinction between dream and reality. As Wolff's *Ontology* puts it, in its Latin (§ 97–98) as in its German (§ 142) version: "Since such an order cannot be found in dreams in which one cannot, basing oneself on experience, indicate any reason why things should be together and would remain next to each other and why their modification should follow, it appears clearly that it is because of order that truth is different from dreams. Truth is thus nothing else than the order of the modifications of things."

A new paradox: this logistic theory of objectivity in which the sensible is granted a status close to that of non-being is never far from the themes dearest to an aesthetics whose object, however, it reduces to nothingness—indeed, in many ways the artwork is but a well-regulated dream. Besides, Leibniz is perfectly aware of the fact that his criterion of objectivity does not permit the tracing of an absolute separation line between an ordered reality, grasped by reason, and the productions of the imagination. After all, the author of the *Monadology* did not wait for Freud to postulate, together with the existence of an unconscious psychic life (that of "small perceptions"), the fact that it's possible to "account for dreams themselves, and for the little linkage with other phenomena." Let's go further: nothing prevents us from presuming, as a hypothesis, the existence of dreams with the particular characteristic of being entirely coherent and well ordered. The demonstration, if demonstration were still needed, of the degree to which the criterion of objectivity is dissociated in Leibniz from the notion of a sensible world external to the subject, is his argument that, under such conditions, we would have to say that those dreams are reality itself: "It is true also that, as long as the phenomena are well linked, it matters not that one call them dreams or not."

If we consider the abyss that separates the point of view of man from that of God, this radical dissociation of sensibility from being becomes more pronounced and even a veritable opposition. To say that human knowledge is limited compared to God's (who "sees everything") is also to affirm that it can never completely liberate itself from sensibility so as to arrive at a clear and distinct cognition of the rational order our senses always hide from us. *It is because we are beings endowed with sensibility that we cannot raise ourselves up to the point of view from which it would be possible to contemplate the totality of what is, the* sine qua non *condition for another perception of the world's intelligible order.* It is surely not without importance in this respect that Leibniz often chooses, in order to express this human finitude and imperfection, aesthetic metaphors like this one, whose every element is meaningful: "Let us consider a very beautiful painting. Let us hide it completely except for a tiny portion: what shall we see there . . . except a confusing swirl of colors without choice, without art? Yet . . . when we consider the entire picture from a proper center of perspective, we will understand that what seemed to be applied to the canvas by happenstance was for the artist the work of a supreme art" (*Of the Radical Origin of Things,* § 13).

The text depends of course on an analogy: before the world, man is similar to a spectator who only sees a minuscule aspect of the work he's contemplating; the point of view of the totality, the only one from which it's possible to arrive at an adequate perspective, is reserved to God. There where we see a multiplicity of the sensible, confused and chaotic, he "sees" only order and reason; there where we think we perceive a succession of events in time, he only sees an atemporal logical connection (God is the only being who places himself at the viewpoint of the end of history); there where the world seems to us to be extended in space and, in that sense, "external" to us, God sees but an intelligible order of the reciprocal situation of beings who are in truth immaterial. As he was in Plato's cave, Leibniz's man is constantly misled by the manifoldness of the sensible world: "And just as the same city, seen from different sides, seems entirely different and is as it were perspectively multiplied, it happens in the same way that, through the infinite multitude of simple substances, there are just as many different universes which are but the perspectives upon a single one according to the

65

different points of view of each monad" (*Monadology*, § 57). God is precisely he of whom we know, not only that he perceives this multiplicity of sensible perspectives for what it is (an intelligible difference between beings), but also that he integrates it (in the mathematical as in the ordinary sense) within an ordered systematic totality; and, once again as in Plato, only this totality, in so far as it is the intelligible world, can be said to be truly being [*étante*], the sensible world's diversity providing at best its distorted reflection in the human imagination.

We can, under such conditions, very well understand why the project which aims to take an interest in the sensible world as such in order to produce, as an "aesthetics" or a "phenomenology," a specific theory, would seem to be particularly badly grounded in a Leibnizian intellectual framework. It is for this reason that the *Aesthetica* invited many misunderstandings which Baumgarten tried, with very relative success, to dissipate in the first paragraphs of his book. However, and as contradictory as that may sound, Leibniz's philosophy, as Bäumler subtly understood, could also open the way to this new preoccupation.

Leibniz's theodicy turns out to be susceptible to, if not two interpretations, at least to two radically opposed research directions. We can first of all, together with Wolff's orthodoxy, consider that it founds a philosophy that takes us away from sensibility. If truth resides within an intelligible order that only God's point of view can grasp, then we have to, as far as we are capable of doing so, raise ourselves towards this truth, following an inexorable movement from the sensible to the intelligible. Ontology and Theology must be the essential disciplines under these conditions. But on the other hand, if we follow a certain conception of continuity which fundamentally opposes Leibniz to Descartes, we cannot turn away definitively from the sensible world. On the contrary, we may even hold that it is there, and not in God, who is inaccessible, that we must seek to discover this rational order which is its objective substructure. At that point it is the scientific disciplines, in so far as they correspond to man's finite viewpoint, which become central. Thanks to astronomy, optics, to the different branches of geometry, etc., we learn to discover the intelligible connections there where they are visible *for us*, that is, at the heart of the sensible world. From God's point of view we go over to man's and, following a logic we have already invoked, it's with this turnabout that the problem of the status of sensibility becomes so crucial that philosophy can no longer evade it even if it were inclined to do so. Witness Lambert's *Phenomenology* and, especially, the *Aesthetica*.

THE AMBIGUITIES OF THE *AESTHETICA*: TOWARDS
THE AUTONOMY OF THE SENSIBLE

Upon first reading, Baumgarten's aesthetics seem to place themselves within the tradition of Wolffian intellectualism. This is borne out notably by the definition of beauty as "perfection perceived by the senses" or *perfectio phenomenon* (§ 662 of the *Metaphysica*)—a very classical definition within the Wolffian school[27] and one Leibniz had already suggested in a passage of his essay on wisdom[28] and which Meier, Baumgarten's main disciple, makes explicit in these terms in section 23 of his *First Principles of All Sciences of the Beautiful* [*Anfangsgründe aller schönen Wissenschaften*], text written in 1748, before the publication of the *Aesthetica*, but in awareness of it since Meier had followed Baumgarten's courses: "That beauty in general is a perfection in as much as this perfection is known in confused or sensible fashion, is today a thing agreed upon by all serious connoisseurs of the beautiful."

The danger of such a conception of the beautiful, based entirely on an assimilation of the sensible to the vague or confused, is obvious, as Mendelssohn, as a good Leibnizian, remarks in his "Essay on Sensations," a "confused or sensible" knowledge of perfection remains in every way inferior to a clear and distinct knowledge of this *same* perfection,[29] so that one could be led to see in paragraph 662 of the *Metaphysica* an obstacle to the very idea of an autonomous discipline entitled "aesthetica."

Baumgarten tries to point out another way with his notion of *analogon rationis*, to which I will return. But this alternative is not without ambiguity on this decisive question of the nature of the beautiful. The title of one of the main chapters, "Aesthetic Truth" [*Veritas aesthetica*], seems to imply a subsumption of aesthetics to logic, of the sensible world to the intelligible world, an impression reinforced when reading the paragraphs consecrated to the definition of this truth which Baumgarten still calls "aesthetico-logical," as if to underline the parallels between the two competing disciplines. The criteria which permit the determination of aesthetic truth are thus strictly borrowed from theoretical philosophy. We can distinguish three: possibility or noncontradiction, conformity to the principle of reason, and unity.

Aesthetic truth requires in effect "the possibility of objects of elegant thought," meaning that in them there should not be "characteristic traits which are mutually contradictory" (§ 431)—where we recognize the Leibnizian definition of *absolute* possibility to which Baumgarten, in quite orthodox fashion, adds *hypothetical* (§ 432) and *moral* (§ 433) possibilities.

To this first requirement, which takes care of the principle of contradiction, is added that which emanates from the principle of sufficient reason and which demands of the beautiful object that it be well grounded and well linked, "according to reasons and consequences" (§ 437). If it is, for example, a narrative, for it to be beautiful its sequences will have to follow the order of reasons, so that nothing in it will appear incoherent; the model in Baumgarten's eyes being Livy's *Coriolanus:* "His very name and the origin of his authority are explained; therefrom his excessive pride before the tribune's power; hence the rabble's anger; the result being Coriolanus's exile . . ." etc. In a word, the *reasons* that explain the action should be completely *perceptible.*

The third and last requirement, of *unity*, is deduced from the first two: the objects of the beautiful thought must possess unity since the characteristics reflection discerns in them are simultaneously noncontradictory and well linked, through which Baumgarten brings together not only the Leibnizian saying that that which is not *one* being is not a *Being*, but also the hallowed classical rule of the three unities: "This unity of objects, which is an aesthetic unity to the extent to which it is found at the level of phenomena, will be unity of internal determinations, and thereby unity of ACTION, if the object of the meditation on the beautiful is an action, or else unity of external determinations and of relations, of circumstances, and thereby unity of PLACE and of TIME" (§ 439).

Reading these texts, one could get the feeling of moving about in a classical framework in which the beautiful is defined as a function of the same criteria which permit picking out the true, beauty being in the end but the *sensible presentation of a logical perfection.* That Baumgarten's philosophical model is, unlike what was the case with the French classicists, Leibnizian rather than Cartesian does not seem to alter this diagnosis in any way; on the contrary, it's as if Leibniz's rationalism, more radical and more complete than that of Descartes, comes into aesthetics only the more to lengthen the list of claims to rationality the beautiful object must make to deserve its name.

Let's say it right off: such a reading of the *Aesthetica,* however accepted it may have been even among Baumgarten's disciples, is not only mistaken, it quite simply misses the general direction of Baumgarten's project, which can be put thus: How, while starting out from Leibniz's and Wolff's philosophy, to nevertheless grant a consistency all its own to the phenomenal sphere of the sensible, and grant therefore to aesthetics its autonomy in relation to its "elder sister," logic (§ 13), and thereby affirm the pertinence of an effective incorporation of the viewpoint of this finite being that is man? Baumgarten's basic idea is that, in so far as man could not perceive the world otherwise than through the categories of sensibility, there exists within him an *analogon rationis,* a faculty or collection of faculties that is the analogue for the sensible world of what reason is for the intelligible world. Correlatively, if we situate ourselves on the side of the object and no longer on that of the faculties of the subject, there must be, on the plane of the sensible world, forms and sequences or relations between these forms which are, not identical, but *analogous* to the rational forms (ideas) and the relations between these forms as reason perceives them on the plane of the intelligible world. It's because of the creation of this notion of *analogon rationis,* at times very difficult to follow through the winding paths of the *Aesthetica,* that Baumgarten eventually distances himself from the orthodox theses of the Wolffian school and even comes to oppose them on certain essential points.

Let's begin at the beginning, the definition of aesthetics given in section 1 of the *Aesthetica.* We cannot understand it correctly if we read it through the Wolff school's glasses: "Aesthetics (theory of the liberal arts, doctrine of inferior knowledge, art of the beautiful thought, art of the analogue of reason) is the science of sensible knowledge." The important thing about this definition—if what we are looking for is its originality—is not the fact that it continues, in Leibniz's and Wolff's wake, to hold that a theory of sensible knowledge is inferior and therefore qualifies aesthetics as *gnoseologia inferior,* but that, by putting in place the concept of *analogon rationis,* the project of a science of the sensible as such becomes possible, thus legitimating the idea that man's point of view as a limited being is also worthy of a particular consideration. This new perspective, inverted in relation to the seventeenth century's, will leave an important inheritance, not only among Baumgarten's immediate disciples—such as Meier, who in 1755 writes his *Observations on the Limits of Human Knowledge* [*Betrachtungen über die Schranken der menschlichen Erkenntnis*]—but also and especially in Lambert's *Phenomenology,* whose project seemed to Kant to be so important that for a while he too thought of giving the *Critique of Pure Reason* the title of "phenomenology."

Baumgarten's aesthetics constitutes in this sense a real paradox, and we can understand how it could have so often lent itself to reductive readings: how, indeed, to interpret an itinerary that begins from a Leibnizian philosophical position that holds the highest theoretical viewpoint, God's, to be by essence above the sensible world, finally to legitimate an interest in knowledge of a sphere, that of sensibility, which everything, it seems, should lead the philosopher to neglect?

Baumgarten is quite aware of the difficulty since the main part of the "prolegomena" to the *Aesthetica* is consecrated to answering the objections an orthodox Wolffian could raise against it. These objections bear upon the subject studying this new discipline as on its object: "To our science, one could object that the impressions of the senses, the products of the imagination, the fables, the disturbances of the passions, etc., are unworthy of philosophers . . . I answer: the philosopher is a man among men," (§ 6) which means that, rather than to try for an impossible coincidence with God's point of view, he ought to take an interest in what constitutes the object or in any case the uncircumventable medium of all his knowledge: the sensible. "One could still object that confusion is the mother of error. My answer is that it is the *sine qua non* condition of the discovery of truth" (§ 7). The *Aesthetica's* paradoxical situation becomes clearer; the philosopher can, no doubt, neglect the knowledge of the senses and turn exclusively towards intellectual, clear and distinct knowledge of the universal; that way he comes closer to God. But if he wishes to remain "among men"—what he can't avoid anyway (§ 557)—he must plunge into the sensible particular and try to seize the individual. That is another consequence of the same principle of continuity: as section 7 of the *Aesthetica* insists upon, confused knowledge is an integral part of true knowledge for "nature does not jump from darkness to clarity. It is thus through dawn that we travel from night to noon."

Throughout these responses to possible objections coming from the Wolffian school we make out, from the very first lines of the *Aesthetica*, the will to grant the sensible an autonomy for which the idea of *analogon rationis* quite exactly defines the nature and limits. The notion of "aesthetico-logical" truth refers back to this idea and not, as one might have thought on first reading, to the confusion of the two domains, even less to a reduction of the first, aesthetics, to the second.

To better grasp what Baumgarten understands by *analogon rationis* we must discern how he distinguishes the inferior faculties that make up this *analogon rationis* from the superior faculties, understanding and reason. Baumgarten in many ways takes up again and extends the domain Wolff, in his *Empirical Psychology* (part 1, § 2), had already designated as that of thinking "similar to reason." But from "similar" to "analogous" is a considerable step, one determined precisely in section 640 of Baumgarten's *Metaphysica*. The inferior faculties—the *analogon rationis*—comprehend "(1) the inferior faculty of knowing what is identical between things; (2) the inferior faculty of knowing what is different between things; (3) the sensitive memory; (4) the poetic faculty [*facultas figendi, Vermögen zu dichten*]; (5) the evaluative faculty [*facultas di judicandi, Beurteilungsvermögen*]; (6) the expectation of similar cases; (7) the sensual faculty of designation [*facultas characteristica sensitiva, das sinnliche Bezeichnungsvermögen*]."

These faculties have in common that they apprehend the relations among the things of the sensible world. Taken together as such they constitute the *analogon rationis:* like reason (and unlike the understanding) they work to produce objectivity by interlinking representations. Here again we need to go back to Wolff's *Empirical Psychology* (§ 29 and § 233), which distinguishes three levels:

—that, first of all, of the inferior faculties (of which Baumgarten would eventually make, as we have seen, through various modifications,[30] the *analogon rationis*): the senses, the imagination, the poetic faculty [*facultas figendi*], memory;

—that of the understanding [*intellectus, Verstand*], which comprehends attention, reflection, the faculty of abstraction and of comparison. The understanding is by nature part of the superior faculties since its representations are distinct (the concept of distinction [clarity] thus traces the dividing line between inferior and superior faculties);

—that, finally, of reason [*ratio, Vernunft*], which is the faculty of connection or linkage [*nexus, Zusammenhang*] between representations and which, as such, engenders objectivity properly speaking—which is why, while the understanding arrives at logical truth, reason introduces us into the sphere of transcendental or metaphysical truths.

The *Aesthetica* works out an original philosophy by taking up this Wolffian classification with the aim of forging its concept of *analogon rationis*. The beautiful will first of all be defined—and it's in this that it corresponds to the faculty, the *analogon rationis*, which will grasp it—as a *sensual linkage of representations* or, to use the future Kantian vocabulary, as a "legality without concept." Hence the formula that comes back again and again under Baumgarten's pen: aesthetics certainly deals with truth, but with truth *quatenus sensitive cognoscendae est*, "in so far as it is known sensually"; which means that there exists a legality proper to the sensible or an "aesthetico-logical" objectivity. The expression enjoys here its full meaning: "The truth of true things in its strictest sense is aesthetic in so far as these things are sensually perceived as true through sensations, images, or even anticipations connected to forebodings, and there ends its domain" (§ 444). Such linkages or representations can only be grasped by a faculty close to reason. But since the linkages are sensual, therefore confused and not intelligible, it cannot be reason itself, and we must here have recourse to an *analogon rationis* as defined by the inferior faculties evoked in section 640 of the *Metaphysica*.

Therefrom a third thesis which also singularly anticipates the main themes of the *Critique of Judgment* and initiates a true synthesis between classicism and the aesthetics of sentiment: the beautiful is halfway between the rational and the ordinary sensible. In its confused aspect it is of course the opposite of reason, but to the extent it is a linkage of representations it nears "metaphysical" truths. *Analogon veritatis,* it can only be grasped by an *analogon rationis*. Beauty is *perfectio cognitionis sensitivae* [perfection of sensual knowledge], a formula perfectly commented on by Bäumler: "*cognitio* refers to unity, *sensitivus* to plenitude (diversity, material richness) and *perfectio* means nothing other than the elevation of these two moments of sensual knowledge as such: this does not at all mean a rationalist/metaphysical theory but simply the fact that sensual knowledge possesses its own perfection. The representations of the imagination and of the senses are capable of having their own unity and their own connections" (ibid., p. 229).*

The beautiful object can thus belong to the domain unknown to Cartesianism for the same reason it ignores the principle of continuity—the domain of the verisimilar:

I think it has already become clear that much of what is represented in the beautiful thought-act is neither completely certain nor can it be perceived as to

---

* Cf. also: "Baumgarten had two great ideas: first, that the aesthetic object is individual (as is "taste"). Thereby the *specific* task of art in relation to (generalizing) science is acknowledged . . . The aesthetic object, so may we clarify the idea, is not a scientific object, but it is all the same an *object*. It is not surrendered to the subject's arbitrariness but to a determination analogous to that of reason. If we bind these two ideas together: the aesthetic object combines individuality with legality. That is the meaning of the formula: beauty is the perfection of sensual knowledge." (Ibid., p. 231.)

its truth under full illumination. Yet from a sensible point of view nothing false can be discovered without repugnance. That in which we cannot arrive at a perfect certainty without for all that discovering falseness there is the verisimilar. In its essential signification, aesthetic truth can thus be said to be verisimilar: it has that degree of truth which, if it does not imply a complete certainty, does not however permit us to discern any type of falseness." (§ 483)

We can therefore better understand that the goal of aesthetics, in so far as its object is sensual perfection, is not so much truth (§ 428), which is necessarily abstract and general (§ 557), as the quest of the individual in its specific diversity and richness. What the aesthetician aims for, as Baumgarten puts it in one of his favorite formulas, is the "most possible determined determination of the individual" or, as expressed in his *Meditations:* he seeks the *extensive clarity* of representations, meaning the most complete possible enumeration of a representation's characteristics,[31] while the scientist aims for *intensive clarity,* obtained by considering only one characteristic and decomposing it into simple elements (the search for truth requiring, according to Leibniz, that we go from composites to simples).

That is one of the decisive aspects through which the *Aesthetica* distances itself from the tasks traditionally assigned to philosophy by Wolff's school of thought. To better grasp its importance, we need to keep in mind the distinction Leibniz makes, in his *Meditationes de veritate, cognitione et ideia,* between clear representations and distinct representations.

Clarity ensues from the enumeration of characteristics: a table may be red, square, big, etc. This type of clarity, called extensive by Baumgarten, is not at all specific to scientific activity. It is on the contrary, intrinsic to ordinary knowledge and permits it to grasp the *individual* to the extent to which one individual stands out from the others the moment we have enumerated, be it at an entirely empirical level, its principal characteristics. The more we elaborate extensive clarity the better do we reach the individual in all its sensual richness and diverseness. This type of clarity will interest the aesthetician for it gives life to the beautiful object.

Distinct knowledge, the intensive clarity intrinsic to scientific knowledge, refers to an inverse procedure that does not aim at enumerating external sensible properties: after having separated out the various characteristics (using attention), it abstracts out inessential traits, singles out shared points and main differences with the intention of hammering out general concepts (species and genera). This faculty permitting us to grasp identities and differences will be named "reflection" by Wolff—reflection being "the mode through which we arrive at distinct knowledge."

This simple classification, apparently quite scholastic, actually has great philosophical importance for aesthetics. It raises first of all a problem whose solution allows us to better understand the exact nature of the *analogon rationis*. In the quest for distinct knowledge, the understanding, which is more or less a *formal* faculty of classification, quickly becomes *reason,* a transcendental faculty generating objectivity. Why this happens in Leibniz's system is easily understood. Once the simple elements have been sorted out and the general concepts have been created, all the work of the understanding, we discover the intelligible foundation of characteristics and the *reason* for their concatenation (for this interlinking which actually constitutes them as objects). Now—and this is the problem I was talking about—if aesthetics is interested in extensive clarity, if therefore it stays with the mere empirical analysis of representations, one fails to see what in it could play the role of an *analogon rationis* or indeed what the need could be for such a faculty. The solution is as follows: The beautiful is no doubt found in the wealth, the variety, the vivacity of characteristic traits; but this wealth is organized, those traits are bound to one another following a legality which is not that of reason but is—or that at least is the fundamental postulate of the *Aesthetica*—intrinsic to the sensible sphere. For example, in a poetical description we certainly come across an enumeration of traits, but the rhetorical modalities of this enumeration are as important as its richness. Or again, when a metaphor substitutes certain characteristics with others, it most certainly creates a symbolic link whose "logic," if we can say that, is not that of reason but that of aesthetics.

The definition of the poem—*oratio sensitiva perfecta est poema*[32]— as the "sensual perfection of discourse" indicates a conception of beauty that integrates two elements: *diversity* (or, vivacity, the richness of the concrete particular brought to a high degree of extensive clarity) and the *interlinkings* of this diversity in their quality of *sensual* linkages (which is why they are cognized by the *analogon rationis* and not by reason).

In certain ways the *Aesthetica* will take the opposite direction from that of philosophy; it cannot and should not abstract out the sensible particular; as the *Meditations* put it, "What is poetical in the poem is the fact of determining the things to be represented as much as possible" (§ 18). And "individual [things and persons] are determined in every way, therefore the particular representations are always poetic" (§ 19).

One passage of the *Aesthetica* expresses in striking fashion this opposition between the theoretical research method leading to the general and the path of aesthetics which, on the contrary, aims at absolute determination, at individuality. Describing how logic arrives at general concepts—activity he judges, of course, excellent as far as it goes—Baumgarten adds:

Yet the question arises as to whether *metaphysical* truth is equivalent to universal concept in so far as it corresponds to the individual object contained in such a concept. In what concerns myself, I think it should be perfectly clear to a philosopher that all that is contained in formal specific perfection in knowledge and in logical truth has only been obtained at the price of a considerable loss in material perfection. To take a comparison: one can transform an irregular block of marble into a ball only at the price of a loss of material substance corresponding at least to the high value of the regular round form. (§ 560; "high value" here meaning as seen from a logical, not an aesthetic, point of view).

A clear-cut consequence comes out of this comparison: "We begin then with the presupposition that efforts to attain aesthetico-logical truth direct themselves especially towards metaphysical material truth and that they thus seek to grasp the objects of a determinate metaphysical truth, as much as is possible, up to the individual" (§ 561).[33] "As much as is possible" because, as Baumgarten well knows, it is impossible to arrive distinctly at the individual for the same reasons that we cannot, as finite beings, grasp the highest logical truths.[34] But the quest for individuality in the sphere of aesthetics does not mean that "everything" need be put into a picture or a poem and that a microscopic realism could be the guarantee of beauty. The *Aesthetica* is not the French New Novel's forerunner. As he reads the *Aeneid,* the aesthetician will "neither think about nor care about the question of knowing with which foot Aeneas first touched Italy; and yet, it is very true, he did touch it with either the left or the right foot, unless he did it with both feet, which is less convenient" (§ 30).[35]

Worth is laid upon the individual, upon that which escapes the concept—for example on the *first name,* which the *Meditations* affirm as poetic for the sole reason that it refers back to a unique representation (§ 89; a theme often reconsidered in German thought up to and including Walter Benjamin)—but the artist should not for all that renounce the aesthetic unity of the various without which the beautiful object would not even be an object. This aspect of the *Aesthetica* opens up to another dimension, the one that is Kant's main concern in the *Critique of Judgment:* the beautiful object, although nonconceptual, must have the potential of being the object of a *communication,* and interest in the individual must not lead, as is too often the case in the aesthetics of sentiment, to a monadic withdrawal of subjectivity into itself. It's because the beautiful object has its own laws and epistemological status [*une légalité propre*] as well as a unity of the diversity of its characteristic traits that it can be communicated. It ceases thereby to be strictly subjective and acquires, if not conceptual objectivity, at least a sensual objectivity which is its exact analogue.

The *Aesthetica* gave a philosophical formulation to the themes already encountered, in a more literary form, in the French debates between classicism and the aesthetics of sentiment. With the artist's search for the *individual* or *particular,* we enter a realm Cartesian reason cannot grasp, which we may call the realm of the irrational or, borrowing from the vocabulary of aesthetics, the realm of "mystery," of delicacy, or of the "I-know-not-what." But with Baumgarten, the mediation between reason and unreason, between the universal and the individual begins to work itself out, thanks not only to the effects of the continuity principle but mainly to the idea of *analogy,* which as we have seen permits us to build a bridge between the sensible and the intelligible worlds. (This is the thesis at the heart of Bäumler's book.) For such a bridge to become a real necessity, however, the separation of the two worlds must also be truly secure. That is a task which Baumgarten, despite his project's boldness and originality, could not accomplish within the framework of a Leibnizian philosophy.

THREE

The Kantian Moment: The Subject of Reflection

U NTIL KANT, modern philosophy remained, despite Baumgarten's and Lambert's efforts, dominated by a Cartesian conception of the inherent limits of human knowledge. Finitude is thought of in relation to an absolute reference: the idea of an omniscience supposedly entirely entrusted to the divinity. It's by reference to this supposed divine omniscience that human knowledge is said to be limited and that the mark of this limit, sensibility, is relativized so that aesthetics can never truly free itself and become autonomous from logic and metaphysics. The Kantian moment is, seen from this angle, a veritable revolution, a switching around of perspectives unprecedented in the history of thought. In the *Critique of Pure Reason,* and especially in its first part, the "Transcendental Aesthetic," Kant invites us to reverse the relation that existed between finiteness and the Absolute since the dawn of modern metaphysics. Instead of *first* positing the Absolute in order to *then* situate the human condition within the order of lesser Being, of limitation, Kant begins with finitude to then go up, but only as a second step, toward the Absolute. In other words, the simple fact that our consciousness is always already sensually limited by a world exterior to it, a world it did not create, is the first fact, the one from which we must set out to envisage anew all of metaphysics' traditional questions. Man is a radically finite being, and without this finitude he would not be endowed with representations and consciousness, if it is true, as Husserl puts it later, that "all consciousness is consciousness of something" which limits it. The ultimate consequence of this reversal: the metaphysical pretention to know the absolute, to grasp the ultimate essence of the cogito or to demonstrate God's existence, is relativized in relation to the initial affirmation of the limited or sensible condition which is necessarily that of human consciousness. It will no longer be possible to relativize sensual knowledge and define it as lesser being, as confusion, in the name of the divine figure of an entirely intelligible Absolute; on the contrary, in the name of the unsurpassable finitude which is the sign of all real, nonillusory knowledge, the divine figure of the Absolute is in turn relativized and brought down to the rank of a simple "Idea" of reason whose objective reality is forever indemonstrable by theory.

In this reversal there are two implications for the status of the divine and for that of the sensible, whose intimate connection we must grasp in order to understand the philosophical foundations of Kant's aesthetic theory.

THE IDEALITY OF THE DIVINE AND THE ARRIVAL OF MAN

The first implication concerns God's status to the extent that his existence as the site of omniscience and eternal truths is, in modern metaphysics, the object of a demonstration. What Kant denounces in rationalist metaphysics is not the definition of God as the holder of an unlimited knowledge. Nothing, indeed, prevents us from thinking out *negatively,* in opposition to our finite understanding, the idea of an infinite understanding for whom being and thought, real and rational, would be but one. What is questioned is "merely" the pretension of demonstrating the existence of such a being through ontological argument. Here we must bring to mind, be it only briefly, the critique that the "Transcendental Dialectic" develops on this topic.

In its most rationalist formulation, the ontological argument, in Kant's presentation of it, takes the following form: the concept of God as perfect and necessary being contains all reality. "Now, in all reality existence [*das Dasein*] is also included: thus existence is contained within the concept of a possible being. If this thing is abolished, abolished as well is the inner possibility of this thing, which is contradictory."[1] According to the ontological argument, we could thus conclude, from the simple analysis of the concept of God, his real existence. Kant's objection is well known. It consists in stating that the logical possibility, that is, a concept's noncontradictory character, does not in any way guarantee its objectivity since, in one of the *Critique*'s celebrated propositions, "Being is evidently no real predicate, meaning a concept of something which could join itself to the concept of a thing" (ibid., p. 400). In other words, admitting the Idea of God as a necessary Idea of human reason, admitting even that the idea of his existence necessarily joins the Idea of God, it is nonetheless the case that this existence remains an ideal existence, an existence only in thought, not a real existence. The fact that I have the idea of a necessarily existing being proves nothing about the real existence of that being. Hence the new meaning accorded to the idea of God by the *Critique of Pure Reason:*

So, the transcendental and only determinate concept of God that speculative reason gives us is, in the strictest sense, deistic: reason never even provides us with the objective validity of such a concept . . . from which it becomes clear that the idea [of such a being], like all speculative ideas, says nothing more than that Reason commands us to regard all connections in the world following principles of a systematic unity, even as if they had all been engendered from one sole all-encompassing Being [*Wesen*] as highest and all-sufficient cause. Hence it is clear that Reason could not have as its goal anything other than its own formal rule in the extension of its empirical use, never an extension *beyond all limits of empirical usage.* (Ibid., pp. 445, 451–52)

The idea of God thus has, from a theoretical point of view, no objectivity. (It would of course be a different matter if we adoped the "practical" standpoint, that of morality.) But such an idea still invites us, as scientists (and no longer as metaphysicians), to look at the universe *as if* it were a systematic, coherent all, created by an intelligent author. The idea of an omniscient understanding, of an achieved knowledge of the universe, maintains a regulating function for our finite knowledge. It's in relation to that idea that scientific progress makes sense, for example. As Kant puts it in an essential text we must quote and comment on: *

I maintain that: transcendental Ideas are never of constitutive usage, so that the concepts of certain things might be given through them, and should they be understood this way they are but sophistical [dialectical] concepts. [*According to the critique of the ontological argument, although it is the necessary idea of a being to which we attribute existence, the idea of God is nonetheless a mere Idea of reason, whose objectivity is rigorously proven by nothing. The ontological argument that would have us believe we can go on from the concept of God to the affirmation of his existence is only a sophism.*] They have on the other hand an outstanding regulative use, which is indispensably necessary for directing the understanding toward a certain aim. With that aim in prospect, the directional lines of all rules of the understanding meet in one point, which serves to give them the greatest unity together with their greatest spread, although that point is only an idea [*focus imaginarius*] from which concepts of

* My commentary is in italics, bracketed.

the understanding do not actually emanate, as it lies completely outside the boundaries of possible experience. (Ibid., pp. 426–27)

In a word, in order to progress, the understanding's activity—the activity of science—needs to refer to the idea of God, to the idea of omniscience, even though we have admitted the nonobjective character of this idea. It does, after all, bestir and direct knowledge by continuously demanding of it, not only that it should seek to render the world more and more intelligible, but also to organize itself, as far as possible, into a more and more coherent and systematic totality. The withdrawal of the divine thus manifests itself by a *secularization of the idea of God in the realm of the theory of knowledge.* Against the background of this secularization we can situate the revalorization of sensibility which will lead Kant to make plain the autonomy of the aesthetic sphere in relation to the intelligible world.

THE AUTONOMY OF AESTHETICS

In the Platonic philosophical tradition, but also within Christianity, sensibility has been systematically denigrated in favor of the intelligible. That is, in any case, the thesis defended, sometimes humorously, by Nietzsche, as in this passage from *The Twilight of the Idols:* "These senses, *which are so immoral in other ways too,* deceive us concerning the *true* world. Moral: let us free ourselves from the deception of the senses, from becoming, from history, from lies; history is nothing but faith in the senses, faith in lies. Moral: let us say 'No!' to all who have faith in the senses." Nietzsche speaks here from Socrates' and Christ's point of view in order to mock them both. His argument against philosophy is a "genealogical" one. It suggests, as the section I've put in italics indicates, that in reality it was because they feared *sensuality* that philosophers and moralists condemned *sensibility* in the name of the primacy of the intelligible. Without following the path of genealogy, the *Critique of Pure Reason* leads, in the "Transcendental Aesthetic" chapter, to a critique of Leibnizian rationalism which in many ways foresees Nietzsche's position.

We have seen how, for Leibniz, from God's point of view, thus from the point of view of an omniscient being, the relations which seem spatio-temporal to us are in truth purely logical and intelligible. From God's viewpoint the sensible has no real existence and space is but a conceptual order, that of the simultaneous coexistence of beings. Similarly, time has for God no real existence. It is only a system of logical, not chronological, relations: the system of the succession of beings—if the term "succession" still makes any sense here (anthropomorphism is difficult to get rid of). For Kant, on the contrary, the point of view of finitude should not be relativized in relation to an infinite divine understanding, for the simple reason that that understanding is only a point of view of human reason, an Idea. Therefore, the principal characteristic of human knowledge, the fact that it is always bound to sensibility, to intuition, should not be relativized and, as such, devalorized, either. Human, sensible reason, is not lesser than that of God; it is the only possible knowledge, which is exactly why divine knowledge, the infinite understanding, is reduced to the status of an Idea of reason. We could say that the withdrawal of the divine and the revalorization of sensibility "express each other"; we begin with the one to arrive at the other and reciprocally. It is because knowledge is always tied to sensible intuition that the notion of omniscience is expelled to the realm of metaphysical illusion, and it's because this latter notion is expelled to the realm of illusion that sense-based knowledge must finally acquire its full entitlement to legitimacy.

As Kant stresses, the *Critique of Pure Reason* can be read both ways, going from the "Aesthetic" to the "Dialectic" or from the "Dialectic" to the "Aesthetic." We therefore have to be very attentive to the way in which Kant, in the "Transcendental Aesthetic," seeks to demonstrate the nonconceptual—sensible and intuitive—character of the notions of space and of time. His argument, aimed directly at Leibniz and at his reduction of sensibility to a "confused intelligible," might seem purely formal, but in fact it touches upon one of the profoundest questions in the history of philosophy, that of the status of the irrational, of the nonconceptual. They divide up into two moments whose meaning and significance we can briefly indicate.

"Space is no discursive or, as it is said, general concept of the relations of things, but a pure intuition. For first of all one can only represent a single space to oneself, and when one speaks of many spaces one understands by that only parts of one and the same space. Furthermore these parts cannot precede this one all-encompassing space as their component parts (so that their aggregate could be possible) but are only thinkable as existing in it" (ibid., p. 53). This first aspect of the argument has to do with the nature of both the totality and the continuity which characterize space (and time). It can be interpreted in the following way. Every concept is, always, a synthesis of preexisting properties or elements; in the concept, totalization and continuity are obtained through the aggregation of parts. For space and for time, on the contrary, it is totality and continuity that precede the parts since, to borrow Husserl's vocabulary, the parts of space are thought of against the *horizon* of an ungraspable totality, as limitations coming after this totality.

The argument's second moment is, so to speak, complementary. It is contained in one formula: "Space is represented as an infinite given magnitude" (ibid.), which sufficiently proves its nonconceptual character: no concept encompasses in its very signification the measure of its extension. The definition of the concept "table" does not inform us of the number of tables existing in the world. But the representation of space is connected to the idea of the infinity of its parts. More than that, the infinity of space is antecedent, coming before the parts "cut out" of it.

This line of argument, which brings Kant to challenge Leibniz's formulation of the Principle of the Identity of Indiscernibles, leads him to introduce irrationality (nonconceptuality) into the heart of human knowledge. What is outside the concept, what radically evades all attempt at rationalization, or even explanation, is the fact that things are given us *hic et nunc*, in space and time. This thesis will find its way into Husserl's and Heidegger's phenomenology. By affirming the sensible's autonomy from the concept, it challenges the most basic presuppositions of traditional metaphysics.

CRITICAL PHILOSOPHY AND PHENOMENOLOGY

The connection that unites the phenomenological tradition to critical philosophy can be made still more useful and exact. It will enable us to better appreciate the importance of Kant's aesthetics within the general history of the link between the autonomization of the sensible and the eclipse of the metaphysical figure of the divine.

In *What is Metaphysics?*, Heidegger distinguishes and opposes two different notions of the totality of beings or of the existent [*seiend, étant*]. As he asks himself about the meaning of nothingness, understood as the "radical negation of the totality of the existent,"[2] Heidegger remarks that the notion of the "totality of the existent" brings up a special problem: "how should we, who are essentially finite, make the whole of beings penetrable in themselves and especially for us? We can of course conjure up the whole of beings in an 'idea.'"

The totality of beings thus appears to be accessible only in the mode of the imaginary, only in the mode of the "Idea." Heidegger uses the term "Idea" here in its Kantian sense: a "thought" or "thinking" of the totality which can never become "knowledge," which can never be "presented." Thus, the negation of such an ideal totality does not put us in the presence of Nothingness or the nothing, but only in the presence of a nothing itself imagined or ideal: "In this way do we attain the formal concept of the imagined nothing but never the nothing itself" (ibid.).

Heidegger does not here develop the reasons why the totality of beings is only accessible in the mode of the Idea. He only indicates that that is how it is for us "finite beings." He does however specify that there is another way of grasping the totality, it consists in "finding oneself in the midst of beings as a whole": "In the end an essential distinction prevails between comprehending the ensemble of beings in themselves and finding oneself in the midst of beings as a whole." This is an allusion to the notion of "Being-in-the-world" that was developed in *Being and Time*. We feel ourselves to be in the midst of the ensemble of beings when we see that each thing "gives" or unveils itself against a background, and this background is in turn unveiled against another background, so that from background to background and from horizon to horizon it is impossible to ever arrive at an ultimate, final foundation. It is in this process that we experience the nothing, the experience of anxiety, this nonpsychological feeling of the radical contingency of beings: "In the slipping away of beings only this 'no hold on things' comes over us and remains. Anxiety reveals the nothing" (ibid.). Thus, it is by virtue of a certain grasp of the totality that we experience the feeling of anxiety, of finitude, of the nothing, of non-being, that is to say, of Being. But at the same time we understand why we "finite beings" can only grasp the ensemble of beings in themselves through an Idea. It is in fact the second way of grasping the totality of beings (the "finding oneself in the midst of beings as a whole") which prevents the first way from being anything other than an Idea (in the Kantian sense).

We can convince ourselves easily that these two notions of totality are borrowed from Kant if we recall, first of all what Kant understands by Idea, then the definitions he gives of "infinite given magnitudes." Kant stated with great clarity in the *Prolegomena to All Future Metaphysics* (1783) the thesis that "the totality of all possible experience is not itself an experience," yet remains for reason "a necessary task [*Aufgabe*] whose mere representation requires concepts entirely different from the pure concepts of the understanding." What the Idea represents can never be given in intuition; it is thus negatively defined as a "necessary concept of reason to which no adequate object can be given through the senses." Positively considered, Ideas only point to a "problem," a task; it's in this that they have a regulative usage aimed at setting up a system defined as the "unity of various fields of knowledge under one Idea."[3] Transcendental ideas thus aim at constituting a system of experience to which they invite the understanding. This systematic totality, which would be made up of the successive accretion of the beings constructed by science itself, always remains an Idea, meaning a "task" to accomplish or, as the third *Critique* puts it, a "principle of reflection."

But there is yet another way of grasping the totality, the one aimed for in the definition of space and time as "infinite given magnitudes." In a chapter of the *Critique of Pure Reason* entitled "On the Amphiboly of the Concepts of Reflection," space and time are categorized as forms of "nothing" [*ens imaginarium*]. They are indeed, for a simple reason, nothing in consciousness. For there to be consciousness there has to be synthesis and therefore application of the categories, and that can only happen if there is already a content in the intuitions. Pure time and pure space are thus never perceived in themselves, but only when there is a content already situated in time. Space and time, as horizons beyond the bounds of any representation, are thus nothings which nevertheless, says Kant, are "something": pure space and time are "certainly something as forms of intuition, but are not themselves intuited objects."

This definition of empty space as nothingness enables us to better understand the notion of infinite given magnitude. It does not at all mean that space is given in totality, in its infinity, *in a representation*. Kant is definitive on this point when he writes in a text against Eberhard that it is impossible "to survey the whole of infinite given space, to ever gather in our representation what never ceases, as if it were some thing which ends somewhere . . . The understanding can encompass the infinite no more than sensibility can." That space is an infinite given magnitude means only that it always already oversteps any representation and, as such, as an overstepping, it is this nothing which is yet "something." This comes down to saying that our finitude is itself unlimited, that we are infinitely finite. If space is an infinite given totality (meaning not constituted by the accretion of parts), it never falls within a representation but rather oversteps all representation. This "overstepping" is called "nothing" by Kant, and this nothing is itself the unlimited sign of our finitude. The totality that the Idea aims for, on the other hand, truly is a representation, but not one that is ever "given." It is only "thought," not "known," since in the final analysis it only represents a task, an invitation to add up indefinitely the beings that science constructs.

These two conceptions of the totality are not unconnected, and we could even say that one forces the other to be only an idea. If it is indeed impossible to survey space, to enclose it in a representation which it always precedes, then the actualization of an achieved system of experience is, also, forever impossible. These "nothings" that are the a priori forms of sensibility always guarantee an exteriority irreducible to representation and, as such, they resist any attempt at a closure of the system of experience.

THE SOLUTION TO THE ANTINOMY OF TASTE:
FROM THE INDIVIDUAL TO THE SUBJECT

This relation of finitude to the rational Idea of system makes especially clear what type of solution Kant wishes to put forth, concerning the antinomy of taste, in his *Critique of the Faculty of Judgment* [or *Critique of Judgment* in the English tradition]. For opposing reasons, both classical rationalism and sensualist empiricism share the same failing: they lead to founding the "common sense" that emerges around the beautiful object in such a fashion that subjectivity becomes, so to speak, reified and thereby negated. Among the classicists, the personality specific to the author of a judgment of taste is dissolved in a universal reason that behaves quite dogmatically toward the particular. Among empiricists, the subject's particularity does seem, at first, to be preserved; but in the end intersubjectivity is reduced to a purely material principle, to the idea of a psychic and organic structure common to a species of individuals. From that point on, the aesthetic experience needs nothing further that is specifically human, the Beautiful is but a variety of the pleasant, and the art of cooking, the model for aesthetics in general.

This is the question raised by the antinomy of taste: how to keep the *idea* of a possible universality of taste, without the principle of this common sense negating a subjectivity conceived of in a nonmetaphysical, non-"anthropological" way, as man's humanity? (I shall come back to the non-"anthropological" character of man's humanity later in this chapter.) In other words, how to think aesthetic intersubjectivity without grounding it either on a dogmatic reason or on a psychophysiological empirical structure? Inversely, how to maintain the absolute particularity of taste without giving in to the formula, "to each his own taste," thus destroying the claim to universality without which mere aesthetic discussion would lose all significance? "Where one can argue, one should also have some hope of agreeing."

Rationalism and empiricism are both built upon a reifying conception of subjectivity; both think the cogito monadically, as a *thing* withdrawn into itself—whereby they both lead, at first, to solipsism, and, in the end, have recourse to the idea of a preestablished harmony (whether harmony of spirits or of bodies) in order to solve the problem of intersubjectivity. The logic behind this solution has to be abolished through the elaboration of a novel way of thinking about the subject which Kant calls *Reflection,* and which is already implicit in the distinction between determinant and reflective judgments on which the entire aesthetic theory developed in the third *Critique* is based:[4]

> Judgment in general is the faculty of thinking the particular as contained under the universal. If the universal (the rule, principle, or law) is given, then the judgment which subsumes the particular under it is *determinant.* (This is so even where such a judgment is transcendental and thereby provides the conditions a priori in conformity with which alone subsumption under that universal can be carried out.) If, however, only the particular is given and the universal has to be found for it, then the judgment is simply *reflective.*[5]

It is in these terms that Kant works out the division between the judgment of cognition, a determinant judgment, and the judgment of taste, a reflective judgment. With this simple distinction Kant shows himself already diametrically opposed to rationalist classicism, which saw aesthetic judgment and cognitive judgment as a confluence. Kant considers it possible to set up a "poetic art," which would be a veritable science of the production of the Beautiful. The originality of the Kantian position is located in the notion of reflection, which therefore has to be made more precise.

The word "reflection"—univocal in Kant, in the *Critique of Pure Reason* as much as in the *Critique of Judgment*—very generally designates an intellectual activity characterized by five sequences or moments. A brief example can serve as illustration as well as prepare for the analysis of the aesthetic judgment.[6] To create the empirical concept of a collection of objects unknown to us—for example, of a kind of tree never before identified—we have to begin with a classification. By comparing likenesses, by abstracting out differences we judge unessential, we can bring together the objects under consideration into a common class, and thus create an empirical concept to which we can attach a name. In this simple operation, the five constitutive moments of reflection—of the reflective judgment—are already present:

1. First of all, the activity of reflection clearly proceeds from the particular to the universal (from the individuals to the general class).

2. The general (or the universal) is not given before the activity of reflection but only through it and after it—wherein the reflective judgment is the opposite of the determinant judgment, which goes from a universal we already have to the particular, and thus constitutes only an application of the universal.

3. Although the general is not given as a concept or as determined laws at the beginning of the reflective operation, there is all the same an indeterminate horizon of expectations serving as clue or, in Kant's expression, *principle* to reflection. In our example this principle comes from the logic of classes. It consists in the expectation or the requirement that the real will let itself be classified and thus conform to logic. The universal then exists, not as a concept, but in the status of Idea, of a regulative principle of reflection.

4. This operation implicitly supposes that it is perfectly contingent whether the real does or does not correspond to the imperatives of logical rationality that we do not impose on it, but to which we submit it; nothing stops us from thinking that the real could very well not satisfy our subjective requirement of logical systematicity, so that finally we could constitute neither genera nor species. To deny this proposition would be to postulate the rationality of the real a priori and, in the final analysis, to once again grant objectivity to the idea of a divine point of view from which the world would be wholly intelligible.

5. The activity of reflection thus turns out to be at the origin of a satisfaction Kant calls aesthetic, and which refers to the notion of finality. Because the real, after the deconstruction of metaphysics and the ontological argument, appears radically contingent when compared to our requirement for rationality, the reflecting subject can experience pleasure when, having had no guarantee of it, he observes an agreement between the real and his requirements.

These five moments of the reflecting activity make up the intimate structure of the judgment of taste. As in the operation which presides over the creation of empirical concepts, it is the Idea of system, the Idea of an entirely intelligible world—the very one God would see—which is the principle of the aesthetic reflection. And that's the reason why the

Kantian definition of the beautiful object as one that reconciles nature and spirit looks forward to the theories of romanticism. The connection between the idea of system as principle of reflection and the definition of the beautiful as the reconciliation of sensibility and intelligence can be stated succinctly: despite the demonstration of the illusoriness of the Idea of God, this Idea continues to play a regulatory role for all intellectual activity. It points to the unsatisfiable but forever present demand for a perfect rationalization of the real, and therefore for a complete subsumption of the sensual matter of knowledge under an intelligible form (the categorial structure). Stated more clearly: in conformity with Leibniz's philosophy, if we could situate ourselves at God's point of view, there would no longer be any distinction for us between the sensible and the intelligible, intuition and concept, particular and universal, nature and spirit, etc. That such a point of view can never be ours, that it cannot, furthermore, relativize man's finite point of view, is the end result of this purely ideal status. It remains nevertheless true that, as a mere requirement of reason, the Idea of God or of system can at times be, if not entirely "fulfilled" (Kant says "presented"), at least partially or "symbolically" evoked by certain objects. The Beautiful is, precisely, one of these objects; as a *partial* reconciliation of nature and spirit, of sensibility and concepts, it functions as a contingent trace—dependent on the real itself—of this necessary Idea of reason. Reflection's five constitutive moments will thus be present in the judgment of taste, which proceeds (1) from the particular (the beautiful object) to the universal (the requirement of a perfect union of the sensible and the intelligible); (2) without a determined concept (this requirement points to nothing which could furnish the substance of a "poetic art"); (3) and this since only the Idea of God or of system can here provide the principle for reflection; (4) the existence of the beautiful object being contingent in relation to this idea; (5) the similarly contingent agreement between a particular real and the universal requirement for systematicity bringing about aesthetic pleasure.

The solution to the antinomy of taste here finds its explanation and its meaning. Unlike what classical rationalism maintains, the judgment of taste is not based on *determinate* concepts (or rules); it is thus impossible to "argue" about it as if it were a judgment of scientific knowledge. Yet it is not thereby confined to the pure empirical subjectivity of feeling, since it rests on the presence of an object which, if it is beautiful (we shall accept that for the sake of argument), will awaken a necessary idea of reason, as such common to humanity. It is through referring to this indeterminate idea (it merely calls for the reconciliation of the sensible and the intelligible without stating what precisely this reconciliation could consist in) that it becomes possible to "argue" about taste and to expand the sphere of subjectivity in order to envision a nondogmatic sharing of the aesthetic experience with an other, in so far as this other is another human.

SCIENCE AND BEAUTY: THE END OF THE CLASSICAL IDEAL OF AN OBJECTIVITY OF TASTE

The exact difference between the judgment of knowledge (the determinant judgment) and the judgment of taste (reflective judgment) should be made more precise in order to bring to light the ultimate ground for the distinction that the solution to the antinomy of taste effects between a *disputatio,* in which subjective particularity is canceled within an imperious rationality, and discussion, in which the same particularity, while remaining particular, aims nonetheless to expand, up to the point of claiming, without demonstration, without the mediation of a concept, universality.

Let us first of all consider the case of a judgment aiming at scientific objectivity. In precritical philosophy, and especially in Cartesianism, the problem of objectivity is, according to Kant, put in the following terms: to ask if our representations of objects are "true" is to try to know if they are adequate to the object as it exists in itself, outside my representation. If we reflect on this carefully we will realize that, put that way, the problem of objectivity is insoluble a priori: *by definition* I can never know what the object is *in itself,* without my observation of it. *By definition,* the object I'm considering is always an object *for me,* an object of *my* representation and, to know what this object is in itself, I would have, so to speak, to leave my consciousness—which is, of course, impossible. In the precritical philosophies, in the philosophies which conceive of the cogito as a subject closed in upon its consciousness, as a monad prisoner of its own representations, the very positioning of the problem of objectivity can only, following Kant, lead to false solutions. One of them consists in having God intervene (the divine guarantee or the preestablished harmony) to assure the connection between the "object for us" and the "thing in itself" (or whatever is designated as such). The other is the skepticism of which Berkeley's philosophy is the most spectacular example. Thus, either we ground intersubjectivity on the dogmatic intervention of a deus ex machina, or we renounce objectivity and accept complete relativism or, as they called it in Kant's day, philosophical "egoism."

As we have seen, the antinomy of taste reproduces this structure in many ways. The *Critique of Pure Reason* argues that we have to carry out a "refutation of idealism," to go beyond the viewpoints of dogmatic or skeptic cogitos and define objectivity independently of the notions of interiority and exteriority to which the monadic conceptions of the subject implicitly refer. Objectivity, in critical philosophy, will no longer designate what is external to representation but rather the universally valid character of propositions which effectuate an association or synthesis of representations.* Subjective and objective will then be opposed as an association of representations valid only for me, and an association of universally valid representations (and here intersubjectivity is definitively placed at the heart of objectivity). We shall have to distinguish between representations valid only for me (subjective) and those which are universally valid (objective) by going to the representations themselves or, rather, to their various syntheses, and no longer through reference to an external "thing-in-itself."

The task is thus, to borrow again Husserl's formula, that of grounding "transcendence" (objectivity, intersubjectivity) within "immanence" (without "exiting from" representations). The determinant scientific judgment aims at such a transcendence. Let us look at the example of a judgment stating there is a causal relation between two phenomena. Two elements come into play which allow us, according to Kant, to claim objectivity in the *link* of the effect to the cause:

—We first have to have a universal rule (the determinant judgment proceeds from the universal to the particular). In this case it is the principle of causality, according to which every effect necessarily has a cause.

—But for it to be truly scientific, and not merely metaphysical, this law must also provide a criterion of application to phenomena. Since phenomena all take place in time, the principle of causality will apply to any succession of which it can be experimentally shown, by isolating variables, that it is *irreversible.*

If I follow this criterion in applying this law, I cannot "freely" associate just any phenomenon to just any other. Or, more exactly, if I

---

* Apparently, one could trace such a definition of objectivity back to Leibniz. But that would be to forget that the demonstration of God's existence requires, in a sense, a leap outside representation, a belief in the in-itself.

associate my representations without taking into account the law and its criterion, the associations I produce will have no objectivity and will remain purely subjective.

We must therefore distinguish, within the sphere of theoretical philosophy, between two types of association: the purely empirical type which has but a subjective meaning, and the objective, which presupposes the intervention of a concept, that is, of a rule of synthesis at the same time determinate and determinant. If, for instance, I'm looking at the wall in front of me while twisting my head from left to right, I could feel, at the purely subjective level of perception, that the wall "exists from left to right." But it is clear that a proposition founded on such a feeling has no objectivity and that, in truth, the parts of the wall exist "simultaneously," that I therefore have to "posit them together," to "synthesize" them, to supersede my particular perception and arrive at objectivity.

The way the judgment of taste functions should be described in relation to these two types of associations (empirical subjective association, conceptual objective association). It in fact participates in both without thereby becoming identical with either. The feeling of beauty—according to the analysis developed in the third *Critique*—and the aesthetic pleasure that accompanies it are born of a "free" association of the imagination: when there is a perception of a beautiful object, the imagination, "the most powerful *sensible* faculty," associated images without this linking up being in any way regulated by a concept. From this point of view, this imaginary interplay is closer to an empirical subjective association than to a regulated synthesis aimed at producing a scientific judgment. But although this interplay is quite free in that it obeys no rule, everything nevertheless takes place *as if* it followed a certain "logic," as if there were, in Kant's own formulation, a "legality of the contingent," a legality without concept. In music, the art seemingly the most distant from the theoretical sphere (because it offers no analogies with vision), the sounds and the associations of images they bring forth in us seem to be organized, seem to be structured as if they had some sense, as if they wanted to say something (which is why music can so easily, without our understanding how, "express feelings"). From this point of view the play of the imagination, although it remains purely within the order of sensibility and has recourse to no concept to regulate its organization, all the same structures itself *as if* it could, of itself, satisfy the requirements of the rules for a judgment of knowledge.

There is thus a free and contingent agreement between the imagination and the understanding, an agreement completely unforeseeable and ungovernable—which is why there can be neither a poetic crafts-manship (*ars poétique*) nor any science of the Beautiful however de-fined. And this agreement of the sensual and the intellectual faculties in turn functions as a *symbolic* trace, as a beginning for the bringing into reality of those Ideas of reason which, as we have seen, to be "pre-sented," need to actualize a perfect reconciliation of the sensible and the intelligible corresponding to the point of view a divine understanding would have upon the world—which can be represented by the accom-panying diagram.

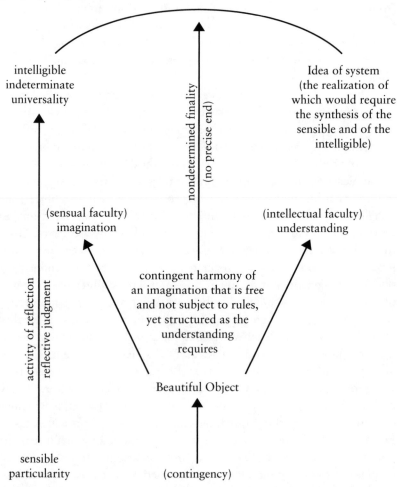

In reflection's ascension from the particular to the indeterminate Idea, the two extreme moments are the essential ones. If the *particular* beautiful object did not *contingently* bring about the agreement of the faculties demanded by the Idea of system, if this agreement were produced in some artificial and voluntarist fashion, the requirement of systematicity included in the Idea of God, understood as regulative principle of reflection, would not at all be fulfilled. Fulfillment comes from the feeling of finality or end-purposiveness called forth in us by the beautiful object in as much as it is exterior to us and contingent in relation to our principles, everything happening *as if* the object only existed to satisfy *of itself* our requirement for rationality (for reconciliation of the sensible and the intelligible). What is pleasing here is that the real should, without our intervention, come to satisfy our entirely subjective demands. Natural Beauty will thus be held to be the model for artistic beauty (which explains the deep significance of the Kantian theory of genius, a subject I'll come back to). On the other hand, if the Ideas of reason, although indeterminate, were not presumed to be common to humanity, the beautiful object, when stirring up these ideas, would summon up no common sense, not even the project, in case of discord, of discussing taste, since, to discuss, "one must at least have the hope of coming to an agreement."

A NEW WAY OF THINKING THE SUBJECT: REFLECTION AND THE COMMON SENSE

Contingency of beauty and universality of the horizon of expectations on which the judgment of taste is based are the two terms between which reflection oscillates. We have already seen how, from a logical point of view, the reflective activity consists first of all in the comparison, following the concepts of identity and difference, of the elements which make up species and genera. This usage of the word, which goes back to Wolff's psychology,[7] has an appendix in a theory of the *Witz*, of the "mind" or "spirit," understood as the capacity to establish unforeseen relations between apparently distant or quite different elements.[8] But to this "expansion of the object," as Kant puts it, corresponds also an "expansion of the subject" through which the latter ceases to be contained within the narrow frontiers of monadical egoism and arrives at the sphere of "the common sense":

Under the *sensus communis* we must understand the Idea of a sense common to all, that is, a faculty of judgment, that in its reflection takes into account in thoughts (a priori) everyone else's mode of representation, in order simultaneously to maintain its judgment within the whole of human reason, and thereby to escape the illusion that, stemming from subjective private conditions which could easily be taken to be objective, would have a disadvantageous influence on the judgment.[9]

Therefrom the fundamental maxim of the reflective faculty of judgment, the maxim of "expanded thinking": "Think in every other one's place" [*An der Stelle jedes anderen denken*].[10]

It's at this point of the Kantian argumentation that the solution to the antinomy of taste is reached, and we must here delineate the exact nature of that which at the same time brings Kant near but also separates him radically from the two points of view which make up the antinomy. Neither dogmatic rationalism nor empiricism aim, strictly speaking, at this common sense. In the former the work of art seeks a universality founded on reason, while in the latter, despite its relativism in principle, the work can achieve, as is the case in Hume, an empirically founded generality, an agreement resulting from sympathy understood in its strict sense, as the fact of sharing the same feeling. Kant's position might seem near to that of rationalism and empiricism in certain ways: isn't the common sense established, in the very passage we have just read, through a very classical reference to "the whole of human reason"? And besides, doesn't this common *sense*, as the expression indicates, have to do with *sensibility*, with *sentiment*? But despite appearances, the difference between the Kantian and the classical rationalist positions is fundamental. If the expansion of reflection that generates a common sense is in fact conceived of in reference to reason, this reason is no longer the Cartesians' determining reason, but the indeterminate Idea of an agreement of the sensible imagination and of the understanding—an Idea itself only contingently and unforeseeably evoked by the emergence of natural or genial beauty. The beautiful thus truly remains a matter of feeling and sensibility. But there again, in contrast with what takes place in empiricism, we must carefully avoid confusing feeling and sympathy, as one of Kant's important *Reflections* points out: "The property man possesses of being able to judge the particular only in the universal is sentiment. Sympathy is entirely different: it has to do only with the particular, although the particular in others [*Sie geht bloß auf des Particulare, obgleich an anderen*]"; in sympathy "we do not at all put ourselves in the Idea, but in the place of others"[11] as simply empirical beings and not as humanity in general. Within empiricist aesthetics, the common sense remains a simple factual generality and its rightful status is, therefore, merely particular (meaning linked to the psychological and physiological particularities of this animal species, itself particular, that is humanity).

We must therefore reject sympathy as much as dogmatic reason when we turn to a reflection on the transcendental conditions of possibility of a truly inter-*subjective* aesthetic common sense. In rationalism as in empiricism the foundation of the "common sense" is not truly an intersubjective foundation since it nullifies the very idea of subjectivity, in the first case absorbed by an impersonal universal, and in the second by a simple material structure, both of them excluding the very possibility of discussion. For discussion, and all criticism with it (including of course art criticism), presumes both admitting a common point of view, and the fact that this point of view is not conceptual but indeterminate. In other words, the linking up of a particular sentiment and a universal Idea as operated by reflection, with the aim of establishing a direct communication between individuals, a non–conceptually-grounded common sense.

"SENSUS COMMUNIS" OR "DIFFERENCE"

It has sometimes been objected against such an interpretation of the *Critique of Judgment* that, "far from permitting a 'direct communication,' the exercise of the reflective judgment gives rise rather to the sentiment of a promised and ever differed community"; that the reflective judgment, unable to achieve a philosophy of the "common sense" and of intersubjectivity, on the contrary sketches out an "inventive procedure which, upon the trace of the unknown, of the unacceptable, breaks the constituted norms, explodes the consensus, reanimates the sense of difference [*du différend*]."[12]

This objection, which claims phenomenological inspiration and refers willingly back to Heidegger's reading of Kant, in fact rests upon a misunderstanding, which can be easily cleared up, and on an error, which jeopardizes in its very principles any interpretation of the third *Critique* aiming to find in it a mere philosophy of "difference."

The misunderstanding has to do with the notion of "direct communication." The expression does not at all mean, as the objection suggests, that the taste judgment could be the object of an instant and easy consensus among individuals. Must we cite Hume once again? "The great variety of Taste, as well as of opinion, which prevails in the world, is too obvious not to have fallen under every one's observation." We could not put it better: insistence on "difference of opinion" in general is banal, but in matters of taste it becomes so trivial we could hardly understand how it could be the object of a philosophical passion. When I evoke the idea of a direct or immediate communication it is obviously not to deny the effectively "uncircumventable" existence of a difference without which there would not even be aesthetic discussion, but to indicate that, unlike what happens in the realms of ethics and science, aesthetic intersubjectivity does not go through the mediation of a determinate law or concept, as Kant himself never ceases to remind us in the most explicit way: "he who judges with taste . . . may take his sentiment to be generally communicable, and this *without the mediation of concepts*" (§ 39); there is also in the judgment of taste a "general communicability of sensation (pleasure or displeasure), and such a one that takes place without a concept" (§ 17); and also, "one could even define taste as the faculty of judgment that makes our feeling about a given representation universally communicable without the mediation of a concept" (§ 40), etc. Short of denying the existence of these texts—and with them the central thesis of Kantian aesthetics—I don't see how one could consider the fact of talking about "immediate" or "direct" communication, when referring to aesthetic communication, to be "the most serious misinterpretation committed by the Neo-Kantians (ibid.).

We can go even further: Kant takes up here, in the aesthetic domain, the famous opposition Rousseau worked out in his *Letter to d'Alembert on Spectacles* between the *theater,* symbol of the monarchy, of the indirect communication which goes through the intermediary of the stage, and the *festival,* symbol of democracy, of the direct communication where the spectators' eyes are not directed toward an external object but rather themselves provide the show, among themselves. "Let us not adopt," as Rousseau wrote,

these exclusive spectacles that lugubriously enclose a small number of persons in an obscure den, that hold them, timorous and immobile, in silence and inaction . . . No, happy peoples, those are not your festivals! It is in the open air, it is under the sky that you must gather together and give yourselves over to the sweet feeling of your happiness . . . But what will be in the end the objects of these spectacles? What will be shown there? Nothing, *if you so will.* Under liberty, everywhere affluence reigns well-being will reign also. Plant a stake crowned with flowers in the middle of a square, gather the people there, and you will have a feast. Do more: make the spectators the spectacle, give the actors: themselves; make every one see and love himself in the others, so that they will all be more united.

That's exactly the theme Kant, mutatis mutandis, transposes into the third *Critique* and which grounds an aesthetic conception of the public sphere as an intersubjective space of free discussion not mediated by a concept or a rule—which in no way means, as we can see, some sort of "abolition of difference" but on the contrary, the articulation of difference with the idea of the common sense.

When thinking about this articulation, the element that makes the third *Critique* so interesting and which radically distinguishes it from a trivial philosophy of difference, we have to be careful and not make a mistake often thought of as something obvious: although the idea of an "ideal community," of a perfect reconciliation of individuals within an undistorted communication, is obviously just that, an Idea, it would be against both the letter and the spirit of the Kantian aesthetic to think that the common sense is nothing but a thoroughly ideal horizon. The problem of the status of the common sense is infinitely more complicated than is suggested by the argument that it is only a "fragile and ever differed community."

If by that is meant that aesthetic discussion aims at a highly hypothetical agreement, that our tastes are not necessarily shared, etc., we fall back on commonplaces that cannot be denied. But if one means by it that the common sense has no other status than an ideal one, a serious mistake would be made concerning the nature of the bond uniting reason and the empirical realm. The Idea of perfect intersubjectivity is a common sense which de facto arrives at a sometimes impressive level of generality, to which the *Critique of Judgment* intends to also accord a *philosophical*, and not merely ideological, status. This is a crucial point, bringing into play as it does the difference in status the universal enjoys vis-à-vis the particular within theoretical philosophy and in aesthetics.

In theoretical philosophy the universal can only behave imperiously toward the particular. Either a law is scientific or it isn't a law, and if Newton had been the only one to think he was right, he would have been right to think so. That is a consequence of the essential nature of the determinant judgment. In the sphere of taste on the other hand, the relation between universal and particular, between idea and empirical realm, is infinitely more nuanced. It is of course always possible that an empirical consensus is in fact ideological; that it is, as they say, a mere fashion. But as *critic* I have to acknowledge that I have at my disposal no absolute universal criterion in the order of the reflective judgment that would allow me to decide in complete certainty and I have to admit, at least by way of hypothesis, that the empirical consensus I observe around those works of art said to be "great" could also, for the same reason, be the sign of a symbolical evocation of the Ideas of reason. Which is why, as mentioned before, only the path of discussion is open to me. In other words, it is of the essence of the reflective judgment that in it the claim to universality behave in an a priori "friendly" way towards the particular, including—and perhaps especially—when the latter spontaneously takes the form of empirical common sense. Not to admit this proposition, and I don't see in what way it implies some sort of "surrender to the ideologies of consensus," is quite simply to forbid oneself to understand what differentiates the *Critique of Pure Reason* from the *Critique of Judgment*.

Kant is quite explicit on this crucial point. On the one hand, it is clear that an empirical consensus is never, all alone, the proof of the apodictic quality of the judgments of taste it is based on, and that from it we can never deduce the necessity of our adherence. Because if the necessity of the aesthetic judgment "is not a theoretical objective necessity, where it can be known a priori that everyone will feel pleasure from the object called beautiful by me . . . much less can [necessity] be concluded from the universality of experience (from a thoroughgoing unanimity of judgments on the beauty of a certain object). It is not just that experience would hardly furnish very many examples; no concept of the necessity of these judgments can be grounded on empirical judgments" (§ 18). Yet an empirical consensus—and we can note in passing that Kant does not absolutely exclude the possibility of aesthetic unanimity—is to be neither held in contempt nor neglected; nor can it be in the framework of the reflective judgment in which it constitutes, if not an absolute a priori criterion, an empirical one, creating, so to speak, a presumption in favor of authenticity which must be criticized as such. Although "there can be no objective rule of taste which would determine through concepts what is beautiful," there remains nonetheless "the general communicability of sensation (of pleasure or displeasure), and such a one that takes place without a concept. It produces the unanimity, as far as is possible, of all epochs and peoples in respect of [the subject's] feelings towards the representations of certain objects. This is the empirical criterion—however weak and, for its presumption, barely sufficient—for the provenance of such a taste, conserved throughout many occasions, from a principle that is deeply hidden and, common to all, of unanimity in the evaluation of the forms in which objects are given them" (§ 17).

Such a text would make no sense in the *Critique of Pure Reason,* since it means, contrary to what the objections we talked about suggest, that the common sense, even though empirical and particular, must at least be taken into consideration in the reflective judgment, since it could be the case that it is itself the symbolic trace of an Idea. That is the reason why Kant can calmly maintain that "beautiful nature contains innumerable things about which we readily admit the harmony of everyone's judgment with our own, and we may even expect it without much risk of being misled"—a text that would be completely unintelligible if it were true that in his eyes the reflective judgment always referred back to the mere *Idea* of a "fragile and ever differed community."

Things are more complicated than that, as we can see, and the common sense cannot be reduced to either a de facto consensus nor to a pure idea. In its empirical generality it constitutes, as it were, a mixture, a symbolic trace of Ideas—at least if it is not ideological. At this point criticism must come in, the discussion must start which can no more be abolished in the name of difference than in that of the universal. For, in the judgment of taste, "one sollicits everyone else's adherence because one possesses a principle common to all; one could always count on this adherence if one could always be sure that the case at hand were correctly subsumed under the principle" (§ 19).

THE SUBLIME AND THE BAROQUE: THE ARTICULATION OF "DIFFERENCE" AND OF THE UNIVERSAL IDEA

It may be objected that the interpretation put forward here is valid in the case of the reflective judgment concerning the beautiful, but that, with the sublime, Kant orients himself resolutely towards thought of the "excess," of the "formless," of "difference" [*différend*], which no longer has any consensual or universalist pretensions. Does he not say explicitly that if, in matters concerning the beautiful, we can often ascribe assent to others, "with our judgments on sublimity in nature we cannot so easily promise ourselves access to others"? (§ 29). And, unlike what happens with the beautiful, do we not have with the sublime a case of "presentation that there is an unpresentable," since the aesthetic feeling of pleasure or pain is not brought about by the agreement of faculties but by their disorder and chaos?

I believe on the contrary that with sublimity, just because there is indeed a problem of the "unpresentable," of that which "surpasses" all representation, Kant carries the project through to its ultimate consequences—not of sketching out a philosophy of difference, but of articulating this difference (that which escapes representation) with Ideas, understood as principles of reflection. We must dwell on this because, if my hypothesis is correct, it's with the philosophy of the sublime that the Kantian aesthetic, and above all the conception of the reflective subject it puts into action, reaches its summit.

Let us begin by examining the Kantian definition of the sublime. Certain passages of the third *Critique* seem to place sublimity either in nature or in the Ideas of reason, or yet again in the very activity of the imagination. The global definition (valid for the "mathematically" as for the "dynamically" sublime) given in the "General Remark on the Exposition of Aesthetic Reflective Judgements" has it that the sublime is "an object (of nature) whose representation [*Vorstellung*] prepares the mind to conceive of the unattainability of nature as a presentation [*Darstellung*] of Ideas (§ 29). The sublime thus calls upon the three terms we have evoked: the object of nature, the mind (imagination), and the Ideas of reason. Through the contemplation of a natural object (for instance the ocean), the imagination is led to the temptation of presenting the Idea of a whole in one single intuition. It fails, and according to Kant this failure functions as a "negative presentation" of an Idea whose adequate presentation is by definition impossible: "the authentic sublime cannot be contained in any sensual form but has to do only with Ideas of reason. Although no adequate presentation of the latter is possible, they can be aroused and brought to mind through this very inadequacy, which allows itself to be sensually presented" (§ 23).

What is presented in the sublime has nothing "objective" about it. Ideas are not evoked here by any intuition, not even a "symbolic" and partial one. It is the very failure of the imagination, in so far as it bears witness that *there is that which is nonpresentable,* that is called upon and which, as such, evokes the Ideas. "The disposition of the mind upon feeling sublimity encourages its receptivity for Ideas; it is in nature's very unsuitability to them, and thereby in their presupposition and in the imagination's endeavors to treat nature as a scheme for them, that lies that which is at once forbidding yet attractive for sensibility" (§ 29).

What is sublime is thus in truth neither the object (it is only the opportunity for a movement of the mind—which is why there will be no "deduction" of the sublime) nor even the Ideas of reason (although they are presupposed), but the movement of the imagination to try and present the Ideas, with all its ambiguity (attempt-failure). "Nothing that may be an object for the senses . . . can be called sublime. But precisely because there is in our imagination an effort towards progression into infinity, and in our reason a demand for an absolute totality as to a real Idea, the very inadequacy of our faculty for evaluating the greatness of the things in the sensible world is for this Idea an arousal of the feeling of a suprasensual faculty in us" (§ 25).

It is the imagination's failure which, as a negative presentation of the Ideas, has a finality and brings about the feeling of the sublime. In short, the sublime "presupposes" or, as Kant puts it, "involves" the Ideas, but it is not reducible to them, if we understand by sublime that which has finality (although, taken in another sense, one could argue that the Ideas of reason are sublime only in so far as they can measure up to the infinitely great. But then the sublime is defined by its content, the absolutely great, and not from the point of view of finality, the point of view the reflective faculty of judgment is interested in).

What is the reason for the imagination's failure in its attempt to present the Idea of a rational All? Kant's answer is explicit: "We are rapidly convinced that neither the unconditioned nor, consequently, absolute magnitude belongs to nature *within space and time.*" In other words, space and time, *sensibility,* are the limits we cannot transgress, and we discover again, at the center of the theory of the sublime, and especially of the mathematical sublime, the conception of radical, transcendental finitude with which the *Critique of Pure Reason* overturned the general perspective of Cartesian philosophy. Reciprocally, it is time and space that we would have to move beyond, "survey as from above," to be able to present an Idea; this is exactly what the imagination tries to do in the case of mathematical sublimity. But Kant does not limit himself to recalling what has been worked out in the first *Critique;* he adds a description of the experience brought about by the attempt to integrate into a representation this *Nothing* that is space ("Nothing" because it is, in fact, nothing, as the chapter on "The Amphiboly of the Concepts of Reflection" in the first *Critique* points out). The problem consists in understanding the equivocal nature of this experience, of this "sentiment of the powerlessness of the imagination to present the idea of a whole" (§ 26).

101

Let us now reconsider the two moments of the sublime: "Our imagination proves, in its greatest effort in view of the comprehension demanded of it, of a given object in a totality of intuition (and thus in view of a presentation of an Idea of reason), its limits and its inadequacy, yet simultaneously its disposition to the actualization of the same (the Idea) as to a law" (§ 27). The two moments are here clearly posited in their difference and their relationship: first of all failure, the feeling of limits, of impotence; this naturally produces a *displeasure* (whose nature is yet to be determined). But this failure hides an attempt which, as such, reveals our destination—displeasure is immediately transformed into *pleasure* (whose nature is also yet to be determined). Pleasure and displeasure thus succeed each other or, as section 27 puts it, "The feeling of sublimity is then a feeling of displeasure due to the inadequacy of the imagination in the aesthetic evaluation of magnitude to evaluation through reason, and of pleasure aroused thereby, due to the concordance of this very judgment, about the inadequacy of this greatest of sensual faculties, with Ideas of reason." To the "negative presentation" corresponds thus a "negative pleasure."

The nature of such a feeling must be made precise. The failure of the imagination comes from the fact that (§ 27) "what nature, as an object of the senses, contains that is for us great, is to be valued as little in comparison with the Ideas of reason." Why? Because nature is contained within the limits of time and space, limits within which there is no absolutely great. Space (along with time), in other words, is here the reason why nature never corresponds to the Ideas, or, put yet another way, that which makes it so that the Ideas remain always only Ideas. To try to climb to an "overhang" over space is, in a way, to experience the "infinite given greatness," an obviously negative experience or, more exactly, a frightening experience of Nothing: "The Overflowing [translating *Das Überschwengliche* literally, to avoid confusion with *Das Transzendent*—L.F.] is for the imagination (driven as it is to it in its attempt to grasp intuition) an abyss in which it fears to lose itself; but for the Idea of Reason of the suprasensible it is not overflowing, but legitimate, to bring about such an effort of the imagination—attractive thereby to the same degree as it was repulsive to the sole sensibility" (§ 27). If the experience of the always "overflowing," that is, of space as nothingness, is frightening, it is because in the effort toward "the aesthetic comprehension towards a greater unity . . . we feel in our minds as though aesthetically enclosed within limits" (§ 27). In its attempt to present the Ideas, the imagination experiences aesthetic limitation, transcendental finitude, and, as it were, overflowing space (= Nothing); it is then plunged into what Kant calls a "frightening abyss." Thus we understand the nature of the pleasure and displeasure making up the two moments of the mathematically sublime: they consist of anguish and its relief, each of those sentiments corresponding to a glance at one of the two types of totality we dealt with earlier on: space (Nothing), in the first case, and system (Idea) in the second.

We can now compare this analysis with the concrete examples evoked by Kant in section 26. The sublime is defined in section 25 as the absolutely great, as that in comparison to which everything else is small. Section 26 then tries to make the notion of absolutely great explicit by showing what type of evaluation of greatness it refers to. Numerical (mathematical) evaluation is thereby immediately eliminated: any number can be greater or lesser than another; a number cannot, as such, pretend to evaluate the absolutely great.

But mathematical evaluation itself presupposes, in order to determine greatness or magnitude, the evaluation Kant calls "aesthetic," meaning the evaluation grounded on a unity of measure grasped "by the eye's judgment." Whereas numerical evaluation can continue indefinitely, aesthetic evaluation soon reaches a limit beyond which I cannot represent anything to myself that is not obscure and confused. This maximum is reached when the imagination, in its work of apprehension or seizure of intuitions, adds up the partial representations and can no longer understand, can no longer simultaneously grasp at an aesthetic level all of these partial representations. What it gains from one side it loses at the other. This limit of aesthetic comprehension is then the "aesthetically greatest fundamental measure of the evaluation of magnitude." It represents a maximum, a subjective (aesthetic) absolutely great, "where it is considered an absolute measure beyond which no greater is possible subjectively . . . it then conveys the idea of the sublime and calls forth that emotion which no mathematical estimation of magnitudes by numbers can evoke" (§ 26).

The connection Kant establishes between the feeling of the sublime and the limits of aesthetic comprehension (the subjective absolutely great) creates certain difficulties. It had seemed that the sublime lay in the attempt the imagination makes to "soar above" space in order to present the Ideas of reason. Indeed, in this attempt the mind experiences both a transcendental finitude (an anguishing experience of the nothingness that is space) and its destination (the presentation of Ideas). But if we believe section 26 of the third *Critique,* the mathematically sublime has nothing to do with a transcendental finitude; space itself is not the uncrossable border between the empirical sensible and the intelligible (the limit that hinders the presentation of Ideas). It would, on the contrary, be a matter of entirely "subjective," "psychological" finitude and limit. Otherwise put, the limit of "aesthetic comprehension" is one within the sensible itself, a limit which, in a sense, separates a clear and distinct sensible from a sensible that becomes obscure and confused (the beyond of the limit, which escapes comprehension, is in fact still the sensible). But then we have the right to ask what is so sublime about this subjective absolutely great. What can evoke the Ideas of reason if, in a way, everything takes place inside the sensible itself?

The difficulty is at its greatest in the example Kant chooses in this very same section 26, the cathedral of St. Peter's in Rome. "On first entering" there, says Kant, the visitor is seized by a "sort of perplexity . . . For here a feeling comes home to him of the inadequacy of his imagination for presenting the idea of a whole within which that imagination attains its maximum, and, in its fruitless efforts to extend this limit, recoils upon itself, but in so doing succumbs to an emotional delight." The problems this example raises are many. The structure of the mathematically sublime does seem to be present. There is, on the one hand, "the Idea of a whole" that one tries to make present, on the other a vain effort of the imagination. But if we look at the example more closely, we shall see (as we might have expected, given the link Kant establishes between the sublime and the subjective limit to aesthetic comprehension) that the whole one is trying to make present, far from being a rational Idea, is a sensible whole, a totality already situated *in* nature: the church of St. Peter in Rome. De jure, then, this totality is presentable, even if de facto it is not presented at one glance; besides, it is not at all inconceivable that this church might be presented in one single intuition (it might just be necessary to find the right viewpoint, to use one's memory, etc.). And furthermore, Kant himself notes that bewilderment seizes the spectator penetrating into this place for the first time. Which leads us to suppose that the second, or perhaps the third time, the feeling would disappear as the (entirely sensual) church would be made present.

In the other example Kant mentions at the beginning of section 26, the pyramids, the whole is, as a matter of fact, presented, as long as we stand neither too close nor too far away. If, to sum up, the limits of aesthetic comprehension are drawn at the interior of the sensible, whatever goes beyond this comprehension is still part of the "presentable" (even if not of the in fact presented), a way of saying that the finitude experienced in the mathematical sublime (if we believe the example) could be qualified as "psychological," in contrast to the transcendental finitude. We could no longer understand what would be so forbidding about it nor how, from such an example, we could again find the sublime that "concerns only the Ideas of reason." If it is true that the sublime "aris[es] from the inadequacy of imagination in the aesthetic estimation of magnitude *to attain to its estimation by reason*," (§ 27) the bond uniting aesthetic with rational estimation here seems to be lost. Instead of observing a transcendental finitude (limit of pure space = nothingness) and a rational totality (Idea), we seem to come across an entirely "subjective," "psychological" finitude (the limits of aesthetic comprehension) and a sensible totality (the church).

But we would be mistaken in concluding that Kant either chose his examples lightly or contradicted himself. One phrase, affirming the linkage between aesthetic and rational estimations, allows us perhaps to solve the difficulty: "the greatest effort of the imagination in the presentation of the unit for the estimation of magnitude involves in itself a reference to something absolutely great . . ." (§ 27). What is the nature of this reference? That is the question Kant invites us to answer in order to understand the meaning of his examples. The following remark from section 26 situates the problem more precisely:

> We get examples of the mathematically sublime of nature in mere intuition in all those instances where our imagination is afforded, not so much a greater numerical concept as a large unit as measure (for shortening the numerical series). A tree judged by the height of man gives, at all events, a standard for the mountain; and, supposing this is, say, a mile high, it can serve as a unit for the number expressing the earth's diameter, so as to make it intuitable; similarly the earth's diameter for the known planetary system; this again for the system of the Milky Way; and the immeasurable host of such systems, which go by the name of nebulae, and most likely in turn themselves form such a system, holds out no prospect of a limit. Now in the aesthetic estimate of such an immeasurable whole, the sublime does not lie so much in the greatness of the number, as in the fact that in our onward advance we always arrive at proportionately greater units.

This kind of example is quite different from the preceding one. Here, space itself explicitly constitutes the unsurpassable limit one would nevertheless have to surpass to present the Ideas. This confirms the first interpretation: the mathematically sublime is indeed an experience of transcendental finitude and not a psychological one. It is even rather surprising that the limit to aesthetic comprehension should not be alluded to here. On the contrary, the progression from a smaller to a larger unit seems to go on indefinitely. What is stressed is the character—itself unlimited, infinite—of our finitude, what could once again be expressed in the proposition: space is an "infinite given magnitude."

Let us get back now to our question: what relation is there between the subjective absolutely great of aesthetic estimation or evaluation and the absolutely great of rational evaluation? The answer is, at first, obvious: between them there is a negative relation, a relation of failure. The first does not come up to the second, it fails in its attempt to be adequate to it. But why? Is it only, as the example of the cathedral might lead us to think, because beyond a certain limit everything would become confused and obscure? That amounts, in the final analysis, to asking another question: why is it that "*everything* that nature, as an object of the senses, contains that is great" is "to be valued as little in comparison with the Ideas of reason" (§ 27)? Why is "*every* measure of sensibility . . . insufficient for the Ideas of reason" (§ 27)? This cannot be guaranteed only by experiencing the limits of aesthetic comprehension (since those limits are located within the sensible). We must add to it the conceptual gain of the "Transcendental Aesthetic" chapter of the *Critique of Pure Reason:* space is an "infinite given magnitude," and nature is in space. Then and only then can the limits of aesthetic comprehension make sense. They are a sort of inferior, psychological way of experiencing spatial aesthetic limitation. The examples in section 26 of the third *Critique* must then be understood as analogues of the true sublime, since the relation between the church and the limit to aesthetic comprehension that brings about the failure of imagination is identical to the relation between the rational Idea and the transcendental limit that space is, in a way that could be represented like this:

$$\frac{\text{CATHEDRAL (sensible whole)}}{\substack{\text{limit of aesthetic comprehension} \\ \text{(psychological finitude)}}} = \frac{\text{IDEA (rational whole)}}{\substack{\text{spatial limit} \\ \text{(transcendental finitude)}}}$$

Thus, only in so far as the limit of aesthetic comprehension refers back to the—transcendental—limits of space can it evoke the Ideas and bring about the sublime.

REASON, SENTIMENT, AND THE BAROQUE:
AESTHETIC HUMANISM

The few pages Kant consecrates to the sublime in the third *Critique* are rich in what they teach us. They show quite precisely how, within Kantian aesthetics, a deconstruction of the system of metaphysics coexists with a radical thinking about finitude, about what forever escapes representation and which in contemporary philosophy goes by the name of "difference." Which explains why Kant's aesthetic, while giving up neither reason nor sentiment, both granted an essential status in the judgment of taste, decidedly orients itself toward the baroque, for as long anyway as this art of excess manages to maintain itself within the bounds of "good taste" and thus conserve a (for sentiment) satisfactory relation with the Ideas (of reason):

But where all that is intended is the maintenance of a free play of the powers of representation (subject, however, to the condition that there is to be nothing for understanding to take exception to), in ornamental gardens, in the decoration of rooms, in all kinds of furniture that shows good taste, etc., regularity in the shape of constraint is to be avoided as far as possible. Thus English taste in gardens, and baroque taste in furniture, push the freedom of imagination to the verge of what is grotesque—the idea being that in this divorce from all constraint of rules the precise instance is being afforded where taste can exhibit its perfection in projects of the imagination to the fullest extent.[13]

It is the task of reflection (or of the reflective judgment) to articulate these three moments—deconstructed reason, sentiment, and the excess that is the nonpresentable—which is what makes it the defining characteristic of the human being as finite being but one nonetheless capable of thinking the infinite. This point has been vigorously disputed.

According to a thesis put forward by Jean-François Lyotard—faithful, or so he thinks, to Heidegger's interpretation and to his polemic against Ernst Cassirer—"Kant's thinking is not a humanism," as the neo-Kantians would have it, and moreover the issues at stake within it are "too important to be left to the Neo-Kantians."[14] Lyotard's argument bases itself essentially on a classic reading of the *Critique of Practical Reason*, and especially of the distinction it establishes between man and reasoning finite beings in general: "Kant comes back to this point again and again; man is not the recipient of the categorical imperative: the latter addresses itself to 'all reasoning finite beings.' As pure principle of practical reason, the moral law is, in the strictest sense, *inhuman*" (ibid.). Let us overlook the formula. Why not simply say nonhuman or suprahuman to designate the sphere of transcendence which—no argument here—rises above empirical man? Let us also overlook the banality of a remark serving merely to remind us that transcendental philosophy is not reducible to psychology or anthropology. We are left with the problem of determining the meaning of the distinction between man and reasoning finite being and of clarifying the extent to which it still authorizes us to speak of a "Kantian humanism" when we evoke the conception of "the subject" dealt with in the theory of the reflective judgment.

No doubt about it, at the level of the *Critique of Judgement,* at the level therefore of aesthetics, it is well and truly man and exclusively man that is under consideration. "The pleasant," Kant writes, "is a significant factor even with irrational animals; *beauty* has purport and significance *only for human beings* [*nur für Menschen*], i.e., for beings at once animal and rational *but not merely for them as rational—intelligent beings—but only for them as at once animal and rational;* whereas the good is good for every rational being in general" (§ 5). This proposition, drawn out at length in section 83 of the third *Critique,* would by itself be enough to legitimize the use of the term "humanism" to qualify Kant's aesthetics.

But we need to go further. The strange thing is that, apropos the *Critique of Practical Reason,* Lyotard attributes to Heidegger a thesis that, in fact, was not only a long-standing position of the neo-Kantians but also the main criticism Cassirer made of the Heideggerian interpretation of Kant. The point merits discussion. Not only does it have philological importance, it also brings us to the crucial question of the status of Kantian aesthetics in relation to the second *Critique.*

The interpretation Heidegger develops in his *Kantbuch* [translated as *Kant and the Problem of Metaphysics*] sets out from the—quite correct—principle that Kant's thought is a thinking out, and the first in modern philosophy, of radical finitude. At whatever level one locates oneself within critical philosophy (sensibility, understanding, theoretical reason, practical reason), the link to an *originary receptivity* must not be broken—the imagination, as faculty at once receptive and spontaneous, being the milieu where this link to receptivity, and therefore to finiteness, is thematized as such. In section 30 of his *Kantbuch,* therefore, Heidegger tries to provide an interpretation of the *Critique of Practical Reason* compatible with the project he discerns in the first

Critique. The goal for him is one of harmonizing a thinking out of radical finitude, tied to the transcendental imagination, with the "practical" thought of the "dignity of the self," of the "fundamental and total possibility of authentic existence." He must thus find within practical reason a conception of receptivity through which the link with finitude can be maintained. Hence his interpretation of respect for the moral law as the analogue, in the practical field, of what pure intuition is in the theoretical field. Far from being secondary in relation to the moral law, its reception by a finite being in the aspect of that nonpsychological feeling that respect is "is neither subsequent nor is it something that takes place only occasionally. Respect for the law . . . is in itself a revelation of myself as the self that acts." [15]

This interpretation, which is disputed by Cassirer (in his 1931 review of the *Kantbuch,* a text that should be read to grasp what the Davos debate between Heidegger and Cassirer was all about), permits Heidegger to find again in the sphere of practical reason the unitary structure, at once spontaneous and receptive, that belongs to the imagination. "The self-submissive, immediate surrender . . . is pure receptivity . . . ; the free self-imposition of the law is pure spontaneity. In themselves, the two are originally one" (ibid., p. 166). The consequence of this interpretation is clear: the moral law should have as destination man, and not finite beings in general. As Heidegger recalls in section 31 of *Kant and the Problem of Metaphysics,* man is, for Kant, but a particular species of reasoning finite being, that in which finitude is tied to *sensibility* (*intuition* at the theoretical level and, according to Heidegger, *respect* at the practical level). But nothing hinders a purely *rational,* nonsensual, conception of finitude, one that would be expressed only in the difference between being [*l'être*] and the ought-to-be [*le devoir-être*], the *is* and the *ought.* For an infinite being the moral law is of the order of Being, for a finite being, of the ought-to-be, without this difference being, for Kant, necessarily tied to sensibility and thus to a specifically human finitude.

Now, what Heidegger regrets about the second edition of the *Critique of Pure Reason* is precisely the emergence of this distinction, which obviously leads Kant to separate finitude and sensual receptivity and thus to relegate the imagination to a secondary level. Heidegger then demonstrates how Kant, obsessed with the idea of separating the ethical from the psychological, unfortunately effects a distinction between men and rational finite beings and posits the moral law as valid also for the latter in general—which makes it independent of respect and abstracts it out of the temporal structure of the transcendental imagination. This is what Heidegger writes about it: "It is incontestable that the distinction between a finite rational being in general and man as a particular example of such a being comes to the fore in the transcendental deduction as the latter appears in the second edition" (ibid., p. 174). And, "In the second edition, Kant has enlarged the concept of a rational finite being to the point where it no longer coincides with the concept of man and thus has posed the problem of finitude with greater comprehensiveness" (ibid., pp. 175–76).

Has this enlargement had, as Cassirer thought (and Lyotard along with him, no doubt), the effect of an "improvement," of a victory against psychologism and "anthropomorphism"? Heidegger's answer to this question is also explicit: "On the contrary, when correctly understood, this edition is even more 'psychological' simply because it is oriented exclusively on pure reason as such" (ibid., p. 176). It is thus not, as Lyotard believes, Cassirer the neo-Kantian, but Heidegger himself who never stopped criticizing the distinction between two kinds of finitude: man's sensible finitude and the purely rational one of the finite being in general. It was furthermore Heidegger who first showed the way in which this distinction, contrary to appearances, could have the second edition of the *Critique* lapse back into anthropology as a consequence, in so far as it leads Kant to "thrust the imagination into the background, thus concealing its transcendental nature completely" (ibid., p. 174).

Is a further proof needed that, to the contrary, it is neo-Kantianism that holds the distinction disapproved of by Heidegger to be crucial, and that maintains the idea that the moral law addresses itself to finite beings in general and not only to man? We need only read the review Cassirer wrote of Heidegger's book on Kant in the 1931 *Kant-Studien*. Kant, he wrote, went to some lengths so that

the meaning of his "transcendental" problematic should not be displaced onto the psychological—nor his observations shoved over into the merely anthropological planes. He tirelessly stresses that any analysis that would set out from the mere "nature of the human being" would miss the transcendental Idea of freedom, and with it the laying-out of the grounds for ethics, in its very principles. It is owing to this preoccupation that the Kantian proposition, so often ill-known and ill-interpreted, was uttered, that one could only arrive at a pure conception of the ethical law if one took care that it should be valid not only for humans but also for "all rational beings in general" [*fur alle Vernunftwesen überhaupt*]. Kant was here not really thinking, as Schopenhauer mockingly reproached him, "of the dear little angels"—here also he was speaking as critic and methodologist, whose concern was not to allow the frontiers between the disciplines to "run into each other," and who accordingly wished to separate, strictly and following principles, the tasks of ethics and those of anthropology. This line of demarcation is given him through the opposition between "appearance" and "thing-in-itself," between time and freedom. And here lies also the authentic and essential objection I must raise against Heidegger's interpretation of Kant.[16]

This text has evidently been forgotten by the very thinkers who today pretend to carry on the inheritance of what they believe to be the Heideggerian interpretation of Kant. It is rather piquant to see Lyotard take up, almost word for word, against neo-Kantism an argument so typically neo-Kantian that Cassirer did not hesitate to make of it the true point of separation from Heidegger. It proves, if proof were needed, that the contempt with which the Heideggerians have always looked upon the neo-Kantians is most often accompanied by ignorance of essential pieces in the record of the ongoing debate. Why such a blunder? Because the imagery around the Davos debate and the *Kantstreit* has it that, in the eyes of an overhasty Heideggerianism, any and all reference to man or to humanism inevitably refers back to the idea of anthropology, and therefore to the metaphysics of subjectivity. And, as is well known, neo-Kantism = positivism = metaphysics of subjectivity, therefore anthropology. Q.E.D.

But beyond the philological mistake, Lyotard's adopted position leads him to miss that in Heidegger's interpretation which, though debatable, may be philosophically fertile. As I have tried to demonstrate elsewhere,[17] the idea of thinking ethics without losing the link to temporality, therefore—Heidegger is right—with *man* as the site of a finitude whose structure is that of the schematizing imagination, has nothing absurd about it. Correctly understood, it finds its most developed formulation in the *Critique of Judgment,* where the Ideas of theoretical and also of practical reason, conceived of as principles of the reflective judgment, maintain an unbreakable, even though symbolic, link with aesthetics, with sensibility and temporality seen as the radical signs of human finitude.

At the end of this analysis, we can see more clearly the way in which the "Kantian moment" can legitimately put itself forward as an impressive attempt to articulate the three most characteristic tendencies of what has here been called the prehistory of aesthetics:

—Rationalism keeps some of the rights it could lay claim to within Boileau's classical tradition: some, but not all. The ideas of reason, in the theory of the beautiful as in that of the sublime, do in the final instance remain the supporting pillars of the common sense. But rationalism itself has, all the same, lost its dogmatic character, and the project of a science of the beautiful, at the source of the *Art poétique*, is invalidated at the same time that the temptation to reduce beauty to a simple sensual presentation of truth vanishes. Inescapable consequence: aesthetics, even when thought of as a philosophical discipline, must once and for all give up the pretension of establishing infallible criteria of good taste. One can, at best, interpret the common sense as a presumption in favor of a work's greatness—supposing it not to be "ideological."

—Sentiment thus finds again the place denied it by dogmatic classicism. While the reference to ideas permits the grounding of the common sense, sensibility becomes the touchstone thanks to which logic and aesthetics can separate *without a reduction of one realm to the other being possible*. Bouhours's argument that the Beautiful is as ineffable as it is unforeseeable recovers its legitimacy—though, as criticism requires, it too must be limited in its relativistic penchants.

—And that also permits us to accord the demands of baroque aesthetics their rightful place. If classical good taste, in its metaphysical horror of excess, "clips the wings of genius," it must no longer hinder it to the point of blocking its flight. The Beautiful is no longer the sensible image of truth, the imitation of what is essential, rational, in nature. It acquires its own structure, an autonomy without which the smallest aesthetic pleasure could not exist, also and perhaps even especially due to its irregularity and its contingency in relation to the necessities inherent in logical thought. Like humor, the veritably beautiful must surprise, otherwise it will never overstep the narrow frame of an aesthetics of perfection where the "well painted" remains, will always remain a thousand miles removed from the trait of genius.

The Kantian moment is thus par excellence the moment of the breach: a breach in the theology of a satellizing divinity that intermediates between monads walled up in themselves; a breach also in the secular reduction of sensibility to a confused perception of the intelligible world, to a deformed copy of ideal truth; a breach, finally, in the conception of man as creature, as a being whose finitude must forever be downgraded when measured against a divinity whose existence "in itself" could be demonstrated.

Hegel's aesthetics tries, with a doubtlessly unequaled grandeur, to wall up this opening through the power of the concept.

FOUR

The Hegelian Moment: The Absolute Subject or the Death of Art

T RUTH IS ONE, yet it is impossible to dispute the fact that there
exists a multitude of mutually contradictory philosophical systems:
"Upon this stands the shallow demonstration which affirms, with a
knowing air, that nothing is obtained from the history of philosophy;
one man proves the other wrong; the very accumulation of philosophies
is proof of the nullity of philosophy as an undertaking."[1] Confound-
ingly banal though it may be, the objection raised by scepticism still
requires an answer. Worse, the philosopher knows all too well, having
once taken it seriously, that the challenge thrown down by nonphilosophy is of the kind that can take you very far away from where you
thought you were going—an observation all the more irritating in that
the problem itself remains one of extraordinary simplicity: if the true
should be the same for everyone, as human reason demands, then what
status should this bothersome plurality be given?

We have to acknowledge it: the "shallow argument" was worrying
Hegel well before his system received the definitive form that alone allowed him to bring to the problem a satisfying answer (meaning in his
own eyes, of course). When in his youth he created in Jena, together
with his friend Schelling, the *Critical Journal of Philosophy* (it appeared
in Tübingen in 1802/1803), the first issue's introduction was devoted to
this delicate question. Bearing the title "On the Essence of Philosophical
Criticism in General and Its Relation to the Present State of Philosophy
in Particular," it intended to set out the conditions under which criticism could legitimately sort out the wheat from the chaff, meaning not
only philosophy from nonphilosophy (mere opinions), but also, at the
very heart of that which deserves the name of philosophy, the true system from the others. The solution Hegel considered in those days is not
without interest. Inspired by Schelling, it consists in the description of
the history of philosophy by analogy with that of art, as the presenta-

tion, in diverse forms, of one and the same idea. Thus art criticism also becomes the model for philosophical criticism. Just as the aesthetic work is the expression of presentation [*Darstellung*] of an idea in a sensual form (colors, sounds, etc.), and just as criticism's aim is the singling out of the idea, of the signified, from the manifest signifier, so one can distinguish within each philosophical system between the content, the "rational kernel," identical in the final analysis among all systems of thought worthy of the name, and the contingent form in which it is expostulated.

The young Hegel could thus believe he was refuting the skeptics' argument by stating that only the form is variable and historically determined, in so far as it depends on each historical period's own culture [*Bildung*]. Philosophical criticism's task consists then in breaking the shell that prevents the inner movement of thought from coming to light. At which point there is no longer any veritable contradiction between the different philosophical systems, since they all, in the last instance, express the same Idea. Their apparent diversity proceeds only from the fact that the philosopher is obligated, following the various periods and cultures, to express his ideas in a relative and contingent form, which must be set aside by placing oneself at the highest philosophical point of view, that is, at the point of view of a philosophy of identity in which the form of the presentation, unburdened, finally, of the particular aspects of such and such a determinate historical culture, is identical to the Idea of philosophy itself. (This harmony of content and form defines the systematicity that, in 1802, Hegel still thought he saw brought to reality in Schelling's philosophy.)

It may perhaps be objected that the grounds for philosophical criticism's claims to objectivity—or art criticism's claims, for that matter—are not easy to grasp. By what right does one authorize oneself to declare that this or that work is a proper expression of the true idea, while that other one is nothing but an embroidery of opinions, without truth? Hegel's answer is, again, borrowed from Schelling; it depends on the argument that one can use the Idea present in the work to disengage it from the form, which is defective because specific and tied to the culture of its time. There would thus be a "need for philosophy," unsatisfied as long as it has not been molded into a systematic form. It is upon this need that criticism can set foot in order to become legitimate; in order, that is, not to be radically external to its object (without which, because unacknowledged, it would behave violently towards it).

It is easy enough to perceive this first solution's shortcomings when set against the standards of the definitive system. First of all, though grounded, criticism does not entirely avoid what Hegel, in the Introduction to the *Phenomenology*, later designates as dogmatism. Criticism is always carried out, in fact, from the viewpoint of a supposedly true knowledge, thus from that of the achieved, completed system—which is why it never really manages to become an internal criticism (the hypothesis of a "need for philosophy" being, so to speak, the dues dogmatism pays to virtue). Even more seriously, the skeptical argument is actually refuted in the context of a vision of the history of philosophy whose inconvenience is merely that of denying historicity as such. If we think about it, we will indeed realize that it is precisely the historical element in each philosophical system that is its inessential component (the part tied up with the historical *Bildung*). If, at bottom, all the systems give expression to the same idea, we hardly see what could be so interesting about the unfolding of their diversity in the course of time, and the criticism that would separate out the content from what is mere contingent form in them has no other finality than that of self-justification.

Herein lies the real analogy with the aesthetic sphere. In 1801, Hegel still conceived of the temporality of the one and eternal philosophical Idea as its expression in a form other than itself (in the *Bildung*), but also as something other than temporality itself, whereas in the definitive system the philosophical Idea enjoys its own development, its own intrinsic evolution during which it unfolds its different moments, contained within it originarily as if within a seed. Historicity has here become a constitutive element of the idea itself, being no longer either contingent, or tied only to the external form, but truly necessary to the life of the Idea.

We should understand clearly this decisive rupture in Hegel's intellectual itinerary, at least in its principle. Although as late as 1801–02 aesthetics and philosophy could to a certain extent be put at the same level, this ceases to be the case beginning with the *Phenomenology* of 1806 (to cite a gigantic but very convenient landmark). Of course, the idea of the beautiful—which is and will remain for Hegel the idea of the truth—will also be "historicized," penetrated through and through by an internal evolution. But the immense difference between aesthetics and philosophy will nevertheless consist in the fact that art, as in 1801, continues to be thought of as alienation (as "presentation" or exposition) of the idea of the true in a form *external* to it (the sensible), while philosophy becomes the expression of the Idea *in thought*, thus, we may say, in itself, in its own element. Art criticism maintains therefore a function identical to what it had in 1801. Its aim is still to single out an intelligible signified "behind" a sensual signifier; the beautiful continues to be, in this sense, an object for interpretation. Philosophy, on the other hand, ignoring this diremption between content and form, between the idea and its expression, definitively disassociates itself from the world of art, forcing the latter back to a superseded phase among the ordered stages of the progress of the spirit. It is indeed hard to see why, if the essential thing is the Idea, the content, we should limit ourselves to grasping it through the distorting form of sensibility rather than apprehending it in and for itself, as it is in itself. The death of art, so spectacularly decreed by Hegel, could well have about it a whiff of Platonism.

But, to be certain of this, it behooves us to grasp the source of the distinction between art and philosophy. Reexamining, in the *Lectures on the History of Philosophy*, the skeptical argument drawn from the plurality of systems, Hegel counters it with an argument the inverse of that developed in 1801: the history of philosophy is no longer conceptualized as the unfolding of the Idea "in its other"—in an external form—but rather as an internal development, as a self-unfolding. This latter presents a ternary structure whose real principle should be grasped (commonplaces about "the three moments of the Hegelian dialectic" being most often screens camouflaging a much more delicate method of thinking than would appear at first sight).

The first moment in this trinity of the idea's development is the *in-itself*, which Hegel willingly compares to Aristotle's *dynamis*, meaning (at the level that interests us here) being as potential, merely virtual being. Following the well-known imagery (itself based on a complex logical argument concerning the category of "becoming"), the in-itself may be compared to the seed, containing *as potential* all the richness of the reality to come. The second moment is that of *being-there* [*Dasein*]. The term quite simply means, in German, "what exists," the particular real of existence. This second stage in the becoming of the Idea is the one where the elements, the determinations contained virtually in the seed, pass over into existence. The third moment is the *for-itself*. It indicates the return to unity, the re-collection into a *system* of the specific determinations of the Idea so far developed. Following the imagery, the for-itself may be compared to the fruit, simultaneously the ultimate result of the development and bearer of new seeds (of new "in-themselves").

Even if we ignore the details, we can easily understand how the application of this logical structure to the problem raised by the skeptical argument provides a solution completely different from that consisting in making of art criticism the model for philosophical criticism, in order to clear the irrational dross away from the idea. Here, not only is the plurality of systems no longer an objection to the idea of truth, but, rather, the real objection would be the absence of such a multiplicity, for the plurality—as the reader will have already intuited—corresponds to the second moment of the unfolding of the idea, the moment of the being-there in which the multiple determinations incarnate into the existence of specific philosophical systems. Once gathered into the "for-itself," this multiplicity finally appears as what it is: a system—or, to be more exact, the system of philosophy in which historicity has been fully incorporated. With Hegel, the history of philosophy accomplishes its task of becoming philosophical, since it purely and simply fuses with the auto-unfolding of the complete system of the determinations of thought. There are indeed—the skeptics are right in a certain sense—various philosophical "systems" that contradict each other; but to that must be added that the true system, the only one worthy of such a prestigious name, is nothing that is external to them. On the contrary, it fuses into their recollection.

The consequence of this temporalization of the idea of truth: if philosophy's history, unlike art's, is no longer the narrative of the sensual incarnations of an idea, if, on the contrary, its different moments are the necessary and logical ones of the auto-unfolding of this idea, then there is no longer any point in *interpreting* the works that signal its development:

About any thing, we can ask about its sense or its meaning: so, with a work of art, about the meaning of its form [*Gestalt*]; with a language, about the meaning of the word; with religion, about the meaning of the image or of the worship; with other types of activity, about their moral value, etc. This meaning or sense is nothing else than the essential or universal substantial content of an object, and this substantial content is the concrete Thought of the object. Here we always have two aspects, an outer and an inner, an outer appearance that is sensually perceptible and intuitable, and a meaning, which is, precisely, the Thought. But where our object is now Thought itself, there are no two aspects at hand: Thought is what is meaningful for itself. [*Indem nun aber unser Gegenstand selbst der Gedanke ist, so ist hier nicht zweierlei vorhanden, sondern der Gedanke ist das Bedeutende für sich selbst.*] (Ibid., p. 95)

Of course, in the final system, the idea of the beautiful will itself be historicized. But art will keep its status as the presentation of the different moments of thought in sensible form and, as such, it cannot pretend to the same dignity as philosophy. Thus, Hegelianism effects, going back before Kant, a certain return to a devalorization, much like Leibniz's, of the sensual world.

THE THEODICY REVISITED

Hegelian aesthetics developed within a metaphysics whose inner core remained prisoner of monadic individualism—a framework that needed to be taken apart, as Baumgarten's *Aesthetics* had already intuited, to preserve the autonomy of the sensible and establish the intellectual room for a true philosophy of art. This is true enough for us to be able to single out, without great difficulty, the five constitutive principles of Leibniz's *Monadology* at work within the system's innermost structure—the affirmation about "the death of art" being thus a priori inscribed into the architectonics of a preestablished harmony no doubt further refined, but on this point not decisively modified, by the introduction of dialectics and historicity. A few indications:

1. The *identity principle*. Understood in its Leibnizian meaning, it secretly continues to define the individuality of what Hegel, in a broader meaning, calls the "determinations" [*Bestimmtheiten*] of thought—whether these be the different configurations of the Spirit, of consciousness, or of the logical categories. We could say, to be entirely explicit, that these determinations within Hegel's system are the exact analogue to the monads in Leibniz's theodicy. Each moment—if we think, for example, about the stages of consciousness in the *Phenomenology*—represents a point of view, a partial perspective upon an ensemble which, contemplated from God's or the philosopher's viewpoint, is seen as integrated (in the mathematical sense of the word) into a harmonious totality.

2. The *principle of sufficient reason*. It regulates the linkage of the monadic determinations down to the smallest detail. The *Phenomenology* can again be the model here: not only does each stage of the naïve consciousness's experience literally produce the next stage, but also when, anguished by the discovery of the contradictions immanent in its worldview, consciousness desperately tries to hold on to its view by systematically exploring all possible fallback positions, it is constantly guided in its operations by the principle that it must not without

reason abandon the knowledge it possesses or thinks it possesses. More generally, we can say that it is the perception of a dialectical contradiction that furnishes sufficient reason for passing from one determination to another.

3. Thus, the *continuity* of the integration of the different moments or points of view is preserved. Just as in the *Monadology* there is no emptiness (nature makes no leaps), so in Hegel's system there are no ruptures and the distance separating one determination from the next is infinitely small.

4. For the same reason, the system cannot unnecessarily multiply entities. We will never find two perfectly identical stages in the divine process of the auto-unfolding of the Idea. Otherwise they would be indistinguishable and would be in reality one sole and unique determination.

5. Like the Leibnizian world, the Hegelian system at every point conforms to the *principle of the best*. The maximum of determinations are integrated within the most economical, the most elegant figure—circularity.

To this comparison it will perhaps be objected that it hides the dimension of History that Hegel obviously adds to the Leibnizian monadology. Objection granted. But that should not obscure the fact that, from an aesthetic point of view, Hegel's conception of temporality concurs with Leibniz's in its common refusal to consider the sensible as something other than a confused intelligible. Here again I will limit myself to pointing out a few indications of this continuity.

I have already alluded to the way Kant grounded the autonomy of sensibility in the theory of pure intuitions. We need to come back to this to better grasp how Hegelian thinking about time remains strangely pre-Kantian. The aim of the "Transcendental Aesthetic" section of the *Critique of Pure Reason* was that of separating, contrary to the Leibnizians (meaning contrary to the principle of indiscernibles), the sensible intuition from the concept. It is with this in mind that Kant defined time (and space) as "infinite given totalities." He, indeed, had to distinguish carefully between aesthetic time and conceptual time. Aesthetic time is characterized by the fact that, in it, the totality precedes the parts (one cannot conceive of a moment in time without immediately thinking of it against the horizon of an indefinite totality of instants). Conceptual time, on the contrary—meaning for example the time of the history of scientific progress—should be conceived of as an addition of parts (the stages in the evolution of science) which, ideally (at the level of Ideas as metaphysics imagines them) should end up constituting a totality. It's through such a distinction, and only through it, that Kant could qualitatively oppose the sensible to the intelligible, there where Leibniz could only make of the first an epiphenomenon of the second. It is also through this distinction, and, again, only through it, that, the autonomy of sensibility secured against the concept, Kant could carry out Baumgarten's project, otherwise unrealizable within Leibnizian metaphysics.

Now, paradoxically—and contrary to the received idea that would have Hegel be the great introducer of historicity in philosophy—the latter's conception of temporality signals a twofold return to the Leibnizian integration of time in the concept:

1. One of the consequences of Kant's distinction between concept and sensibility was that time and space had to be thought of as empty frames, though they could never be perceived as such. In his wish to recapture the totality of what is in the concept, Hegel, as opposed to Kant, comes back to the idea that time, in Leibniz's famous formula, "is only conceivable through the detail of what changes." This thesis becomes visible within the entirety of the system at the point at which temporality is defined as "the concept being there." Temporality is thus reduced to the "intelligible" development of the various determinations of the Idea so that, as with Leibniz, from God's point of view or *für uns,* for us philosophers who know the truth, it is but an appearance. It is, in essence, just the confused way in which the finite subject, the reflective subject, apprehends the development of determinations that in themselves exist since and for all eternity. Establishing as it does the distinction between the effectively real and the contingent, this thesis is also found at a key moment of the logical dialectic, since it undergirds the first fundamental category of the logic of Being: the category of becoming. It is because pure becoming is nonthinkable (or aesthetic, nonconceptual time, if one prefers) that it must immediately be conceptualized as the becoming of *something*. Right from the beginning, from its very first pages, Hegel's *Science of Logic* rehabilitates the Leibnizian conception of aesthetic time as a pure illusion of finitude destined to be superseded in the perfection of the divine point of view.

2. But we can go further, we can find the entire ontological structure of Leibniz's Theodicy in the Hegelian philosophy of history. Hegel himself never made any secret of it: *Reason in History* will go so far as to define the whole of the system as a working out of what was already

contained in embryo in Leibniz: "Our meditation will therefore be a theodicy, the justification of God that Leibniz had attempted metaphysically, after his fashion and with as yet indeterminate categories."

This upgrading of God's point of view in relation to man's results in two consequences that are basic in aiding us to grasp the inferior status of aesthetics in Hegel's oeuvre:

1. Hegel, paradoxically, does not escape from the monadological configuration of modern individualism. It is thus not at all accidental not only that his philosophy of history locates its metaphysical origins in the Leibnizian theodicy but also that its perfect expression, in the sphere of political theory, is the liberals' famous "invisible hand." That the liberal state may have been elsewhere criticized by Hegel in no way affects the structural similarity between the "cunning of reason" and the "invisible hand"; aesthetic communication thus once again becomes a *mediated* communication. It is in the aesthetic idea—itself related to truth—that the spectators can recognize themselves and each other, and it is through the mediation of a system (i.e., of a preestablished harmony) that they can communicate among themselves.

2. Sensibility's autonomy over against the concept also vanishes, if it isn't altogether fused with pure and simple contingency. As the "Preliminary Concept" in Hegel's *Encyclopaedia* states, intuition is a faculty in embryo, capable only of grasping confusedly what reason alone can veritably think. Art, corelatively, can only be an equally inferior means of grasping the truth of the idea; it is, in a word, a *gnoseologia inferior*. Under these conditions, the tendency of Hegelian thinking will be to challenge the *Critique of Judgment*'s effort to break with classicism, which in the end leads, as we shall soon see, to Hegel's affirmation of the superiority of the artistic over the natural Beauty.

THE COPERNICAN COUNTERREVOLUTION: ARTISTIC BEAUTY OR NATURAL BEAUTY?

Kant has often been taken to task for his relative lack of interest in, and even want of taste for, artistic beauty. Frederick the Great's verses, quoted in section 49 of the *Critique of Judgment* as an instance of artistic genius, make us smile even in their original French. The passages given over to the classification of the fine arts are profound, but in vain would we look for the traces of an authentic aesthetic culture therein. On this point, no doubt of it, Hegel's *Lectures on Aesthetics* are quite superior to the third *Critique*. Besides, the way Kant links "the advantage of natural beauty over artistic beauty" with the fact that it is "in harmony with the purified and serious way of thinking of all human beings who have cultivated the moral sentiment" (§ 42) seems today, to put it kindly, antiquated. Even worse, from the point of view of transcendental philosophy itself, the argument looks to be entirely empirical and rather feeble in this regard. The world is full of quite serious and quite respectable people who would place artistic beauty well above natural beauty. Any number of interpreters have thought to see in this point the Achilles' heel of Kant's aesthetics.

And that began with Hegel himself. The Kantian position is countered from the very first page of the introduction to the *Lectures*. Hegel stresses there that the object of aesthetics is not the realm of the beautiful in general but only that of artistic beauty. It is not even certain that the qualifier "beautiful" can properly be used of natural entities. And even if we allow ourselves this poetic license, we shall have to assert anyway that "the beauty of art is *higher* than nature." Hegel's justification for this reversal of Kantism is not without interest. If artistic beauty is the only valuable one, it is because it is "beauty born of the spirit and born again"; therefore "the higher the spirit and its productions stand above nature and its phenomena, the higher too is the beauty of art above that of nature. Indeed, considered formally, even a useless notion that enters a man's head is higher than any product of nature, because in such a notion spirituality and freedom are always present." Who could dispute that the human is superior to the inhuman and that, in that condition, it must have been through a strange naïveté or through a surprising disinterest for culture that the *Critique of Judgment* did not perceive the obvious superiority of art over nature?

But the problem of the relation between the two types of beauty is much more complicated than it seems. If we judge too hastily we risk missing the target and not seeing, for example, that he who truly holds art in contempt is not the one we think, and that nature's "advantage" is perhaps, in a paradoxical way that merits dwelling upon, the best if not the only way of saving art from the inevitable handicap it suffers in classicism. If beauty is but the sensible expression of truth, and if this expression is itself fully mastered by a subject (the artist), art will doubtless be superior to nature because more adequate to the ends thereby assigned to beauty. But in that case we don't see how art could avoid having a status lower than that of science and philosophy, supposed to provide a more direct and more reliable access to "the thing itself." When nature is accorded pride of place over artifice a certain portion of beauty is, indeed, taken away from the power of the spirit, but that is also the way aesthetics can hope not to be reduced to a "theory of inferior knowledge" nor to a simple formula indicating the means capable of communicating to the common understanding truths too abstract to be grasped by it at the level which is, nonetheless, the only level befitting them: that of true speculation.

The better to grasp this paradox, we must keep in mind the motives leading Kant to the position that beauty must, above everything else, contain a natural element, independent of the human mind. The beautiful object, as we know, is one which, though purely sensible (natural), brings about in us an intellectual agreement of the faculties analogous to what would be required for the Ideas finally to be actualized. What reason demands, in fact, is for nature and spirit to be reconciled as they would be seen from the point of view of a completed science or—what comes down to the same thing—of an infinite, omniscient understanding, as the divine understanding must be. *But for it to be of any interest, this reconciliation of nature and spirit must proceed from nature itself.* We may say of the beautiful object that it is that which evokes in us the idea of God. But for this Idea to be "revived in us," as Kant puts it, it is important that this accord between nature and spirit that reason demands not be fabricated. It should not be artificially produced, otherwise it would lose all that makes for its charm, namely its contingency, its naturalness, the fact that it is not a product of our will. What reason finds pleasant about the beautiful has to do precisely with this contingency; it is because reason's demand is that nature should, in the end, conform to the laws of the understanding that it is, so to speak, happy to see certain objects manifesting, independently of us, *without being forced*, something like a "trace" (§ 42) or the beginning of a satisfaction of this uncancelable stipulation. The beautiful is like humor, it can never be completely "intended."

What is at stake is not negligible. At the philosophical level, the difference between reflection and determination is here at play. The reflective judgment always presuppoß that the agreement between nature and spirit is in principle *contingent*, therefore natural since it proceeds from the particular to the general and not the contrary. Only at that price can the beautiful object remain for us always a surprise. At the aesthetic level, in the sense of a specific intellectual discipline, it's the key problematic of classicism that is set aside along the way. Since beauty is not of the domain of the determining judgment, there can be no "poetics of art" [*art poétique*], no science of the beautiful that would once and for all determine both the general rules of the production of beauty and their correct criteria of application.

That is what the famous examples where Kant denounces imitation as inaesthetic are trying to illustrate. Like Leibniz, Kant admires the beauty of flowers and of insects. In the symmetrical designs of rare complexity sometimes adorning beetle or butterfly wings, in the extraordinary variety of colors, nature has all the appearances of art. One would say it means to do it, in purposive fashion, and, precisely because that is not the case (nature has no intentions), human reason can experience a certain pleasure in seeing some of its most unrealizable demands confirmed just a little bit. It is indeed truly remarkable that if we had "secretly gone behind" the lover of the beautiful and "planted artificial flowers (which can be prepared so as to closely resemble the natural ones) in the earth, or had placed artificially carved birds on the branches of trees, and he had thereupon discovered the deceit, the immediate interest he had previously taken in these things would in an instant disappear," for only "the notion that nature produced this beauty" (§ 42) is capable of grounding out immediate interest in the very existence of the beautiful thing. Kant insists upon this several times: "But this interest that we have in beauty quite requires that it be beauty of nature; it disappears entirely as soon as one notices one has been deceived" (ibid.). Thus, "what could be more valued of poets than the enchantingly beautiful song of the nightingale, in a lonesome bush, on a quiet summer evening, but the soft light of the moon?" (ibid.). But if we learn that some "kid who knows how to imitate this song" of the nightingale has been deceiving us, what seemed beautiful to us a few moments before is now "not to be supported" (ibid.).

The example of the nightingale is no doubt one of the most celebrated passages in the third *Critique,* and perhaps one of the least understood. Hegel commented upon it, and many after him agreed in seeing in it the mark of great naïveté, or of a regretable lack of taste, as if the important thing here were the biographical aspect. As if the aim here had been to display all the culture of an art historian! The intention is entirely different: what it aims to testify to is the fact that only what is external to human subjectivity, and therefore *natural,* can be said to be beautiful, at least if we refuse purely and simply to fuse beauty with truth, art with science. The passage is also, negatively, about art, and about its irreducibility to either an imitation of nature or to the application of a mere technique permitting the perfect accomplishment of a purpose to be illustrated. Authentic art must thus contain an element of naturalness, an element that escapes from the control of subjectivity and of its consciousness of the objectives it can assign itself in art. If we wish to avoid the reefs of a classicism à la Boileau, we must (and this is the deeper meaning of the allusion to the nightingale) resolve the following paradox: how can art at the same time set itself conscious ends, explicitly aim at the bringing into reality of a certain form of beauty, yet still belong to nature so as not to be reduced to the technically successful actualization of a "good idea" (of one or another "truth of reason")?

The theory of the genius responds to this strange equation. In Kant's anticlassical perspective, art confronts us with this dilemma: "It is either such an imitation of nature that it passes for a mistaking of it, and then it has the same effect as the natural beauty (that was mistaken for it); or else it is an art intentionally aiming at our satisfaction [*Wohlgefallen*]. Immediate satisfaction through taste will then indeed take place, but there will be nothing other than a mediated interest in its original cause, that is to say, an art that may be of interest through its goal but never in itself" (§ 42). Kant intends to free art from this alternative by introducing in it, through his conception of geniality as a natural talent, the predominance of nature over a mind conscious of itself and of the rules it is supposed to apply. Zeuxis' grapes, of which Plato tells us they were so well imitated that the thrushes flew down to pick at them, have no beauty, if they have any, except as copies, in which case it's easy to understand why one might prefer the original—unless one takes art to be a simple technical performance. But art is not better off in the other situation evoked in the above-cited passage. If indeed the aim is, as in classicism, "above all to please" by elegantly presenting beautiful moral ideas, then, clearly, art's finality and value are once again external to it; it is yet again an instrument, the vehicle, itself secondary in importance, of a communication whose terms are played out elsewhere.

This is the essence of Kant's position on art: "Nature was beautiful when it simultaneously looked like art; and art can only be called beautiful when we are conscious it is art, yet it nevertheless looks like nature to us" (§ 45). He could hardly be clearer: since beauty resides in a certain reconciliation of nature and the mind, since this reconciliation is of no interest to human reason unless it is a happy surprise, an unforeseeable and contingent harmony, then, when it comes to natural beauty, nature must astonish us in resembling the mind, and therefore in having the appearance of art; when it comes to artistic beauty, we must be able to, through genius, recognize the *work of nature* in the finished product: "Thus, finality/purposiveness [*Zweckmäßigkeit*] in the products of the fine arts must not seem intentional although it is intentional . . . the 'school form' must not shine through, that is, it must show no trace that rules floated in front of the artist's eyes and laid chains upon the powers of his mind" (§ 45). Contrary to what the French classicists thought, art has nothing to do with the concept of perfection: the point is not to present correctly a good idea, but to *unconsciously create* an unprecedented piece of work, radically new yet immediately gifted with significance for everyone.

We can better understand under these conditions why Kant meets up again with certain aspects of the aesthetics of feeling, and even with baroque art. Not only is the true genius unconscious—which invests him with a component of naturalness without which the fine arts would be nothing but applied arts—but the rules he invents as he applies them are as mysterious for him as they are for the spectator. "The creator of an [artistic] product, for which he must thank his genius, does not himself know how the ideas within him found their way to that product" (§ 46). The "aesthetic Idea" that guides genius can be neither conceived nor stated clearly, "no expression can be found for it that indicates a determined concept; it allows then, besides the concept, much that is unnameable, the feeling for which animates the faculty of knowledge and to language, as mere letters, joins spirit" (§ 49). The artist of genius therefore does not follow rules, he invents them, and the miracle of art consists in the happenstance that this unconscious, and therefore *natural,* invention immediately makes sense to others, and this because of the same principles that made of natural beauty a symbolic trace of the ideas of reason. The artistic Beautiful thus turns out to be, in man, the exact analogue of the natural Beautiful. This is why it is of the essence to maintain, against classicism, that the rule for art, supposing there is one, "cannot be written down in any formula that would serve as prescription" (§ 47).

Making all due allowance for their obvious differences, art turns out to be much like humor: it proceeds from a natural gift that cannot be taught, yet is communicative in that it immediately makes "common sense." We can learn every particular art's technique just as we can learn to tell "funny stories," but this workmanlike accomplishment is not going to transform anyone into an artist or a comedian. Between bringing out what is stored in the memory and having, as is so well said, a *sense* of humor, there is a chasm no amount of effort is ever going to bridge. The advantage of the artificial over the natural, in its very Cartesian will to recuperate the beautiful into the orbit of the powers of the spirit, risks making us forget this "aesthetic truth." Criticizing Kant would inevitably lead Hegelian aesthetics down the path of a renewed classicism.

TOWARDS A NEW CLASSICISM: ART'S TRIPLE HISTORICITY AS SENSIBLE PRESENTATION OF THE TRUE

Let us first of all avoid a misunderstanding connected to the ambiguity of the word "classicism." I don't mean by the term to designate either ancient Greek art, as Hegel himself does, nor even the most significant works of the French seventeenth century, but rather the *aesthetic doctrine* of Cartesian origin that holds that art's main function is to represent the truths of reason in this element, external to them but accessible to the common understanding, that sensibility is. In classicism thus understood the key moment of the beautiful is clearly the *idea*, the sensual element being but the—in its essence inadequate—medium within which truth becomes *perceptible* in *pleasant* fashion. We have already seen how Boileau's *Art poétique* was one of the first great intellectual thematizations of this very "classical" precedence of art's ideal content over its sensual form. We have also already pointed out how, for Boileau, this representation of the beautiful is accompanied by art's claim to eternity: since truth can only be one and atemporal, since the humanity it addresses itself to by way of the various aesthetic forms possesses an intangible, invariable essence, art cannot and should not undergo the kind of historical progress that agitates the scientific world.

The originality of Hegel's aesthetics lies in the very inversion of this postulate. It is because truth has a history—or, better, is itself history—that art, as sensual presentation of this truth, must also enter into the sphere of historicity. There will therefore be "stages" in art's development, as there are in the unfolding of the configurations of consciousness described in the *Phenomenology of Spirit*, or in the working out of the logical idea or of the various forms of spirit (to which, besides, art belongs). But—and this is the thesis I want to make explicit here—the classicism that Kant's aesthetics had tried to tear down is not at all modified *in its principles*. However historical it may have become, truth still remains the essential moment in the work of art, which is still conceived of as a sensible presentation of the true; so that we could say of Hegelianism that if, on the metaphysical level, it consists in a historicization of Leibniz's theodicy, on the aesthetic level it reveals itself to be a *historicized classicism.*

But a formula cannot replace an explanation. The modalities of this historicization of the Beautiful in Hegelian aesthetics are of such great depth that by following them we can truly understand the ultimate position art can aspire to within a metaphysical system in which it is destined to hold an inferior status. Baumgarten's *Aesthetics* and Kant's *Critique of Judgment* tried, in opposition to Leibniz's reduction of the sensible to a confused intelligible, in opposition to the primacy of God's point of view over that of human finitude, to ennoble aesthetics. For that, it was necessary to guarantee it the autonomy of its object. With the introduction of historicity into truth, Hegel intended to reestablish this primacy of the divine and the intelligible. The aesthetic sphere, born out of the legitimation of the sensible, must thereby be reintegrated into the whole of the system. The philosophy of art must thus embrace its object the better to kill it—or, to be fairer, the better to secure it in the subordinate role it never should have left.

That Hegel's aesthetics takes up again the fundamental theme of classicism is confirmed by the mode in which it defines art's supreme destination. According to the introduction to the *Lectures on Aesthetics,* art has reached this point

when it has placed itself in the same sphere as religion and philosophy, and when it is simply one way of bringing to our minds and expressing the *Divine,* the deepest interests of mankind, and the most comprehensive truths of the spirit . . . Art shares this vocation with religion and philosophy, but in a special way, namely by displaying even the highest reality sensuously, bringing it thereby nearer to the senses, to feeling, and to nature's mode of appearance.[2]

Hegel never ceased to repeat that art's object is the presentation of truth. Far from being a pure illusion, as a certain Platonic tradition would have it, art's aim is identical to that of religion and philosophy, even if the truth is presented therein in the form of *phenomena,* of the sensual manifestations that works of art are. "Thus, far from being mere pure appearance, a higher reality [*Realität*] and truer existence [*Dasein*] is to be ascribed to the phenomena of art in comparison with those of ordinary reality [*Wirklichkeit*]" (1:22/9). For, as Hegel often insisted throughout his lectures, the sensual presentation of truth in the beautiful work of art must be made in such a way that the two moments present in it not be brought together arbitrarily but, on the contrary, in the strongest, fittest fashion. "It has already been said that the content of art is the Idea, while its form is the configuration of sensuous material. Now art has to harmonize these two sides and bring them into a free reconciled totality" (1:100/70). Within the variety of modes of such a reconciliation Hegel locates the principle of a *chronological* hierarchy, not only of the different apprehensions of the concept of beauty, but of the various arts themselves. Before making this principle explicit—which will allow us to understand exactly how Hegelianism, in however grandiose a fashion, goes back on some of the advances of Kantian aesthetics—we should grasp how this simple definition of art implies a threefold return to classicism:

1. It is, first of all, the case that a certain "Cartesian" conception of the mind is reactivated here. I do not of course mean to suggest that the Hegelian concept of Spirit is a mere continuation of the *Metaphysical Meditations;* from Cartesian consciousness to Hegelian Spirit the distance is clearly great and is not about to be negated. Nevertheless, as in Descartes, and unlike what was the case with Kant's theory of genius, the spirit is once again granted unlimited mastery of itself. At least in its ultimate moment, when it finally conforms with its concept, there cannot subsist within it the least obscurity, not the smallest portion of the naturalness that Kant did not hesitate to attribute to the artist's creative powers. There is for Hegel no doubt about this point: true beauty is a creation of the spirit, and if there is something we cannot deny, it is "that the spirit is capable of considering itself, and of possessing a consciousness, a *thinking* consciousness, of itself and of everything originating in itself. Thinking is precisely what constitutes the inmost essential nature of spirit . . . Now art and works of art, by springing from and being created by the spirit, are themselves of a spiritual kind, even if their presentation assumes an appearance of sensuousness and pervades the sensuous with the spirit." (1:27/12.)

2. We can understand, in this case, why Hegelian philosophy should be diametrically opposed to the aesthetics of sentiment; it's as a connoisseur of this tradition that Hegel can distance himself from those authors—notably "French" ones—who, against Cartesian classicism, have defended the irrationality of the "heart," of the "je-ne-sais-quoi" that for Bouhours and Dubos constituted, as we have seen, "the soul of delicacy." He indeed wishes to put an end to "these scruples, and others

like them, against a truly scientific preoccupation with fine art" that one can read "in older books, especially French ones, about beauty" (1:19/ 6–7)—but also, as we must point out, in Baumgarten and even in the *Critique of Judgment*.

3. Hegel must therefore resolutely argue—and here we measure the extent to which he moves away from Kant and rejoins the orbit of classical aesthetics—not only that the fine arts are worthy of generating philosophical reflection, but especially (going much further) that they are an adequate topic for strictly scientific treatment (1:18/5). This is an important nuance: it means that art is not an irrational object which philosophical reflection could choose to work on, as if from the outside, but that it is intrinsically part of science's development, that is to say, of the spirit's self-unfolding in all its systematicity.

It's from this aspect that art fully appears to be what it is: a moment of truth, possessing its own (internal) development (its own historicity); but also, and precisely to the extent it is but a moment, its *external* historicity. Within the complete system of science there is a *before* of art (in this case, and for reasons we won't go into here, the State) and an *after* (religion and philosophy, as we will perhaps better understand in subsequent pages): "But just as art has its 'before' in nature and the finite spheres of life, so too it has an 'after,' i.e., a region which in turn transcends art's way of apprehending and representing the Absolute. For art has still a limit in itself and therefore passes over into higher forms of consciousness" (1:141/102).

In this key passage, Hegel gives us the principle of an aesthetics that will essentially consist of an ordering into a chronological hierarchy of the stages of art's autodissolution into religion, then into philosophy. We now know the nature of the limit art contains within itself; it has nothing to do, as the aesthetics of feeling would naïvely have us believe (seeing in it, second naïveté, a supposed superiority of beauty over truth), in the fact that art allegedly contains an irrational element, or would itself belong to some other realm than that of reason. The limit Hegel evokes is obviously that of the sensibility in which truth expresses itself—a sensibility that from the philosophical, from the divine point of view, has no more ontological validity within the *system* than it does within the Leibnizian theodicy.

The task then becomes one of understanding how the introduction of historicity into art, as the sensuous presentation of a truth that is itself historical, is not the contrary of classicism but the surest method

FOUR

towards its completion, towards its finally conforming to its concept—to what was true and just in it from the very beginning of its struggle against the baroque and the sentimental. The triple historicity of the beautiful that structures all of the *Lectures* achieves its full significance at this nodal point of the Hegelian aesthetic. Let us attempt to formulate it adequately.

1. *The First Historicity:*
Symbolism, Classicism, Romanticism

Let us look again at the way Hegel defines the *articulation* between the two constitutive moments of the concept of artistic beauty. We find, "first, a content, an aim, a meaning; and secondly the expression, appearance, and realization of this content. But, thirdly, both aspects are so penetrated by one another that the external, the particular, appears exclusively as a presentation of the inner" (1:132/95). Though art is structured like a language, with, as we would say nowadays, a signifier and a signified, it remains nonetheless very different from ordinary language in that the signifier, the sensuous form, should in principle cede nothing to arbitrariness: "In the work of art nothing is there except what has an essential relation to the content and is an expression of it" (ibid.). There are other ways of stating a truth than the aesthetic mode; what characterizes it among all others is that, though sensible, the form of the expression leaves strictly nothing to contingency. (1:101/71.)

The principle for the hierarchization of art's great forms is deducible from this simple remark: to the extent that "art has the task of presenting the Idea to immediate perception in a sensuous shape and not in the form of thinking and pure spirituality as such, and, since this presenting has its value and dignity in the correspondence and unity of both sides, i.e., the Idea and its outward shape, it follows that the loftiness and excellence of art in attaining a reality adequate to its Concept will depend on the degree of inwardness and unity in which Idea and shape appear fused into one" (1:103/72). The hierarchy principle thus unfolds itself into two:

—An art form's superiority will first of all be measured by its capacity to adequately, *though sensuously*, express the truth of the idea; art seeks what Hegel, following Kant, calls the "ideal," meaning individuality defined as the synthesis of the universal contained in the idea and of the particular inherent in the sensuous form it takes, "for the *Idea as such* is indeed the absolute truth itself, but the truth only is its not yet objectified universality," while, as idea of the beautiful, sensually incarnated therefore or *individualized* by its union with a particular form, it approaches the ideal. We can say that the demand expressed in art is "that the Idea and its configuration as a concrete reality shall be made completely adequate to one another" (1 : 104–5/73–74). It's by referring back to this demand that we shall have to judge the "advances" along the history of aesthetics.

—But it goes without saying that, thus formulated, the principle of hierarchization remains quite insufficient ("abstract"). For the value of art—and here again Hegel's classicism comes through—depends also (we shall see that it is, in fact, all one thing) upon the richness and the depth (the "concreteness") of the idea. And this latter in turn refers back to a *historicity:* "For, before reaching the true Concept of its absolute essence, the spirit has to go through a course of stages, a series grounded in this Concept itself; and to this course of the content which the spirit gives to itself there corresponds a course, immediately connected therewith, of configurations of art, in the form of which the spirit, as artist, gives itself a consciousness of itself" (1 : 103/72).

As the reader will have anticipated, it's at this point that Hegel succeeds in fully reconciling classicism and historicity, the latter conferring its maximum potency on the former. Far from, as with Dubos, the history of art constituting an argument against the position that defends art as a sensuous manifestation of the truth, it, on the contrary, magisterially confirms this position; it is because the "true" truth is itself historical (and not "eternal," at least not in the naïve meaning the seventeenth-century classicists "still" gave the term) that there is necessarily also a history of the sensuous manifestations of this truth. There is thus nothing there to urge the abandonment of the project of transforming art into an object for science; also nothing to argue in favor of an "insurmountability" of art. On the contrary—and the two themes are strongly bound up to each other—because it is, *within the realm of sensibility,* a historical manifestation of a truth itself historical that it will become necessary to surmount or supersede art for expressions better suited to the spirituality of a content that, in the last instance, repudiates sensuousness, even though it can take pleasure in it for a while.

Since art is not a language similar to other languages, the connection within it between form and content, signifier and signified having nothing to do with arbitrariness, the historicity of the content is also that of the forms. We can, in other words, complete the principle for the hierarchization of the arts by stressing the fact that imperfection of form is, in the aesthetic sphere, radically dependent on imperfection of the content: "the defectiveness of a work of art is not always to be regarded as due, as may be supposed, to the artist's lack of skill; on the contrary, defectiveness of form results from defectiveness of content." Hegel illustrates his assertion in cultural terms: if "the Chinese, Indians, and Egyptians" produced images of God that "never get beyond formlessness or a bad and untrue definiteness of form," it's because their "mythological ideas" are themselves indeterminate and abstract (1: 105/74). It is thus only thanks to the development of the idea that "artistic beauty acquires a totality of particular stages and forms"; the three great moments *symbolic, classical,* and *romantic,* therefore "are nothing but the different relations of meaning and shape, relations which proceed from the Idea itself and therefore provide the true basis for the division of this sphere" (1:107/75).

This triple partition of the great genre forms, that manifests itself as the first relation of art to historicity, is (relatively) well known. Within the perspective of a history of aesthetics defined as history of subjectivity it offers the immense interest of bearing witness, though *negatively,* to the intimate connection binding aesthetics to what could be called the *philosophical secularism* inherent, in Kant, to the withdrawal of the divine. Because Hegel truly carries out Leibniz's project of a perfect systematicity, because, along the way, he is led to making of philosophy man's attempt to go beyond the point of view of human finitude (of *reflective subjectivity*) towards the point of view of God (of the *absolute subject* or knowledge), that his ordering of artforms into a hierarchy not only takes the form of a chronology, of a logic of temporality, but that it also turns into the killing off of art. The ordering can in fact be read two ways: as the auto-unfolding of art through the different stages that the gradual complication of the idea imposes on the diversity of forms; but also as art's auto-disintegration, since, as the process goes on, it must inevitably realize, at the very moment it attains perfection in its genre, that it is not the most adequate means of expression of the idea, that it is inferior to the representation of the divine in religion and, in the end, in philosophical thought itself. We must grasp this paradoxical structure of art before going into the other two forms of historicity that will also come to affect and complete this structure of auto-unfolding and of supersession of itself.

Art begins, then, by being *symbolic.* This first moment presents no particular difficulty, so easy is it, following the principle of hierarchization, to detect its double defect: "The symbolic shape is imperfect because, (i) in it the Idea is presented to consciousness only as indeterminate or determined *abstractly,* and, (ii) for this reason the correspondence of meaning and shape is always defective and must itself remain purely abstract" (1 : 109/77). Two *visible* consequences result from this.

Since the idea is as yet too indeterminate to itself concretely indicate the form it should receive, symbolic art, as its name suggests, often limits itself to using natural objects as simple *representatives* of the content to be expressed; one can, for example, symbolize force with the image of a lion. We then think *as if* the idea were present in the form that the natural object has become, but, quite obviously, the relation between art's two moments here remains completely external. The idea is not in fact found in the natural object and the relation between the two remains—one could hardly put it better—merely symbolic.

The idea cannot be satisfied with such an external relation to its form, and it is with this dissatisfaction, that is for Hegel the moment of the sublime, that symbolic art begins to bring itself to ruin, that its self-unfolding becomes self-supersession. What connection can be established between the symbolic and the sublime? Sublime, in German, is *erhaben,* that which rises *above.* In the dissatisfied quest for an adequate form the idea experiences its own sublimity, the fact of its being *above* all the sensuous forms clumsily being attached to it. The idea thus becomes tyrannical toward the natural phenomena, literally torturing them and finally rejecting them in the very attempt to appropriate them. Symbolic art will therefore express itself both in giants and colossi, effortfully trying, through their monumental, grandiose character, to convey this superiority of an as yet indeterminate and abstract idea, and in Indian statues with a hundred arms and chests, whose tortured diversity and artificial richness correspond to the same unfulfilled aspiration.

Classical art is the crowning achievement of this still vain effort. If the ideal is to be defined as the perfect adequacy between form and content, sensuous presentation and idea, then only with classical art do we reach it, thus penetrating into the sphere of perfect beauty. It is important, from our perspective, to fully understand the paradox constitutive of this second stage. It will seem, within the Hegelian system, to be the highest perfection of a limited order, to be perfect art, but, after all, still an art, therefore inadequate to the idea, since the idea, being such, can never be fully satisfied at being incarnate in a sensible form, even if the latter were, unlike what is the case with symbolic art, the most adequate possible, the most intrinsically determined by its content. What, indeed, happens in the passage from the symbolic to the classic? Following the hierarchy principle, the idea must simultaneously determine itself, become richer and more concrete, but also, by doing this, produce, so to speak, its own form, determine not only its content but also the only expression fully fit for it. Classical art can no longer fulfill itself by borrowing from *external* nature forms symbolizing the idea and spirituality. And yet it must remain an art, and, as such, a sensual, and therefore, in a way, a natural presentation of the truth: "Consequently, to suit such a content we must try to find out what in nature belongs to the spiritual in and for itself" (1:110/78).

The only natural form that answers to this equation is the human form, and, for Hegel, classical art is essentially incarnated in Greek sculpture, which presents the visible unity of the human and the divine. The human body, and particularly the face, thus appears as the "only sensuous appearance appropriate to spirit." But of course, in this new stage of aesthetic life, unlike what took place in the symbolic, the body "counts in classical art no longer as a merely sensuous existent, but only as the existence and natural shape of the spirit, and it must therefore be exempt from all the deficiency of the purely sensuous and from the contingent finitude of the phenomenal world" (1:110/78). That is what Greek art, more than any other, manages to express in the calm and serenity of its bodies and faces. It thus arrives at the ideal since, on the one hand, the idea is sufficiently developed to perceive itself as subjective, and, on the other, this subjectivity finds in man an expression that has nothing arbitrary about it. But it's exactly at this point that art's paradox bursts into daylight.

This is because the subjectivity that expresses itself in the most perfect art is still only a finite, human subjectivity, for this very reason assigned to a natural, therefore *aesthetic* (sensible) body. Art, in a sense, cannot help it: how could it break free from all reference to sensibility and, thereby, to finitude, since its very essence is to present the idea in sensuous form? In another sense, it is precisely that which condemns it at the very moment of achieving perfection. Beforehand this limit could still have been ascribed to an accidental, temporary, imperfection; this is no longer possible when we finally have the ideal before us. This is the reason why Hegel evokes in very reserved terms what we must resign outselves to calling the anthropomorphism of the most perfect art: "Of course personification and anthropomorphism have often been maligned as a degradation of the spiritual, but in so far as art's task is to bring the spiritual before our eyes in a sensuous manner, it must get involved in this anthropomorphism" (1:110/78). The true idea is indeed the unity of human and divine that the Greek statue represents;

but, at the same time, the fact that this representation remains within the realm of the aesthetic, of sensuousness, since it expresses itself in the human body, is a limitation that in return inevitably affects the conception of spirituality itself. "Therefore here the spirit is at once determined as particular and human, not as purely absolute and eternal." Classical form, despite its perfection, can thus not sustain itself either: "The classical form of art has attained the pinnacle of what illustration by art could achieve, and if there is something defective in it, the defect is just art itself and the restrictedness of the sphere of art" (1:111/79). "Just" art . . . The formulation is not without interest: it confirms if confirmation had been needed, the degree to which the history of aesthetics is, within a metaphysics of reason, the history of its own supersession or transcendence. The transition from classicism to romanticism bears witness to this even more explicitly.

Indeed, with the romantic period we enter into what could be called "the art that leads out of art" [*l'art de la sortie de l'art*]; romanticism is in fact defined as "the self-transcendence of art but within its own sphere and in the form of art itself" (1:113/80). The paradox merits contemplation. It becomes clearer if we take into account the double structure (content/form) of the hierarchization principle.

The content of romanticist art is, on the one hand, one degree higher than that of classical art. The latter had arrived at the true idea that the spirit is a synthesis of the finite and the infinite, the human and the divine, a union that Greek sculpture presented *ideally* within sensibility. But, among the Greeks, this unity of finite and infinite remains an *in-itself*, an immediate unity, undeveloped and indeterminate. It's precisely for this reason, as a function of its limitation, that this spiritual content can still find a perfectly adequate expression in sensuousness. In romanticist art, by contrast, this in-itself becomes for-itself: the spirit becomes *conscious* that it is unity of divine and human, infinite and finite. From the Greek god we go over to the Christian God who is spirit, therefore *interiority, inwardness, for-itself.*

This modification of the content must inevitably affect the form. In these new conditions, "the *true* element for the realization of this content is no longer the sensuous immediate existence of the spiritual in the bodily form of man, but instead the inwardness of *self-consciousness*. Now Christianity brings God before our imagination *as spirit*, not as an individual, particular spirit, but as absolute in spirit and in truth. For this reason it retreats from the sensuousness of imagination into spiritual inwardness and makes this, and not the body, the medium and the existence [*Dasein*] of truth's content" (1:112/80), unlike what was the case with the classical Greek representation of the divine. We can better understand the paradoxical situation of romanticist art: having finally arrived at a correct, spiritual representation of the divine, it realizes it can no longer present it in a sensuous material that would particularize it and thereby deform it through individuation. "The new content, thus won, is on this account not tied to sensuous presentation, as if that corresponded to it, but is freed from this immediate existence which must be set down as negative, overcome, and reflected into the spiritual unity" (1:113/80). The content of romanticist art becomes from that point on the *internal world*, whose presentation is the new task at hand.

And therein lies the paradox. However romanticist it may be, art does not stop being art and, as such, inherently tied to the sensuous, and thereby in some way or another to externality. The problem, as far as form is concerned, is that of knowing how a content that is pure interiority (consciousness, for-itself) can be adequately presented in sensuous exteriority. In romanticism, "inwardness celebrates its triumph over the external and manifests its victory in and on the external itself" (ibid.). Romantic art will consequently be an art of the internal sense, of feeling, and, if one considers the forms of sensibility, of time rather than space. One observes here the degree to which aesthetics, in Hegel, receives the odd mission of superseding sensibility, the extent to which romantic art is, in this sense, truly the art that leads out of art and the entryway to religion. The idea it has raised itself to is that of spirit, no longer externalized in beautiful Greek individuality but self-conscious, and although rationally superior to classical art it must in some way or another become aesthetically inferior to it. Its task can no longer be one of finding again a perfect adequacy with a sensuousness that is from now on considered the enemy.

Such is the reason why romantic art must resolve itself to abandoning classical perfection and taking up again the bothersome separation of form and content characteristic of the symbolic. The moment is somewhat analogous to that of the sublime since the Idea is once again above the sensuous, but, in this case, for a radically inverse reason: it must once again distance itself from form because it has become too rich and too concrete for it, and not because it might still be indeterminate.

Thereby the separation of Idea and shape, their indifference and inadequacy to each other, come to the fore again, as in symbolic art, but with this essential difference, that, in romantic art, the Idea, the deficiency of which in the symbol brought with it deficiency of shape, now has to appear perfected in itself as spirit and heart. Because of this higher perfection, it is not susceptible of an adequate union with the external, since its true reality and manifestation it can seek and achieve only within itself. (1:114/81)

The three moments (symbolism, classicism, romanticism) of the Idea's relation with its form thus reveal themselves to be the three instances of a process consisting in "the striving for, the attainment, and the transcendence of the Ideal as the true Idea of beauty." This first historicity resolves itself in another, more particular one, within which aesthetics' intrinsically untenable—thus by essence provisional—character is better defined.

2. The Second Historicity: Architecture, Sculpture, Painting, Music, and Poetry

The examination of the diverse individual arts' *chronological*—in the strong sense, as in the first historicity—hierarchy is rich with lessons. To understand its profoundest meaning, we have to grasp how this new division of aesthetics is distinct from the first though referring back to it directly. The trinity of art's great forms—symbolism/classicism/romanticism—is the most general, the one that exposes the moments of the idea of the beautiful itself. Now, when taking into account the specific arts, the goal is to analyze the concrete way these great stages of the concept of beauty incarnate themselves in "external being-there [*Dasein*]" in the form of specific works. There will therefore be an intimate connection between the different artistic genres and the idea of the beautiful since the former are, in the final analysis, the sensuous actualization of the latter (1:114/82). After what has been said on the subject of romantic art, the second hierarchy's principle should be easy to grasp: following the paradox inherent in art as "sensible presentation" of an intelligible truth, Hegel logically posits that the highest art is, quite simply, that which manages to maximally liberate itself from the sensuous sphere, therefore, in certain ways, from *what constitutes art as such*. Reciprocally, the more an art remains stuck in the *externality* of bodily matter, the more it will deserve to be placed on the inferior rungs of the ladder.

The object then is to be emancipated above all from *spatiality* as being the form par excellence of sensuousness (of externality), in which case we can comprehend why, according to Hegel, the first artistic

139

genre, going of course from bottom to top, is architecture; not only is it displayed in the realm of the three dimensions of space, but, besides, the materials it uses to represent the idea—or perhaps we ought to say, to house it, since its favorite exercise is the building of temples—are entirely borrowed from inorganic nature. It is furthest away from true spirituality, which is why it is called upon, by essence, to correspond to symbolic art.

It is precisely in the project of rendering the sensible material more adequate to the idea, less external to it, that we go from architecture to sculpture. The latter is still, of course, situated within tridimensionality, but it has stopped seeing sensuous material merely mechanically and tries to give it an organic and, thereby, an individual form. Sculpture turns out to be quite adequate to the classical ideal, "by architecture, the inorganic external world has been purified, set in order symmetrically, and made akin to spirit, and the god's temple, the house of his community, stands there ready. Then into this temple, *secondly,* the god enters himself as the lightning-flash of individuality striking and permeating the inert mass" (1:118/84) by giving the infinite spirit the form of the organized human body.

Once art has taken it upon itself to build the divine temple, once it has invited in God himself as individuality incarnate in the sculptural organization of matter, the community of the faithful remains to be dealt with. We could say that, in this third stage, God humanizes himself; he becomes spirit reflected in the multiplicity of those who make up its invisible church. "The compact unity in itself which the god has in sculpture disperses into the plurality of the inner lives of individuals whose unity is not sensuous but purely ideal." In a movement of internalization analogous to that by way of which we passed from classicism to romanticism, sculpture gives way to three arts that lead out of art, to the three stages during which the project of putting an end to spatiality will truly accomplish itself.

It begins with painting. Not only does this art manage to do without inorganic matter (or nearly, materiality, strictly speaking, is mostly not of the essence in the pictorial realm), it also spiritualizes the act of making visible by breaking free of the constraints of the third dimension. In Hegel's happy formula: "The visibility and the making visible which belong to painting . . . free art from the *complete sensuous spatiality* of material things by being restricted to the dimensions of a *plane* surface" [*von der sinnlich-räumlichen Vollständigkeit:* in the German text, the terms for sensuousness and for spatiality are inseparably linked—L.F.] (1:121/87). As a compensation for the loss of the "completeness" of external volume, this new artistic genre we have come to can allow itself a first expression of subjective feelings, a first approach to interiority: "Whatever can find room in the human breast as feeling, idea, and purpose, whatever it is capable of shaping into act, all this multiplex material can constitute the variegated content of painting" (ibid.).

Music penetrates further into this interiority, since it is the first amid the other aesthetic genres to completely rid itself of spatiality: "Its material, though still sensuous, proceeds to still deeper subjectivity and particularization" (1:121/87). Sound, indeed, transcends "the indifferent self-externality of space" (ibid.) and allows penetration into the realm of temporality or, to speak like Kant, into the realm of *internal* sense. Musical notes can be considered like *points:* just as in going from architecture to sculpture to painting we had passed from volume to surface, we pass here from line to point. And, always following the same trade-off, what is lost in exteriority is gained in interiority. Music is the first art truly appropriate to the expression of the human soul's infinite variety of feelings and passions.

This internalizing movement, characteristic of romantic arts, ends with poetry. Sound, in music, is still tied to sensibility, even if the latter no longer takes the form of exteriority but is, rather, embodied in the time of consciousness. To put it very simply, musical sonorities are *intrinsically feeling-bound* [*sentimentales*]. In poetry, on the other hand, sound distances itself from this form of spiritualized sensuousness; it becomes *arbitrary,* in the sense used in linguistics today of the "arbitrariness of the sign." "Sound in this way becomes a *word* as a voice inherently articulated, the meaning of which is to indicate ideas and thoughts" (1:122/88). It thus becomes a "point of the spirit," for "this sensuous element, which in music was still immediately one with inwardness, is here cut free from the content of consciousness, while spirit determines this content on its own account and in itself and makes it into ideas. To express these it uses sound indeed, but only as a sign in itself without value or content" (1:122–23/89).

Poetry is the art that leaves art behind to which the history of aesthetics had aspired since its beginnings; it is the art within which—at least in Hegel's vision—sensibility has erased itself to the point that it gives way to spirituality represented in subjective consciousness. If we keep in mind that the idea that is to be exhibited is that of the divine, we will understand that the end of art can only mean the transition to a superior sphere of the spirit; we shall also grasp that this sphere can only consist in *religion*—always defined by Hegel as the apprehension of the divine in the mode of *representation*. But with this observation we enter a third form of historicity. The first two—leading from symbolism to romanticism, then from architecture to poetry—were *internal* to aesthetics itself. As we leave its domain, we can situate aesthetics within the temporality that encompasses it; situate it, therefore, in relation to what precedes it and what follows it within the system as a whole.

3. The Third Historicity:
Art's Dissolution into Religion

Here, Hegel's famous affirmation that art belongs, from now on, to a bygone era in human history gains its full meaning. When Hegel calmly asserts that "art, considered in its highest vocation, is and remains for us a thing of the past [*ein Vergangenes*]," that "it has lost for us genuine truth and life" (1:25/11), the asseveration should be understood at two successive levels of depth.

It is, of course, clear that the "for us" is intended first of all in a historical sense and means "for us, moderns," we who have left humanity's childhood behind. The time gone by is here measured from Greek antiquity: "The beautiful days of Greek art, like the golden age of the later Middle Ages, are gone" (1:24/10), and if they are, it's because we live in a culture of "reflection" or even of reason, which allows us to go beyond the framework of sensuousness when we seek to think the truth. "Consequently the conditions of our present time are not favorable to art" (ibid.). Whereas Greek culture had above all been an aesthetic culture, a religion of beauty, Christian modernity has so well spiritualized the religious that our cultural environment has been able to distance itself from art. To be convinced of this it suffices to consider the difference separating the ancient divinity, as it is ideally manifested in classical art, from Christian spirituality: "The Greek god is not abstract but individual, closely related to the natural human form. The Christian God too is indeed a concrete personality, but is *pure* spirituality and is to be known as *spirit* and in spirit. His element of existence [*Dasein*] is therefore essentially inner knowledge and not the external natural form through which he can be represented only imperfectly and not in the whole profundity of his nature" (1:103/72).

The "for us" becomes more precise. It now means for us, philosophers of Christian culture, who have come to understand that the divinity does not need a sensuous form, does not, therefore, need art, to be represented to consciousness. Since it is pure spirituality, it is only through a kind of fundamental naïveté that the aesthetic vision of the world can come to think we could remain at a sensible apprehension of the absolute. *It is thus because of his classicism, because of the idea that art's mission is the sensuous presentation of truth, that Hegel is inevitably led to affirm art's dissolution into religion—the latter being itself conceptualized as a mere mode (superior of course, because less sensuous) of the presentation of truth.* The logic we had witnessed at work in the transition from Leibniz to Kant via Baumgarten is simultaneously inverted and confirmed. In establishing, as Leibniz had, the autonomy of sensibility, Kant had been led to making of the divine a simple idea, and of religion a modest "practical faith," directed in the end by reason's requirements. He thus brought us into the sphere of *philosophical secularism.* In reestablishing the legitimacy of God's viewpoint, in reassuming the concept of an absolute subject as truth, and not as mere idea of human reason, Hegel eventually had to take up again for his own purposes Leibniz's old thesis about the sensible being the "kingdom of the confused intelligible." It's not an accident, then, if, traveling backward along Kant's road, Hegel invites us to supersede the sphere of sensibility, meaning aesthetic reflection's point of view, and enter that of religion. A procedure that renders art's "third historicity" more explicit.

It is, indeed, in the Greek world that art's own limits begin to be manifest:

> For us art counts no longer as the highest mode in which truth fashions an existence for itself. In general it was early in history that thought passed judgment against art as a mode of illustrating the idea of the Divine; this happened with the Jews and Muhammadans, for example, and indeed even with the Greeks, for Plato opposed the gods of Homer and Hesiod starkly enough. With the advance of civilization a time generally comes in the case of every people when art points beyond itself. (1:141–42/103)

Hegel holds that that time came in Europe when, with the Reformation, Christianity, which had itself made use of art, finally had to give it up, God's representation having achieved too high a degree of spirituality to be any longer thus debased: "when the urge for knowledge and research, and the need for inner spirituality, instigated the Reformation, religious ideas were drawn away from their wrapping in the element of sense and brought back to the inwardness of heart and thinking. Thus the 'after' of art consists in the fact that there dwells in

FOUR

the spirit the need to satisfy itself solely in its own inner self as the true form for truth to take" (1:142/103).

One could hardly be plainer, and this passage through the Reformation summarily expresses all that religion adds to art by adopting the form of *representation*. With the latter, "the Absolute has removed from the objectivity of art into the inwardness of the subject," so that Hegel can speak of an "*advance* from art to religion" (1:142–43/103).

This advance, as is well known, comes to its fulfillment in philosophy, which can alone think inwardness in a way fully adequate to the nature of absolute spirit. However much it may have internalized him, religion does not thereby cease representing God as an object external to consciousness—truth to tell, this is inherent in the very structure of *representation as such*. The latter is in fact always reflective; it therefore remains always within finite consciousness, for which every object remains, one way or another, in a certain exteriority. Only speculative philosophy, which comes to understand that the reflection of finite consciousness is but a moment in the unfolding of absolute subjectivity, and that it is in this sense that authentic spirit cannot express itself in any form other than pure thought, is able to reconcile art's objectivity and religion's subjectivity.

The modalities of this strange reconciliation are not our concern here (besides, we would have to mobilize all of the more general theses of the Hegelian system to justify the possibility of a reconciliation—assuming, of course, we even managed to get there). The important thing to grasp, on the other hand, is that with it the Kantian idea that beauty, artistic or natural, is not reducible to the powers of the spirit is also "superseded." Kant wanted to critique the metaphysics of subjectivity, and his critique's culminating point was, no doubt, in aesthetics. Whether or not the Hegelian "supersession" of this attempt is philosophically legitimate is another question, one of determining the extent to which Kant can also be a post-Hegelian. I have elsewhere tried to answer it. What can, in any case, be but little doubted, is that aesthetics' subsequent progeny will—for quite a long time, even to our own days perhaps—not stop hesitating between these two models. Nietzsche's own aesthetics can, in their reassertion of the autonomy of the sensible, to a certain extent be considered as a kind of "return to Kant." But what will radically differentiate them from Kantian aesthetics, as from Hegelianism, is their willful determination to put an end to the idea that art is a *world*.

OF ART AS "HISTORICAL WORLD"

If there is one thesis Kant thinks it important to hold onto, it is the one that maintains there exists a *world* of beauty. Not only does beauty not make sense except in relation to the *cosmological* idea—alone capable, it must again be stressed, of granting it a certain "objectivity," that of the "common sense"—but, besides, the artistic beautiful itself, although a product of the human spirit, preserves an aspect of naturalness without which it could not pretend to by right belong to the sphere of aesthetics. As we have seen, that's the meaning and significance of the theory of the genius.

It is, to that extent, not inexact to think that Hegel's challenge to this theory, by way of the assertion of the superiority of the artistic over the natural beautiful, is a decisive blow to art's worldliness [*mondanéité*]. The aspect of naturalness in the Hegelian genius is, so to speak, in the process of extinction. It tends in fact towards non-being, and art as a whole is thus given over to the powers of subjectivity and of history—metaphysics recommences its triumphal march. Yet, seen from another side, Hegel, since he is a "classicist"—that is, a rationalist, as was here defined—cannot but continue to consider the universe of the beautiful as a world, even if it has become since Kant thoroughly ideal and historical. Hegel thus explains how, in the third part of the *Aesthetics,* dealing with particular arts, "we have to deal with the beauty of art as it unfolds itself, in the arts and their productions, into a *world* [word underlined by Hegel himself—L.F.] of actualized beauty" (1: 115/83). And this is the description Hegel gives of it in a text that merits being quoted at length:

The content of this world is the beautiful, and the true beautiful, as we saw, is spirituality given shape, the Ideal, and, more precisely, absolute spirit, the truth itself. This region of divine truth, artistically represented for contemplation and feeling, forms the center of the whole world of art. It is the independent, free, and divine shape which has completely mastered the externality of form and material and wears it only as a manifestation of itself. Still, since the beautiful develops itself in this region as *objective* reality [*Wirklichkeit*] and therefore distinguishes within itself its single aspects and factors, granting them independent particularity, it follows that this center now arrays its extremes, realized in their appropriate actuality, as contrasted with itself. One of these extremes therefore forms a still *spiritless objectivity,* the merely natural environment of God. Here the external as such takes shape as something having its spiritual end and content not in itself but in another.

The other extreme is the Divine as inward, as something known, as the variously particularized subjective existence [Dasein] of the Deity. (1 : 115–16/83)

A first observation: it's easy once again to find in this description of the world of beauty, or of beauty as world, the principle behind the three hierarchies, the three forms of historicity, that we have seen at work inside as well as on the immediate outside of art. As with them, art's intimate essence (the ideal) is at the center, preceded by the more natural and followed by the more spiritual. We should then observe that, as in Kant, it is the idea of the divine that structures worldliness, that makes up its infrastructure or framework, so to speak. Without it, there could be no systematic unity, and without that, there could be no world either, so obvious is it, for Kant as for Hegel, that what is not *One* world is not a *World*. But the immense difference separating these two visions of art as intrinsically tied to worldliness is easy to discern, though its implications run deep. It is still the case with Kant that the idea of world is only evoked by art (as by beauty in general) because of the former's contingency and naturalness, that is, because of that in which it is not integrally dominated by subjectivity. And it is also to that extent that it can claim a universal, that is, in a certain sense an atemporal and *ahistorical* validity. If the little nightingale's song, once imitated by man, no longer evokes the idea of the world, if it isn't beautiful, nor even touching in some way, it is because we now know it to be dominated by subjectivity and, from that point on, nothing in it can evoke the cosmos.

Though, for Hegel, art remains a world, this world has all the same ceased to be external to subjectivity *conceived of as absolute subjectivity*. It is so well integrated that it finds itself to be historicized through and through, since this absolute subjectivity itself can only unfold within temporality. At which point we may be truly allowed to ask whether Hegelianism does not, despite itself, open up the way for what is going to happen in Nietzsche's aesthetics, namely the world's explosion in an infinity of *historical* points of view, of "perspectives" for which, in the famous Nietzschean formulation, "there are no facts, only interpretations."

The answer to this question is actually more complicated than it would seem. Hegel's historicism is of a very strange kind, not to say, quite simply, that it is repelled by the historicity it embraces the better to annihilate. Everybody today thinks it's perfectly obvious that Hegelianism was the first philosophical taking-into-account of the problem of historicity, that transcendental philosophy, "structuralist" before its time, supposedly neglected. It's something of a commonplace, not to say a banality since it's not to be doubted that in every part of the Hegelian system one finds successive "stages," whether they be of consciousness, of the logical Idea, of universal history in the proper sense or, as we have just seen, of aesthetics. But, seen another way, we must not be afraid to assert that this proposition is an error—to the degree that the term has any meaning in philosophy. The Hegelian project is not at all one of opening philosophy up to history, *but of absorbing historicity back into the concept,* which task, until proof to the contrary, is not the same thing. The project, a direct descendant of Leibniz's (whose influence on Hegel is, decidedly, too little acknowledged in Hegelian studies), is to demonstrate that temporality, at the opposite end of what Kant held, *is nothing outside of the concept;* that it is, in the *Phenomenology*'s famous formula, but the "Concept in existence" [*der daseinde Begriff*].

And it is in that way that Hegel, we might say, still resists Nietzsche. If he can hold onto the idea of a unique, *though historical,* world, it is not by making of history, as Kant did, a reality external to the concept and of the world an Idea of reason, but, on the contrary, through—more or less successfully—integrating historicity into the system so it will not cause any more disorder. It is therefore this very Leibnizian systematicity, this unification of finite points of view into a superior harmony now carrying the name "absolute subject," that Nietzsche will have to destroy as a first step, in order to liberate the historicist potentialities contained in Hegelianism. Then and only then will the era of the nonworld burst forth, the period of the pure dispersion of the volitional atoms, whose expression could only be a new art configuration.

FIVE

The Nietzschean Moment: The Shattered Subject and the Onset of Contemporary Aesthetics

ACCORDING TO ONE INTERPRETATION, dominant in France since Foucault's and Deleuze's work in the sixties, Nietzsche is supposedly the anti-Hegelian philosopher par excellence. We have to "take seriously the resolutely antidialectical character of Nietzsche's philosophy," for "if we do not discover its target the whole of Nietzsche's philosophy remains abstract and barely comprehensible." The target is, essentially, Hegel, since, as Deleuze goes on to write in his excellent book, *Nietzsche and Philosophy,* "Anti-Hegelianism runs through Nietzsche's work as its cutting edge."[1] In the manner of practicing deconstruction called "genealogy," the philosophy of "difference" is allegedly already at work against the categories of identity which have marked, in the hackneyed expression, "all philosophy since Plato."

We shall see, following a line of argument Heidegger developed with great conviction, that there is a subterranean continuity between Nietzsche's and Hegel's work. But it remains true that, at least at first sight, everything opposes the tragic conception of the irreducible multiplicity of Life to the philosophy of reconciliation that is Hegelianism. Through the virtues of the dialectic, conflicts and contradictions are forever destined to be overcome within a harmonious synthesis. Nietzsche does not merely assert the impossibility or even the mendacious character of this, he also, from a genealogical point of view, denounces the "nihilist" meaning of any antitragic philosophy. Beginning with *The Birth of Tragedy,* he comes up with the hypothesis that "if ancient tragedy had been pushed off its path by the dialectical drive towards knowledge and the optimism of science, we would have to conclude from this fact that there is an eternal struggle between the theoretical and the tragic world-views."[2] Theory's passionate antitragedism is brought to a high point by dialectics, which makes of all "difference," of all contradiction, a mere moment of transition towards the identity of the final reconciliation.

This "war between the gods" in which the tragic and the theoretical confront each other underlies the two critiques Nietzsche never fails to make of Hegelian dialectics. The first may seem trivial: it aims at "the philosopher's submission to reality," that "dialectical fatalism"[3] implicit in the illusive identification of the rational with the real. Hegel is suspected here of having "planted in the generations he leavened that admiration before the 'power of history' that, in practice, transforms itself at every moment into a bare admiration of success and leads to the idolatry of the factual."[4] We should not be misled: Nietzsche does not here take up on his own account the objections already formulated by the neo-Kantians. Nor does he echo Marx's *Theses on Feuerbach*. His intention is obviously not that of rehabilitating any kind of "moral vision of the world" over against the dialectic's fatalism. In this confusion of the real and the rational, what genealogical analysis aims at is not at all to eliminate the notion of an ideal, but, quite the contrary, the fact that Hegel, instead of giving himself over to the idea that what is should be, still seeks to demonstrate that what should be, is. As the outstanding example of the theoretical man, he saw in history the progressive incarnation of the divine, whereas to the genealogist's more practiced eye, it goes without saying that "God has only been created by history" (ibid.). If "the Hegelian worship of the real as the rational" comes down to a "divinization of success" (ibid., p. 169), it is thus not due to "immoralism," as the Kantians so dully think, but, on the contrary, due to an excess of moralism, to the fact that Hegel sustains at all costs the idea that the "is" and the "ought" must be reconciled, and that this reconciliation cannot, of course, be effected from any basis other than the "ought" (the ideal: that is, reason).

Nietzsche's second criticism against the systematic form Hegelianism takes must be understood from within the same perspective; "psychological nihilism" also sets in when one "has supposed a *totality*, a *systematization*, even an *organization* in every event and among all events, so that the soul that thirsts for something to admire and to honor revels in the all-encompassing notion of a supreme form of mastery and domination (if it is the soul of a logician, absolute logical consistency and a dialectics of the real suffice to reconcile him with everything). One imagines a kind of unity, any form of "monism," and following this belief, the human being feels a deep togetherness with and dependence from a whole that infinitely surpasses him, one of the divinity's *modes*."[5]

The will to system is but the ultimate aspect adopted by the metaphysics inherited from Platonism. It, paradoxically, restores the Platonic duality between appearance and truth since, in order to maintain the illusion of monism, it must be constantly demonstrated that plurality reintegrates unity, that the particular enters into the universal—the "philosophical laborer's" work that definitively assures the victory of the theoretical over the tragic. Through the dialectic, Hegel establishes "history in the place of the other spiritual powers, art and religion, as sole sovereign, insofar as it is the 'self-realizing concept,' the 'dialectic of the spirit of nations,' and the 'universal judgment.'"[6] It is this vision of the world that leads to the affirmation of "the death of art"; it must be overcome if aesthetics is finally to be put in its proper place.

AGAINST DIALECTICS:
THE REVALORIZATION OF AESTHETICS

If its Greek, or, rather, "Socratic" origins are examined, dialectics appears to be not only antitragic, but—a constant theme with Nietzsche—inaesthetic: "With Socrates, Greek taste changes towards dialectics: what exactly has taken place? It is, above all, a distinguished taste that is vanquished; with dialectics it is the populace that gains the upper hand. Before Socrates, dialectical manners were avoided in good society. They were considered bad manners."[7]

As is often the case with Nietzsche, the terse judgment conceals a form of argumentation; the latter must be reconstituted to grasp exactly dialectics' antiaesthetic essence, and to understand how the reversal of Platonism Nietzsche aspires to should culminate in a simultaneous rehabilitation of both the sensuous realm and of art. In a sense further to be defined, the "Nietzschean moment" in philosophy maintains a relation with the dialectical, Platonico-Hegelian negation of art *analogous* (which does not mean identical) to that which the "Kantian moment" has with classical rationalism. Even if the paths that are followed are quite different here and there, the aim in both cases is to conquer or reconquer sensibility's autonomy—for Kant, over against the "concept," for Nietzsche, against the dialectical "will to truth"—and thus to open up the space necessary to the very existence of aesthetics.

What, first of all, does dialectics' "popularity" and, thereby, its inelegance, consist of (Nietzsche compares the dialectician to someone who would eat with his hands)? The answer can be put concisely: if the Socratic method takes the path of dialogue, it is the better to refute the adversary's positions with the purpose of arriving at a truth which will be that of the Idea (of the intelligible). But, unlike error, which is, as is generally known, multiple, truth pretends to be unique. It claims to be valid at all times and in every place, for everybody. In that, it is "democratic," "plebian," even, in the sense Nietzsche gives to the term, "reactionary," since it cannot but react against the forces of falsehood and of illusion, especially, therefore, against art—which for these reasons is denounced by Plato in one of the most famous passages of the *Republic*.

By opposition to the dialectician, who is the theoretical man (learned man or philosopher), animated always by the will to truth, the artist appears as an aristocratic character. Still living in the predemocratic world of tradition (for example, the universe of the "great Hellenes" before Socrates), he posits values without discussion, without arguments, *with* authority. The forces he plays with are not reactive: unlike the truth, they don't need to deny other forces to posit themselves. We can therefore better understand this decisive assertion made against dialectics: "What needs to be proven in the first place is not worth much. Everywhere authority is sure of itself, everywhere one does not demonstrate, one commands, the dialectician is a sort of buffoon" (ibid.). And if Socrates is the "buffoon who managed to make himself be taken seriously," it's because, drawing his "ferocity" out of a deep "popular resentment" (ibid., § 7) against aesthetic aristocratism, he successfully set out to inject a "bad conscience" among his interlocutors by constantly placing them in contradiction with themselves. With his "sick man's malevolence," armed with dialectics and the "slashing knife of the syllogism" (ibid.), he succeeded in doing away with the illusive temptations of sensuous beauty in favor of truth. His ugliness and his lowly origins are, in quite precise fashion, inseparably linked, as Nietzsche does not fail to stress: "By his very origin Socrates belonged to the lowest of the low folk: Socrates was the populace. We know, we can even see how ugly he was," which should make us doubt that he was really Greek (ibid., § 3).

And here is the essential: dialectics can only exert themselves within the framework of a theory of the Ideas that maintains the sensible world must be denied in order to favor the intelligible world. Everyone knows that sensuousness is deceitful, that it shows us the same realities under different aspects (we can, for instance, bring to mind the various forms of a piece of wax), and that, consequently, it offends the most sacred rules of logic, and first of all the famous principle of identity. True ideas, on the contrary, are stable: they are what remains under the contingency of changes that never cease to affect the sensible world. All of which is well known, and Nietzsche, despite a received opinion to the contrary, does not merely inverse the terms of the opposition between the temporal and the eternal, the sensible and the intelligible. Before anything else, it is with the eyes of the genealogist that he looks upon the negation of aesthetics that Platonism is as prototype of all theory: "These senses, *which are, besides, so immoral*—these senses deceive us about the *true* world." This is, in the style of Nietzschean irony, the core of the scientific-technological discourse. The "besides," of course, has nothing gratuitous about it: it is, in truth, out of fear of *sensuality* (always "immoral") that *sensibility* (always "erring") comes to be depreciated. In the eyes of the "genealogist" (as, later on, in those of the psychoanalyst), philosophical theses are nothing but "rationalizations," "symptoms" as Nietzsche already put it (ibid., § 2), the fetishized expression of a certain pathos, perhaps even of a pathology.

If, as Nietzsche states in a famous aphorism, "my philosophy is an *inverse Platonism*," what is the result of this inversion as far as the establishment (or re-establishment) of aesthetics is concerned? The answer is given us in a section of *Twilight of the Idols* titled: "How the 'True World' Finally Became a Fable." Heidegger has made an impeccable commentary on it, of which I shall recall only the main conclusion. The key theme of Nietzsche's text is crystal clear, it seeks to demonstrate how the "true world," as opposed to the "apparent world"—the way the intelligible world is opposed to the sensible world—itself turns out to be, at the end of a long history that begins with Plato and finishes with Zarathustra, the illusion par excellence. But what is most important to note is that at the end of this process the point is not at all that appearance (the sensuous) should be valorized as such, but rather that we must eliminate the idea that there is something like appearance: "The true world—we have abolished. What world has remained? The apparent one perhaps? But no! With the true world we have also abolished the apparent one."

Only at this price will the conditions of possibility be created that will permit art to take precedence over philosophy. For the liberation of the sensuous and of appearance that the genealogy of the true world brings about is just as much a liberation of art, since the latter "affirms precisely that which the application of the supposedly true world denies."[8]

Art is indeed but "the will to appearance in the aspect of the sensible" (ibid.), and since this appearance, as we have just seen, is not "really" one, we have to say with Nietzsche that "the will to appearance, to illusion, to deception, to becoming and changing is deeper, more 'metaphysical' than the will to truth, to reality, to being." It is in this that art, by essence anti-Platonic, "has greater value than truth," that it is the most transparent expression of life, of that will to power that forms "the most intimate essence of Being." As *The Birth of Tragedy* had already laconically put it: "Only possible life: in art. Otherwise, we turn away from life"—and we sense here that the genealogical deconstruction of Platonic truth does not do away with every notion of truth, that there is perhaps a truth deeper than that of ideas, more "real," if we may say so, than that animating philosophic or scientific rationalism, truth that perhaps only art could do justice to, just as, at this level, only the senses cease lying to us "in as far as they show us becoming, disappearance, change." There are thus at least two truths and two lies, one kind beneficial and quite real, the other reactive and unreal, and this duality matches that between theory (false truth and bad lie) and art (good truth and good lie).

NIETZSCHE AS ANTI-HEGELIAN? THREE THESES ON NIETZSCHE

The whole problem, of course, consists first of all in determining the extent to which this "inversion of Platonism" remains, or not, dependent on what it seeks to overturn—a phenomenon that would not be contradicted by the other great "overturning" of the nineteenth century, Hegel's by Marx. Contrary to Deleuze and to Foucault (on this precise point, we mean; Heidegger's influence, on Foucault at least, being decisive in other realms), Heidegger has brought to light a certain continuity between Nietzsche and the metaphysics with which the latter pretended to have definitively broken. I will, without going into the details of this interpretation that makes of Nietzsche the thinker of technology, briefly retrace its principle before putting forward three theses on Nietzscheanism as the foundation not so much of our technologized world, as of a contemporary aesthetics from which Heidegger himself is perhaps not as distant as he himself thought.

Heidegger never ceased to urge thinking of technology beginning with its essence, which, in his eyes, is to be found in the completion of modern metaphysics as a "metaphysics of subjectivity." The notes titled "Overcoming Metaphysics," written between 1936 and 1946, set out to show that, understood from the standpoint of its essence, the term "technology" is equivalent to "completed metaphysics," and that the latter finally finds adequate expression in Nietzsche's theory of the "will to power." Going right to the essential: it could be maintained that, since Descartes, metaphysics has been, according to Heidegger, an anthropology, a way of thinking about man as a *foundation* or *ground* following the two traditional axes of philosophical questioning, the theoretical and the practical. Modern metaphysics, as a theoretical anthropology, consists in a conception of the real as obedient to the principles constitutive of the human spirit, transferring, for example (in Leibniz), the principle of sufficient reason (a logical or "subjective" principle) to the real itself and, ontologizing it, positing that *nihil est sine ratione* [nothing is without reason]. But such a theoretical anthropology, which reaches its summit with Hegel's affirmation of the identity between the real and the rational, does not by itself alone, undergird technology's domination as "completed metaphysics."

In order to apprehend the presence of "completed metaphysics" in the technologized relation to the world, we have to take into account the practical aspect of the metaphysics of subjectivity. As a practical anthropology, it represents beings to itself not only as existents subject to rationality's subjective principles, but as "objects for the will." Throughout the modern intensification of the essence of subjectivity as will, the existent, the totality of beings [*l'etant*], has tended more and more to have no reality except as object, manipulatable by the subject under the aspect of accomplishing his ends, uniformly at the disposal of the will whether as instrument or as beings. From this viewpoint, Kant's reinterpretation of the *I think* as an *I want*, and especially his doctrine of the autonomy of the will, were decisive steps towards the technic interpretation of the world that Nietzsche's philosophy makes a theme of. Up until then, the will had been subordinated to something other than itself, to the ends it was supposed to pursue. But with Kant, on the other hand, practical reason wills nothing other than itself, it wills itself as freedom. In "Kant's concept of practical reason as pure will," what is taking place is the very completion of the idea of will, "the completion of the being of will," which becomes will unconditioned by anything other than itself, "absolute will" or, since it wills nothing other than itself, "will to will."

Essential link in the process of the technologization of the real, the "autonomy of the will" in Kant's sense would not, truth to tell, be separated from the ultimate absolutization of the will save for one, still indispensable, mediation, that of the Nietzschean theory of the will to power as the "second to the last stage of the will's development." With Nietzsche's will to power a new figure of the will comes forward explicitly, one which in appearance still wants something other than itself (power), but which—following an interpretation constructed, from 1936 on, during Heidegger's courses on Nietzsche—in fact wills more power (more domination) only the better to experience itself indefinitely as will ruling the real; in a word, "The being of the will to power can only be understood in terms of the will to will,"[9] in terms of this unconditioned will through which the Cartesian project of mastery and possession of nature comes to completion. We can thereby better understand how Heidegger could have thought that, with the advent of the reign of technology, it is "the development of the unconditional dominance of metaphysics" that truly begins, when it finally finds a historical period adequate to itself (ibid., p. 90). Along the road leading from Descartes to Nietzsche, reason's becoming and its fate—and here Heidegger's analysis is rather close to Max Weber's—will have consisted in no longer establishing objectives itself, in transforming itself from the objective reason it attempted to be into purely instrumental reason.

The will is, in parallel fashion, itself no longer assigned to any end. The mastery over the world no longer aims, as it did with Descartes or during the age of Enlightenment, at emancipating human beings or at obtaining their happiness; it becomes the quest for mastery for the sake of mastery or, put another way, for brute force for the sake of brute force. And yet this rupture with Cartesianism is, still according to Heidegger, more apparent than real, since in liberating the will from any subordination to ends Nietzsche does nothing more than fulfill the essence of willing, raising it up to the level of its concept, thus bringing to completion the conception of the subject that was, in the final analysis, still only embryonic in Cartesianism. It is thus as a metaphysician that Nietzsche, following a central theme in his aesthetics, conceptualizes art more in terms of the *artist*, that is, of the *creator* (of his *will*) than in terms of the work of art itself; it is still in direct continuity with this metaphysics of subjectivity he was supposed to have overturned through his genealogical critique of the Platonic-Hegelian dialectic that his philosophy of art takes the form of a "physiology," or a theory of the "vital forces" at the beginning of creative activity. That is why Nietzsche, according to this interpretation, "thinks through and through in the modern way [*durchaus neuzeitlich denkt*] despite his high estimation of the early Greek, pre-Platonic thinking."[10]

The force of Heidegger's reading can hardly be denied, even though it leads to the strange paradox that, in it, genealogy is less distant from dialectics than seems at first to be the case. And yet it also seems to me difficult to deny that Nietzsche's thought is already far closer to Heidegger's than the latter cares to admit. After all, this subjectivity that Heidegger is pleased to discover in the concept of will to power no longer quite possesses, to say the least, the habitual characteristics of the metaphysical subject. Consciousness, rationality, identity, auto-transparency, etc., are so absent here that we hardly see how we could still speak about "subjectivity." And this will to power which, Nietzsche maintains, identifies itself with Life in order to constitute the most intimate essence of Being is characterized by such diversity that it becomes difficult to put it in relation with the durability of any kind of substance. We could, furthermore, with good reason state about Life that it *is* multiplicity and difference, so that between Heidegger's Being and the sort of radical splintering-up Nietzsche tries to conceptualize, the distance might be, here again, smaller than Heidegger wishes to suggest. As so often with the latter thinker, his interpretation of Modern Times as being uniformly destined to working out the different stages of metaphysics' activity in the world leads him to neglect the task of retracing the history, not of the metaphysical subject, but of the various modern conceptions of subjectivity. Heidegger's book on Nietzsche is admirable, at times even grandiose, but I'm not sure it gains anything from squeezing the Nietzschean conception of the subject into that of Descartes.

And thus the first thesis I would like to put forward, before developing the arguments to support it in the following pages: Nietzsche's aesthetics—which is to say, finally, his philosophy (since art is life's most adequate expression)—are not so much a result of the "metaphysics of subjectivity" as a newly opened door onto a *new, radically original form of individualism*. Heidegger himself has quite exactly pointed to what is perhaps the specific trait of such an individualism. Commenting on one of *The Will to Power*'s aphorisms, which states that "perspectivism" is a property of Being itself, Heidegger makes this decisive observation: "No drawn-out proof is needed to show that this conception of the existent is the very one Leibniz held, except that Nietzsche excludes its theological metaphysics, that is, Platonism" (ibid., p. 245). In other words: Nietzsche = Leibniz, less harmony, less God, understood, that is, as the monad of monads that brings into accord the different individual monads' multiple perspectives so that they may form a world, a universe, meaning a coherent totality and not, as in Nietzsche, a radically chaotic multiplicity. One could hardly put it better. But we have yet to determine the meaning to be given to an individualism—or, if one prefers, a monadology—in which the notion of the individual is shattered (the subject is no longer closed in on the identity of his consciousness as it was for seventeenth-century thinkers) at the same time that the idea of a reconciling harmony has vanished—whether this latter be called, as in political philosophy, the "invisible hand," or, as in speculative philosophy, "theodicy," "the cunning of reason," "system," etc.

The second thesis can only be put in the form of a foreshadowing of what will hereafter follow, since it specifies the content of this new figure of individualism. A reading of the texts Nietzsche consecrated to the concept of individual, when compared to those, much more numerous and better known, concerning aesthetics properly speaking, makes a central duality become clearly apparent:

—On the one hand, the abandonment of any and all "dialectical" project, aimed at integrating life's radical multiplicity (what is *tragic* in existence) into some sort of system, makes of Nietzschean individualism the prototype of the contemporary era, in that it takes the form of a historicism and of a relativism such as had never before been seen in the entire history of philosophy. The famous assertion that "there are no facts, only interpretations," can and should be understood not only, as Deleuze and Foucault did, as a genealogical critique of metaphysical or scientistic rationalism, but also and perhaps above all as the inauguration of what could be called an "ultra-individualism," with every one from now on possessing the "right" (the quotation marks becoming necessary here, since the term no longer has any meaning) to express what is, strictly and properly speaking, his "point of view." Nothing any longer constrains the various perspectives to unwillingly align themselves with some sort of order. There is thus nothing surprising, when seen from this aspect, at the fact that Nietzsche should have become the thinker-in-fashion for an intellectual generation that felt itself to be close to the various libertarian/liberationist movements that marked the intellectual and political life of the sixties and seventies.

—Yet, on the other hand, nothing would be more absurd than to see in Nietzsche a thinker of the "liberation of mores." Well-known are his taste for classical rigor and his aversion to anything that closely or distantly resembles a surging up of the passions, and first of all, of course, to romanticism. However, it goes without saying that Nietzsche is not a classicist in the "Cartesian" sense of the expression, in which, as is still the case with Hegel, the goal of art is to give expression to reason. And yet, despite everything, it is in fact a case of the *same* classicism: art continues for Nietzsche to maintain a direct link to *truth*. The true has naturally ceased to be defined as identity, transparency, and harmony in order to become the pure *difference* that is the multiplicity of vital forces. But what the Nietzschean "physiology" of art teaches us is that beauty is nothing other than the wisely hierarchized (in the "grand style") expression of this multiplicity. To create a symmetry with ultra-individualism, we could speak of a hyperclassicism (the use of this term will be justified in the next chapter) since it is more than ever art's task to translate truth into sensuousness—though it must be made clear that this new classicism is, so to speak, a classicism of "difference" and no longer one of harmonious identity.

And it is under this aspect—third thesis, which will be developed in the next chapter—that Nietzsche can be considered the true thinker of avant-gardism. Not that he himself wrote about the subject or belonged to any kind of movement that could have been considered to be "avant-garde." Nor did he evidence any special kind of daring in his own artistic tastes. But, less anecdotally, Nietzsche announces the duality that is the basis for all of the avant-garde movements that have left their imprint on the twentieth century's aesthetics up to the end of the sixties: ultra-individualism on one side, which, while pursuing the revolutionary values of the individual emancipation from tradition, consecrates innovation as the supreme criterion of the aesthetic judgment, and thus causes the latter to fall into the sphere of historicity; the other side being a hyperclassical concern that art should be assigned a truth-function, or even that it should be aligned upon science's progress so that it may translate a reality which, unlike what was the case in the original classicism (the seventeenth-century one), is no longer rational, harmonious, *Euclidean,* but illogical, chaotic, shapeless, and non-Euclidean.

THE INDIVIDUAL: AN AMBIGUOUS CONCEPT

Nietzsche's theory of art as the only honest perspective on life was a particularly important contribution to the internal logic of philosophical individualism as it developed, in the history of aesthetics, through the conflict between sentimentalism and rationalism—two aspects of individualism about which we have already discussed how each in its own way took the form of a *monadology,* where individuals commu-

nicate with each other only mediately, whether through the intermediation of a common psychological structure (Hume) or of a system of
harmony (Leibniz, Hegel). I should here like to indicate how Nietzsche
at the same time takes up again and overturns what had truly emerged
with Leibniz: ontologically, the installation of individuality as the principle of the real (with the affirmation that the real is, in its most intimate
core, a tissue of monads), and, axiologically, the promotion of the values of independence and personal creativity.

But this hypothesis—of Nietzsche completing philosophical individualism—is obviously paradoxical. Not only does it run against the
idea that Nietzsche, as is widely known, was a forerunner of Freud's
critique of philosophies of consciousness and therefore, it would seem,
of philosophical individualism (Nietzsche never stopped attacking the
idea of monad or atom, and its relevance to the theorization of the idea
of subject); it also exposes itself to a certain number of "factual" problems that cannot be underestimated. To put it in a nutshell, when the
texts Nietzsche dedicated to the notions of individualism or the individual are surveyed, they appear to be shot through by a constant tension that seems to forbid a priori any project that would try for a
somewhat concordant reading.

Quite obviously, Nietzsche makes of the individual an absolute
value, and first of all an ontological principle. For example, we read
in *The Will to Power* that there are no species, "only different individuals"—a sort of reformulation of the principle of indiscernibles by
reference to which Nietzsche presents, in various well-known texts,
concepts and words (reason and language) as processes of the homogenization of differences, of obliteration of individuality and, in this
sense, as figures of the loss of the real understood as the interplay of
"pure differentiations," according to the formulation used in another
fragment.

Following the logic of this ontological individualism, Nietzsche
puts forward an axiological individualism that reaches its high point
with the defence of the values issued out of originality against what he
sometimes calls "vulgarity,"[11] meaning the dissolution of the differentiated individual element within the flattened-out average. Certain
memorable moments in the Nietzschean discourse are part of this critique of vulgarity, moments I recall only to aid the memory a bit:

—The genealogy of the values stemming from gregariousness and
from the civilization of the herd, whose succeeding stages Nietzsche
reconstitutes by following a line that goes from Judaism to socialism,

by way of Socrates, Christianity, Rousseau, the French Revolution and democracy.

—The critical analysis of the genesis of *consciousness* and of *language*, a genesis ascribed to a certain evolution of life. It is the very important section 354 of *The Gay Science*, titled "On the 'genius of the species,'" that here develops in a particularly brilliant way the idea that the birth of consciousness in this living being that is man (its emergence, then its valorization) did not happen by itself, it was not fated to be, but was rather connected to the requirements (themselves not fated to be) posed by communication and by language. A certain type of human being could not, Nietzsche explains, face up to life's necessities without needing other human beings, without, that is, substituting the values proper to independence with those corresponding to mutual help and solidarity. This need for the other at the same time brought to the surface the need to express and to communicate this need, for, that is, "mutual understanding," and first of all for the necessity of arriving at the consciousness of this need. Such is, according to Nietzsche, the reason why consciousness is born at the same time as language: "Consciousness has developed only under the pressure of the need for communication." The result is that man only became conscious of what was communicable, shareable with another, and therefore *common*, and, from this point of view, what gains access to consciousness and to language is never the individual but all that is gregarious and vulgar:

My idea is, as you see, that consciousness does not really belong to man's individual existence but rather to his social or herd nature; that, as follows from this, it has developed subtlety only insofar as this is required by social or herd utility. Consequently, given the best will in the world to understand ourselves as individually as possible, "to know ourselves," each of us will always succeed in becoming conscious only of what is not individual but "average."[12]

Earlier, Nietzsche argues that "the thinking that rises to *consciousness* is only the smallest part of all thinking—the most superficial and worst part"—meaning the part that corresponds to individuality. Even though "fundamentally, all our actions are altogether incomparably personal, unique, and infinitely individual," consciousness and language stem from this "great . . . falsification" consisting of a "generalization" and, as such, a "reduction to superficialities" of what is.

Here we can perceive how a theme as important to Nietzsche as the critique of consciousness and language fits readily into the framework of a revalorization of individuality. If generalization is falsification, rendering superficial, the *true* (the nonfalsified) and the profound (the non-superficial) must truly reside in the affirmation of the individual as such. This is one, first line of analysis in which Nietzsche's thought takes on tones similar to those of certain anarchistic young Hegelians. Its conclusion is, quite logically, a critique of modernity as a civilization in which, the values of consciousness having imposed themselves through cogito philosophy and its scientific appendices, the individual is dissolved in the general, defined as gregariousness. Modernity as the triumph of the "genius of the species" over the individual, over the great individualities incarnated by, for example, the Greeks (the ones before Socrates, of course), and, in parallel fashion, democracy, supreme value of the modern world, scientific and therefore "of the commoners," in that it aims at a truth that is "valid for all," democracy as the equalization of men, and therefore as the obliteration of the differences constitutive of individuality: this is, without a doubt, one first approach of Nietzsche's thought, that coheres around the erection of the individual as true reality and absolute value—what is well resumed by this fragment from the posthumous writings of the *Will to Power* period, "nothing is so opposed to these herd instincts as the sovereignty of the individual [*das Einzelnen*]."[13]

The difficulty, as always with Nietzsche, is that other texts, just as numerous and as important, contradict the first ones and put forward a radical criticism of the notion of individual and, correlatively, of individualism. Nietzsche insists upon it many times. In reality, the notion of individual is no more valid than that of species or, as a fragment from the left-behind writings of the 1880s puts it: "The concepts 'individual' [*Individuum*] and 'species' are equally false and merely apparent" (ibid., § 521)—a statement that, now, seems to issue out of an ontological anti-individualism (the individual as mere appearance and no longer as the basis of what is) to which corresponds an axiological anti-individualism: "The 'welfare of the individual' is just as imaginary as the 'welfare of the species'" (ibid., § 552). Thus, the individual is neither a good ontological principle nor a legitimate axiological principle—all of which seems to be in perfect contradiction with the passages we have just looked at.

In fact, when Nietzsche describes the notion of the individual as an "error" (the expression used in *The Twilight of the Idols*), he is aiming at a quite precise particularity of individuality. On this point, the texts are in agreement:

—*Twilight of the Idols:* "The single one, the 'individual,' as hith-

FIVE

erto understood by the people and the philosophers alike, is an error
after all: he is nothing by himself, no atom, no 'link in the chain,' nothing merely inherited from former times; he is the whole single line of
humanity up to himself." [14]

The value of the individual varies, therefore, according to whether
he "represents the rising line of life" or "the descending development,
decline, chronic degeneracy, illness." The individual can thus not be
considered *by himself*, neither ontologically nor axiologically. Neither
does he exist in isolation nor is his worth independent of the processes
that come to achievement within him. The "moment" that individuality
is will be valued highly if it is a moment of intensification and increase
of the will to power—and devalued if it consists in a moment of ex-
tenuation or exhaustion.

—*The Will to Power* contains a parallel text (§ 785): the concept
"individual" must be refuted, Nietzsche explains, in order to perceive
that in fact "every single creature constitutes the entire process in its
entire course (not merely as 'inherited,' but the process itself)," that he
is in fact "all of life up to now in *one* line and *not* its result" (§ 379).

To be correctly interpreted, these assertions, which may seem
strange when compared to the Nietzschean valorization of individualism that we have elsewhere observed, have to be set side by side with
the critiques of the notions of atom and of monad such as Nietzsche
understands them. In the important fragment from the *Will to Power*
cited above (§ 785), Nietzsche evokes the construction of the notion
of subject by designating it as a "false substantialization of the ego"
through which it has been artificially "pried out of becoming," posited
"as something that is a being" (the motor of this fetishization being "the
faith in individual immortality"). Such a substantialization of the ego is
also described by Nietzsche as a "declaration that it exists in and for
itself," that it has been considered "in an atomistic sense."

What thus turns out to be erroneous in the notion of individuality
is not the concept of individual in general but a particular conception
of the individual, that of the individual made *autonomous* in relation
to the world and to becoming, and posited as atom or "monad," [15]—
as, that is, an ultimate, stable, durable, even indestructible (immortal)
unity, the original source of its own acts and its own representations.
Against such a vision of individuality, a passage from *The Will to Power*
(§ 715) asserts that "there are no durable ultimate units, no atoms, no
monads"; that "'units' are nowhere present in the nature of becoming";

162

that there is no "will" that could be the ultimate and self-identical source of what it itself posits, etc. The "autonomization of the individual in atomistic form" in truth refers back to the stabilized images of the world that religion, metaphysics, and science have constructed simultaneously by inventing, instead of the chaotic play of "pure difference" and pure successions of states, a "true world" of *beings, causes, unities*, etc. (in physics, for example, "a firm systematization of atoms in necessary motion, the same for all beings") (§ 636).

Before Heidegger, therefore, but heading in the same direction, it is the "metaphysical" individual that Nietzsche criticizes, meaning the individual centered on the values of unity (atomic or monadic) and autonomy, where in reality reigns within every man a plurality of force-centers, at every instant combining and fighting each other (the unity of the "I" being but a fiction), and what we call the will is the ultimate expression of an uncontrollable conflict between force-centers rather than "free" will, in the sense of a will positing its own laws (autonomy is an illusion).

In a manner parallel to these texts, which work out a critique of metaphysical individuality that is in many ways a forerunner of Heideggerian deconstruction, Nietzsche sketches out an interesting critical challenge to individualism. These passages in his work are quite astonishing on first reading when put next to his high valorization of the individual against the herd, since he here explicitly denounces individualism as being one of the characteristic components of a civilization of gregariousness. We can for example quote from two of *The Will to Power*'s fragments:

—"Individualism is a modest and still unconscious form of the 'will to power'" (§ 784): a strange statement, if we recall how Nietzsche elsewhere makes of the individual's sovereignty the value that is most opposed to those of the herd.

—"My philosophy aims at an ordering of rank: not at an individualistic morality" (§ 287): but we might have thought that the affirmation of the individual's sovereignty is, in point of fact, the principle of an authentic individualistic morality against the morality of the herd.

Along the same lines, we might be troubled at seeing Christianity—in Nietzsche's eyes one of the most characteristic expressions of herd values—credited with the valorization of the individual. "In fact, it was Christianity that first invited the individual to play the judge of everything and everyone; megalomania almost became a duty: one has to enforce *eternal* rights against everything temporal and conditioned!" (§ 765). Nietzsche describes how Christianity thus contributed to the genesis of individualism by making us accustomed to the superstitious concept "of the 'soul,' the 'immortal soul,' soul-monads that really are at home somewhere else" and whose being is therefore not at all conditioned by earthly things (ibid.). There is of course a return, in this description of the Christian contribution, of the monadic version of individuality whose Nietzschean critique we have already seen, but we are still somewhat surprised that in a sense that is yet to be precisely defined individualism should be put on the same shelf as the Christianity whose plebeian, anti-aristocratic evaluations must be overcome.

This puzzlement obligates us to a closer examination of that which Nietzsche intends to genealogize when he criticizes negative individualism. The key text in this context might well be this fragment from *The Will to Power*: "The modern European is characterized by two apparently opposite traits: individualism and the demand for equal rights; that I have at last come to understand" (§ 783).

What has Nietzsche come to understand? That, in reality, *modern* individualism is inseparable from the *egalitarianism* through which it expresses and fulfills itself. This bond (quite paradoxical, since individualism should be the affirmation of *difference* and of *otherness,* and not the valorization of identity or of equality) and its origin are explained by Nietzsche thus: modern individuality is weak and fearful ("for the individual is an extremely vulnerable piece of vanity"); in order not to suffer from differences, the modern individual will set out to deny them; the only way for him to defend the worth of his own existence is for "this vanity [to] demand that every other shall count as its equal, that it should be only *inter pares*"; therefore "the principle of the individual rejects very great human beings and demands, among men approximately equal, the subtlest eye and the speediest recognition of a talent" (ibid.). The appreciation of individuality and of its "little differences" will thus take place against the background of a foregoing equalization and homogenization; against the background, in this context, of a certain *depersonalization.* Against the individualism of the moderns Nietzsche opposes what he calls the "personalism of the Ancients,"[16] for whom individuality was appreciated as such, in its distance and its difference.

The opposition between ancient and modern, or, if one prefers, between tradition and democracy, brings out the following structure:

1. Modern individualism, valuing equality more than difference: and it is through this quality that it marches hand in hand with Christianity (equality before God) and democracy (equality before the law); and it is also "the *most modest* stage of the will to power," the individual only asserting himself within it by holding himself to be equal to others instead of positing his difference with authority, without comparisons or arguments, as is clearly pointed out by this fragment of *The Will to Power:*

> *Individualism* is a modest and still unconscious form of the "will to power"; here it seems sufficient to the individual to get free from an overpowering domination by society (whether that of the state or of the church). He does not oppose them *as a person* but only as an individual; he represents all individuals against the totality. That means: he instinctively posits himself as *equal* to all other individuals; what he gains in this struggle he gains for himself not as a person but as a representative of individuals against the totality. (§ 784)

For that reason, Nietzsche assimilates modern individualism to a form of "individual egoism" (ibid.), to the risible wish to see oneself as in isolation from society and from humanity in its totality. No accident, then, if this figure of individualism is, on the metaphysical level, associated with the illusion of the "I," of the monadic subject transparent to itself or at least ultimate origin of its own actions and ideas. For the truth of this individual as "isolated man"—of this "error," in fact— truly is individualism as the ego's will to egoistically separate itself, to posit itself "against the totality." The goal here is not the authentic cultivation of one's own originality, the creative affirmation of self, but, in this still embryonic, or rather "degraded," "decadent" version of the will to power, only the positing of self as a "one" against the "all." Zero degree of life, therefore, since this emancipation from the whole takes place under the aegis of the equalization of all. By positing myself as identical to all the others, following the Kantian/liberal conception of the law, by positing all the others as being my equals, I install a society—the democratic society—in which, by way of the theme of the individual's rights (of the universal suffrage Nietzsche abhors) that minimum of independence is assured within which the will to power finds its least sophisticated expression.

Nietzsche's analysis of modern individualism as being intrinsically tied to the appearance of the democratic universe can't help bringing to mind Tocqueville's analysis, except that, in its essential arguments, and despite whatever Tocquevillian nostalgias, its signs are inverted. Modernity here exhibits no "progress," it is to be read, of course, rather as a decadence, as a regress towards a withered form of life: "One desires *freedom* [meaning differentiation from the all through identification with all] so long as one does not possess power. Once one does possess it, one desires to overpower."

We would however be mistaken if we were too hastily to liken Nietzsche's critique of liberal individualism (defined as the "egoism" of the "isolated man") to the Marxian critique. Despite the similarity of the formulas used—and although denouncing individualism was already quite well looked upon in the nineteenth century—Nietzsche subtly associates liberalism and socialism in the same rejection. Using terms near to those employed by Tocqueville when the latter saw in the birth of a "tutelary" state one of modern individualism's possible horizons, he explains that, in fact, socialism is "merely a means of agitation employed by individualism," insofar as "the instinct of socialists" is not at all to make "a social order as the goal of the individual" but of using society "as a means for making possible many individuals"—the socialist state being conceived as the one that must provide individuals with *equal* access to the greatest possible happiness, fulfilling a demand that turns out to be the very one made by "individual egoism" (ibid.).

2. Against the modern individualism (democratic, Christian, and socialist), Nietzsche rates highly the attitude that consists in asserting oneself, not as an individual against the all, but as a person in one's *incomparable* difference (because to compare is already to presuppose terms of comparison, and consequently *identities*). This is the "personalism of the Ancients" that corresponds not to the spirit of democracy but to that of aristocracy; what is then highly valued is no longer equality, but distance and hierarchy, the model being found by Nietzsche in what he calls the "great individualities" he discovers among the pre-Socratic Greeks and during the Renaissance.[17] The supreme value is no longer the autonomy of individuals from the whole, but a self-assertion that is wholly independent from consideration of the others. Particularly important in this respect are the fragments where Nietzsche evokes his morality's principle,[18] the antisocial "individuation" that "denies universal equality and equivalence among men."[19] Contrary to what takes place in modern individualism, the point is "to say 'me' oftener and louder than the majority," to dominate the others, "by making them submit or sacrificing them," if one's independence can only be brought about at that price (ibid., § 196).

THE TRUE NIETZSCHEAN BREAK: FROM MODERN INDIVIDUALISM
TO CONTEMPORARY OR POSTMODERN INDIVIDUALISM

The ambiguities in the notion of individualism, as Nietzsche uses it, are of twofold interest for the analysis and the understanding of his philosophy as a philosophy of art. It is first of all clear that the concept of individuality can be taken in many ways and, notably, quite unlike what happens for example in Tocqueville's analysis, it can be understood as designating an ancient reality, a premodern state of the will to power that is, late in the day, weakened by the birth of egalitarianism. But what exactly is at stake for Nietzschean thought in this opposition of the ancient and the modern has to be clearly understood. As usual among the contemporaries (and this goes just as well for Heidegger or for Leo Strauss), the revalorization of the ancient over the modern is not an end in itself, but a strategic disposition senseless outside the perspective of a *post*modernity. If Nietzsche's "observations" are so "unmodern" it is because they shock egalitarian "democratic" modernity, but also because they are thereby more modern than modernity itself, because they prepare a future that sees itself as unprecedented. In the case at hand, since we are dealing most of all with philosophy, they prepare for the transformation of the philosopher's status, which—following a theme constant in Nietzsche's thinking—should go from that of worker to that of artist.

Within this perspective ancient individualism should be of use, if not as model, then at least as a guide in the search for a new figuration of individualism; if the latter should find its most complete expression in art, taken in its most general sense as the most adequate manifestation of the will to power, it is because, in a universe that is now wholly perspectival, in a world once again become infinite in that it offers the possibility of an infinity of interpretations, only art presents itself authentically as what it is: an evaluation that makes no pretence of truth. The assertion that Nietzsche's philosophy takes the form of a monadology with neither subject nor system is here once again verified. Neither monads (individuals in the modern meaning), nor unique viewpoint from which, as in Leibniz or Hegel, the various perspectives could be synthetized following a harmony (that this harmony be thought of as dialectical or not in the end matters little): such could be the formula for Nietzschean, postmodern individualism, through which art becomes the will to power's mode of being for itself.

This kind of individualism is still "monadological" though in a radically new sense, since out of the Leibnizian-Hegelian theodicy it keeps only the idea of a multiplicity of points of view, which it gives up trying to integrate into the unity of a harmonious synthesis. To better outline this individualism we need to consider two types of clue, the first concerning that which Nietzsche holds to be specifically German in philosophy from Leibniz to Hegel, the second the nature of his perspectivism as an unprecedented form of relativism or historicism.

THE FRACTURE OF THE SUBJECT

The very interesting section 357 of *The Gay Science,* titled "On the old problem: 'What is German?'," is consecrated to the analysis of three of Germanity's typically representative thinkers: Leibniz, Kant, and Hegel. With Nietzsche, criticism of these authors for being within the tradition of Platonic rationalism is usually de rigueur. But what makes this text stand out is the very fact that in it he takes, for once, an extolling attitude; and that through his homage to the German philosophers the features of an aesthetic individualism sustained by a new theory of subjectivity are sketched out step by step.

What Nietzsche judges to be indeed 'positive' in the philosophical work of the Germans is its *depth,* understood here in its strict meaning as the capacity for bringing "hidden worlds" to light. This oeuvre bears witness to the fact, as Nietzsche puts it when discussing Leibniz, that "our inner world is much richer, more comprehensive, more concealed" than had been thought until then. It is here that the genealogist's task begins to become visible, at the same time that the modern, metaphysical vision of the subject begins to deconstruct itself—a flatly individualist vision that grants an entirely unjustified primacy to *surface,* to *consciousness.*

To faithfully understand what Nietzsche here credits Leibniz, Kant, and Hegel with, we have to comprehend the significance that the project of going beyond appearances, of rendering the hidden worlds visible, has for him—as opposed to what takes place in every philosophy of Platonic inspiration. Such a will to parousia may seem paradoxical. We have in fact seen how one of the principal reproaches addressed to Platonism, as well as to Christianity, the former's popular version, had to do with its effort to deny the sensible world in the name of an intelligible world—the first being designated as the appearance in relation to which the second plays the role of the demystifying "world-behind" or hidden world (if we follow the famous myth of the cave). Why, in such circumstances, should that which is negative in Plato (the critique of appearances in the name of a hidden world, only accessible to philosophical reflection) become positive when it comes to the Germans? Aren't we dealing in both cases with a relativization of the real world in the name of a hidden world?

Actually, "appearance" has changed position so much in the itinerary from Plato to the Germans that it is no longer the same illusion being denounced in the one and the other case. Whereas in Plato and Christianity (this "horror of touching") it is the sensible world that is criticized from the standpoint of a beyond whose model is provided by the theory of the Ideas, in Leibniz, Kant, and Hegel it is, on the contrary, Platonic truth that takes the place of appearance. The critique of Platonism will, for Nietzsche as later for Heidegger, find its natural extension in a deconstruction of modern science, which limits itself to developing and fulfilling what is already embryonic in metaphysics. The various scientific disciplines indeed tirelessly pursue the goal of denouncing naïve, *sensuous,* opinions in the name of a hidden truth, only accessible to the scholar's and the scientist's reason. Only the inversion of Platonism can create the conditions of possibility for genealogy. The latter will no longer attempt to "spare the phenomena," to unveil the immutable clarity of ideas under the confusing chaos of sensuous images. On the contrary, true depth consists in revealing, under the superficial appearance of the light of the intelligible, that obscure and mad world the young Nietzsche had called "dyonisiac." In this, such an "archeological" activity is typically germanic.

Beginning with Leibniz: what are profoundly challenged are the supposed "self-evidences" of Cartesian philosophy and, especially, the primacy of consciousness, in the name of which "interior" life should be identified with clear and distinct life. Leibniz is in fact the first to introduce the concept of the unconscious into philosophy through his notorious "small perceptions" that, because of the principle of continuity, must necessarily precede the appearance of clear consciousness, that is, they must connect a zero degree of consciousness to a degree N. He thus came up with "the incomparable insight that has been vindicated not only against Descartes but against everybody who had philosophized before him—that consciousness is merely an *accidens* of experience and *not* its necessary and essential attribute; that, in other words, what we call consciousness constitutes only one state of our spiritual and psychic world (perhaps a pathological state) and not by any means the whole of it" (*The Gay Science,* § 357).

The parenthesis is, of course, Nietzsche's own addition; it points to what still separates Leibniz's "discovery" from a true genealogy. For it seems clear that, though having "discovered the unconscious," Leibniz still thinks in terms of modern individualism. The subject is defined as a monad/substance and consciousness, though partially challenged, remains the philosopher's ideal at the same time that the intelligible realm remains the truth of a sensible no more autonomous than it was for Plato. Nevertheless, there are, according to Nietzsche, reasons to think "that no Latin could easily have thought of this reversal of appearances," and that germanic depth has here opened up the path towards an authentic *genealogy of the subject*. The metaphysical background of modern individualism has been subverted.

As far as Kant is concerned, it is scientific as well as philosophical reason, no less, whose secular supremacy is contested: we must here recall the "tremendous question mark that he placed after the concept of 'causality'—without, like Hume, doubting its legitimacy altogether. Rather, Kant began cautiously to delimit the realm within which this concept makes sense (and to this day we are not done with this fixing of limits)" (ibid.).

A nice example of Nietzsche's style. We would have expected him to prefer Hume to Kant, to appreciate the doubt that scepticism hangs over the very category of causality (over the legitimacy of its use as much as over its capacity to go beyond the stage of "belief" and reach that of truth). And yet he judges the Kantian critique to be profounder than the empiricist one: for if Kant, unlike Hume, admits a certain validity for the principles of reason, it is only to immediately relativize it through his famous postulate that the law of causality applies only to phenomena, the sphere of practice being perhaps outside its domain. Thus, "As Germans, we doubt with Kant the ultimate validity of the knowledge attained by the natural sciences and altogether everything that *can* be known *causaliter;* whatever is know*able* immediately seems to us *less* valuable on that account" (ibid.).

Finally, it is "the astonishing stroke of Hegel" that must be credited to German depth. Its merit is twofold: it consists, first of all, in putting an end to the primacy of identity, of accepting the idea of contradiction within the very heart of logic; second and above all, it consists in the fact of introducing historicity into the categories of reason and thus marking a break away from the Platonist theory of eternal, stable ideas.

These breakthroughs towards true genealogy quite obviously remain fleeting, and modern individualism's dependence on traditional metaphysics is still obvious in all three cases: in Kant, because the primacy accorded practical reason still refers back to Platonism and to the rationalist tradition; in Leibniz and Hegel, because the discoveries of the unconscious and of history are still put to the service of a systematization of the existent so that, in the one as in the other case, the "discoveries" are soon cancelled—the unconscious is recaptured by consciousness and history by Reason, rather than the reverse.

But it remains highly significant that the judgment carried out by Nietzsche on the value of what is German indicates a new age, one in which individualism adapts itself to the disappearance of subject and object and their replacement by a pure perspectivism, by an absolute dispersal of the various points of view in a radical historicism.

What is at stake in Leibniz's unveiling of the unconscious is in fact the enfeeblement of the subject—an enfeeblement that finally works itself out in the advent of a "burst" individual, no longer aspiring to self-mastery or to autonomy. This is the reason why the word "subject" does not, in the final analysis, refer to anything more than to "the term for our belief in a *unity* underlying all the different impulses of the highest feeling of reality: we understand this belief as the effect of one cause,"[20] and through this hypostatization of identity we come to believe that the ego is an ultimate substratum of our representations. The Cartesian cogito turns out to be only an effect of what Nietzsche calls the trap of words or "our grammatical custom" (ibid., § 484). Actually, "'the subject' is the fiction that many similar states in us are the effect of *one* substratum: but it is *we* who first created the 'similarity' of these states" (ibid., § 485).

This fiction is well and truly shaken by the hypothesis of an unconscious since, as Nietzsche goes on to explain, we now have to resolve ourselves to consider consciousness as a mere epiphenomenon of life, and in no way as life itself: "consciousness of me," "self-consciousness," from then on looks only like "the last trait added to the organism when it already functions to perfection; it is almost superfluous"—so that if the fiction of the unity of the ego contains some sort of truth, it is not, in any case, at the level of consciousness, as all of Platonic-Cartesian philosophy has naïvely believed: "If there is any unity within me, it surely does not consist in my conscious me," which is nothing more than a "terminal phenomenon" whose causes are entirely unknown to me, but in what Nietzsche designates as "the organism's wisdom."[21] There is thus, in the Marxist sense of the word, a fetishism of the subject, that genealogy literally dissolves by showing that the "I" is but a "created entity," "a simplification with the object of defining the force which posits, invents, thinks, as distinct from all individual positing, inventing, thinking as such."[22] We thus think we exhibit a real faculty in the "ego," but, in truth, this faculty is nothing, or, more exactly, it is only the concretion, the reification of an activity that always only exists as a particular activity.

The eradication of the subject, through which Nietzsche links up again with the "personalism of the Ancients," is accompanied by the inevitable disappearance of the object, as a key passage in the *Will to Power* suggests following a subtle line of argument (ibid.). It is first of all clear that the elimination of the subject/substance (of Cartesian consciousness) leads to thinking of the world as of a tissue of interpretations, irreducible to any kind of unity (they lack any *stable* substratum); in all rigor, therefore, "One may not ask: 'who then interprets?' for the interpretation itself is a form of the will to power, exists (but not as a 'being' but as a process, a becoming) as an affect." And if interpretation alone constitutes the core of what is, then it is not only the subject that is an illusion, an effect of fetishism, but also the idea that there is an "in itself" of "facts," independent of interpretation: "A 'thing-in-itself' just as perverse as a 'sense-in-itself,' a 'meaning-in-itself.' There are no 'facts-in-themselves.'"

From this point on, just as it is vain to look—in the metaphysical sense—for a "subject" of interpretation, and just as one must give up—again, in the metaphysical meaning—the question "who interprets?," one also must resolve oneself to abandon asking the question "what is that?"—for it itself is but "an imposition of meaning from some other viewpoint . . . At the bottom of it there always lies 'what is that for *me?*' (for us, for all that lives, etc.)"—the parenthesis aimed at making it understood that the "me" is, here, no longer taken in the sense of a metaphysical subject identical with itself in the transparency of its consciousness, but as a fractured subject [*un sujet brisé*], as an interpretative force among others, as a pure point of view: "In short: the essence of a thing is only an *opinion* about the 'thing.' Or rather: 'it is considered' is the real 'it is,' the sole 'this is.'"

Nietzsche never stops insisting on this: if "there are no facts" but only interpretations, it is because, as the *Twilight of the Idols* puts it, "every judgment is a symptom," or, as it is phrased in a fragment from *The Will to Power*, all evaluation is senseless outside of "a definite perspective: that of the preservation of the individual, a community, a race, a state, a church, a faith, a culture." We simply "forget that valuation is always from a perspective" (§ 259). In short: "there is no 'thing-in-itself'" (§ 557) because, unlike what happens in Leibniz or Hegel, the multiplicity of viewpoints proves to be irreducible in the postmodern individualism that is here inaugurated, and that for the very good reason that there is no longer a subject capable of establishing in itself any kind of systematic recollection.

That this extreme form of individualism was explicitly adopted by Nietzsche is not to be doubted if we look again at the way it extends the critique of science he perceives, or thinks he perceives, in Kant. It is not only the sphere of scientific truth that is deprived of all objectivity, but also the sphere of signification or meaning. There where Kant tries, especially in the aesthetic domain, to maintain the possibility of a "common sense," of a contingent agreement between subjectivities or sensibilities outside the conceptual rules of objectivity, Nietzsche postulates a radical heterogeneity: "Our values are interpreted *into* things. Is there then any *meaning* in the in-itself? Is meaning not necessarily relative meaning and perspective?" (§ 590).

But the core nature of Nietzschean individualism also determines itself using Hegel as a reference. In the Hegelian supersession of Leibniz and Kant—still too Platonist—relativism reveals its true meaning to be that of a radical historicism, as this fragment suggests: "What separates us from Kant, as from Plato and Leibniz, is that we believe only in becoming . . . We are *historians* through and through" and here Nietzsche evokes the names of Lamarck and of Hegel, of whom Darwin is but a later avatar.

We have already pointed out Nietzsche's distance from the systematic, reconciling spirit of the Hegelian dialectic. Deleuze is no doubt right in insisting upon it. Yet his interpretation, unlike Heidegger's, underestimates the kinship between these two thinkers even though it was acknowledged by Nietzsche himself, for whom the reference to history permits dealing a fatal blow to Platonic idealism. As Leo Strauss quite correctly remarks, until Hegel, "all ideals pretended to have an objective basis: nature, God, or reason. The historical sense destroys this pretention and, with it, all known ideals."[23] It is this potential that Nietzsche greets in Hegelianism before drawing out all its consequences, which evidently implies that historicity be unburdened of its systematic harness. According to Strauss, the various ideals and cultures "are no longer arranged, in Nietzsche, into a system," because it has become impossible to operate "a veritable synthesis" (p. 96). Following in Heidegger's wake, Strauss invites us to see in Nietzschean perspec-

FIVE

tivism more a prolongation of Hegelianism than its refutation, in that
(1) in it, everything finally becomes historical, and (2) the basis for every
ideal (to the extent that the term still makes any sense) is subjectivity
understood as will to power: "The transvaluation of all values Nietzsche tries to carry out is justified in the end by the fact that its root is
the greatest will to power—a will to power greater than that which gave
birth to all the previous values;" or, to take up Heidegger's terminology:
a triumph of the metaphysics of subjectivity rather than its overcoming; or, using the formulation adopted in this work: a triumph of postmodern individualism, since with Nietzsche we witness "the end of the
domination of chance," man for the first time becoming "master of his
destiny" in an apology of artistic creativity that no longer acknowledges
substantial limitations.

THE "PHYSIOLOGY OF ART": A NEW ASPECT OF HISTORICISM

To radicalize Hegelian historicism one has to, as has been indicated,
remove history from the dialectical framework it still belongs to for
Hegel. Only this way can one put into place a perfect relativism, a relativism that is characterized in Nietzsche's work by two particularly decisive traits:

1. By the fact, first of all, that there can be no exteriority, no transcendence to the perpetual *becoming* that life is (which is why vitalism
is a historicism). Becoming still had an end-goal for Hegel, and reason encompassed history more than it was produced by it. Elsewhere, I
have already had the opportunity to analyse this fundamental aspect of
Nietzschean thought[24] and to indicate how this definition of Being as
life or as "will to power" implies an inevitable rejection of rights and
laws—indeed, of any question of the *Quid juris?* type. It is this very
position of principle that Nietzsche designates with the term "physiology," as we can see particularly well in the quite explicit section 2 of
the "The Problem of Socrates" chapter in *Twilight of the Idols*. Nietzsche there argues that the "consensus of the sages" around Platonism
proves nothing about their having been right; it indicates at best that
"these wisest men agreed in some *physiological* respect, and hence
adopted the same negative attitude to life—*had to* adopt it." Furthermore, not only is the Platonic dualism of a sensible and an intelligible
world unfriendly towards life (it is a forerunner of the latter's depreca-
tion by Christianity in the name of the beyond), but, especially, it is
based on a "stupidity" that is, alas, consubstantial with it, the belief

174

that one can *judge* life, where in fact all our judgments upon life are in all obviousness expressions of life, so that "judgments of value, concerning life, for it or against it, can, in the end, never be true." Since "the value of life cannot be estimated. Not by the living, for they are an interested party, even a bone of contention, and not judges; not by the dead, for a different reason," there is in the Platonic pretention to judge life here on earth a veritable hermeneutic circle. To understand this circle is to also understand that no philosophical utterance can escape history (can escape life *as* historicity), that there is no "metalanguage" in whatever sense of the term: "judgments of value . . . concerning life . . . have value only as symptoms, they are worthy of consideration only as symptoms."

But the essential point would go by us if we did not perceive that this historicist vitalism is a direct consequence of the "fracture of the subject" [*brisure du sujet*]—which thus distinguishes it from older forms of relativism. One of the consequences of this "fracture" is, precisely, that our evaluations, our points of view, our interpretations of the world can never be grounded on any kind of reference to an *absolute* knowledge in its strict meaning (that is, unrelated to life's historicity). This is how we should understand section 374 of *The Gay Science*, with the title "Our new 'infinite,'" which asserts that "the world [has] become 'infinite' for us all over again, inasmuch as we cannot reject the possibility that *it may include infinite interpretations.*" Under such circumstances, there can be no objectivity either; there can be, to borrow the vocabulary from another domain, no more signified, only signifier, or, as Foucault quite lucidly put it in a commentary on Nietzsche: "if interpretation can never come to an end, it is quite simply because there is nothing to interpret . . . for, in the end, everything already is interpretation."[25]

2. At this point, the philosopher ends up merging with the genealogist in the most radical sense, with, that is, him who sees that behind the evaluations there is no ground, but an abyss, that behind the hidden worlds themselves there are but other hidden worlds, forever ungraspable because having no existence in themselves except as hypostases of an interpretation itself forever ungraspable. Foucault was right in insisting on this as well: "genealogy does not stand in opposition to history as if it were the lofty and profound view of the philosopher against the mole's perspective of the scholar. On the contrary: it is opposed to the metahistorical display of ideal significations" and moreover, "it needs history to drive away the chimaera of origin" (ibid.). The genealogist,

then, a typical character of postmodern individualism, is a "loner" or "hermit." Being marginal to the herd, the anguishing task of looking into the abyss falls to him:

> The hermit . . . will doubt whether a philosopher could *possibly* have "ultimate and real" opinions, whether behind every one of his caves there is not, must not be, another deeper cave—a more comprehensive, stranger, richer world beyond the surface, an abysmally deep ground behind every ground, under every attempt to furnish "grounds." Every philosophy is a foreground philosophy that is a hermit's judgment . . . Every philosophy also *conceals* a philosophy; every opinion is also a hideout, every word also a mask.[26]

The hermit's cave is no longer Plato's.

Historicism and relativism had always taken the shape, in modern philosophy, of a *subjectivism* (even if the subject is constantly reduced to the isolated atom consisting of the individual of the empiricists as well as that of the dogmatic rationalists). If relativism there was—in, for instance, the aesthetics of feeling, or in the various kinds of sceptical empiricism—it was precisely because the individual's subjectivity was so strongly asserted that it rendered any hope of finding acceptable criteria for the objectivity of taste (or of truth, or of morality) impossible. No such thing in Nietzsche's thought where, as we have seen, historicism assumes the form of a perspectivism with neither subject nor object, of a perspectivism at whose extreme—an extreme we have to remain at—exists only interpretation as such, independently of any conception of a subject that interprets as of an object that is interpreted.

The Nietzschean theory of art as being the will to power's only adequate expression is the site par excellence where the new conception of relativity, where the *new individualism with neither subject nor object* finds its most authentic translation. The problem with Nietzsche's texts is that, through their relativist appearance, they borrow from the form and vocabulary of the sceptical subjectivism inherent to modern individualism, whereas, at bottom, they on the contrary imply a radical critique of all the forms of subjectivity hitherto known—which is why it seems to me that a distinction must be made between this contemporary individualism and the "metaphysics of subjectivity."

As a first approach, we must of course cite the famous dictum in *Nietzsche contra Wagner* that "aesthetics is nothing but a kind of applied physiology" ("Where I Offer Objections"); in the development of this argument Nietzsche has recourse to psychology and biology so often that he at times seems like an eighteenth-century French materialist. The conclusions that "physiology" arrives at have to be understood within the perspective of this *apparent* subjectivism (in the sense of a rejection of the very notion of an objective criterion of taste), and especially the one that holds that the beautiful and the ugly do not at all exist "in themselves," but only as "symptoms" of certain "aesthetic states" more or less useful in the development and intensification of life: "That which is instinctively *repugnant* to us, aesthetically, is proved by mankind's longest experience to be harmful, dangerous, worthy of suspicion: the suddenly vocal aesthetic instinct (e.g., in disgust) contains a *judgment*. To this extent the beautiful stands within the general category of the biological values of what is useful, beneficent, life-enhancing."[27] As for Hume, it would seem, the beautiful is relative to a material structure, in this case to an instinctual structure whose potency it intensifies.

This relativistic "materialism" always shows two aspects—a biological one (reference to the body) and a psychological one (reference to unconscious drives), a duality which quite naturally finds its unity in the concept of life, about which Heidegger was right to stress that it is, in Nietzsche, a metaphysical (ontological) concept and not at all a scientific notion:[28]

—Nietzsche follows the first aspect of the duality when he writes in *The Will to Power* that "all art exercises the power of suggestion over the muscles and senses" (§ 809) since "every inner movement (feeling, thought, affect) is accompanied by vascular changes and consequently by changes in color, temperature, and secretion," phenomena he goes on to put into relation with "the suggestive power of music, its *suggestion mentale*" (§ 811). It is in the same spirit that we are invited to this strange refutation of the Aristotelean conception of tragedy: "On repeated occasions I have laid my finger on Aristotle's great misunderstanding in believing the tragic affects to be two *depressive* affects, terror and pity . . . One can refute this theory in the most cold-blooded way: namely, by measuring the effects of a tragic emotion with a dynamometer. And one would discover as a result what ultimately only the absolute mendaciousness of a systematizer could misunderstand—that tragedy is a *tonic*" (§ 851). In short, everything here seems to be purely material, to such an extent that, according to Nietzsche, "art reminds us of states of animal vigor; it is on the one hand an excess and overflow of blooming physicality into the world of images and desires; on the other, an excitation of the animal functions through the images and desires of intensified life—an enhancement of the feeling of life, a stimulant to it" (§ 802). Not a "tranquilizer," as Schopenhauer so insipidly thought.

—Nor does the psychology of artistic drives offer any kind of opening to the emergence of some sort of objective criterion of the beautiful, and Nietzsche's relativism is, here once again, radical: it quite simply leads to making artistic creation the effect of excessive sensuality. One of *The Will to Power*'s fragments thus explains that "artists, if they are any good, are (physically as well) strong, full of surplus energy, powerful animals, sensual; without a certain overheating of the sexual system a Raphael is unthinkable" (§ 800). One version—at first sight, a rather flat one—of Freudian theory emerges here, holding artistic creation to be analogous to sexual activity: "Making music is another way of making children" (ibid.). This is the source of the theme that is developed at length in the aphorisms dedicated to the physiology of art, that there is a sort of zero-sum game in the relation between the two types of creation (sexual and artistic), the artist having to stay chaste if he wishes to conserve all of his aesthetic energy, "chastity is merely the economy of an artist—and in any event, even with artists fruitfulness ceases when potency ceases" (ibid., § 800).

As in Hume, once again, "*The* beautiful exists just as little as does *the* good, or *the* true" (ibid., § 804). There is no beauty "in itself," no "objective" beauty, since everything is reducible to evaluations, themselves dependent on the individual or, to speak as Nietzsche does, on the "type of man" who does the evaluating: "thus the *herd man* will experience the value feeling of the beautiful in the presence of different things than will the *exceptional* or over-man," for "it is not possible to remain objective, or to suspend the interpretive, additive, interpolating, poetizing power (the latter is the forging of the chain of affirmations of beauty)" (ibid.).

The ambiguity of postmodern individualism becomes here luminously visible: historicism, on the one hand, seems to blend into a form of subjectivity since one of its principal characteristics is that of rejecting the "objectivity" of the beautiful, of having it depend radically upon the "type of man" who evaluates—which suggests that the beautiful remains prisoner of a certain form of "subjectivity." Yet we have seen how the condemnation of modern individualism, though it makes room for another type of individualism, that which Nietzsche attributes to the ancients, is based on a rejection, on a veritable "deconstruction" (in the Heideggerian sense) of the Cartesian, metaphysical, conception of subjectivity. If the criteria for beauty can therefore not be "objective," this

cannot mean that they go back to conscious choices effected by an autonomous subject, endowed with the free capacity of voluntary decision
making that modern philosophy habitually designates with the expression "freedom of the will" [*libre arbitre*].

Nietzsche never tires of pointing it out: the notion of freedom of
the will implies that of *causa sui*. It contains the idea that the conscious
subject, the cogito, should be considered as a "substance," as the unique
and ultimate substratum of decisions and choices whose roots are to be
found, so to speak, in themselves: "The desire for 'freedom of the will'
in the superlative metaphysical sense, which still holds sway, unfortunately, in the minds of the half-educated; the desire to bear the entire
and ultimate responsibility for one's actions oneself, and to absolve
God, the world, ancestors, chance, and society involves nothing less
than to be precisely this *causa sui*." [29] But this idea is quite simply
absurd: "The *causa sui* is the best self-contradiction that has been conceived so far, it is a sort of rape and perversion of logic," comparable,
minus the wit, to Baron Münchhausen's extravagant stories, in attempting, "with more than Münchhausen's audacity, to pull oneself up into
existence by the hair, out of the swamps of nothingness" (ibid.). The
Nietzschean genealogy of this is well known; it consists in showing how
the illusion of freedom of the will stems from the reification of the concepts of cause and effect in their application to the will, where in fact
"in real life it is only a matter of *strong* and *weak* wills," but not of
"free" will in the sense of *autonomy*.

Though Nietzsche's individualism, taken in the sense of a reac-
tivation of ancient individualism, denounces belief in objectivity in
general, this cannot be on the basis of any kind of metaphysical conception, whether empiricist or rationalist, of subjectivity. But in order
to denounce objectivity, in order also to conserve some sort of meaning,
however minimal, in the notion of individuality, the possibility of a reference to subjectivity must be preserved. Of what nature? This is the
question we must answer if we wish to interpret correctly the new individualism expressed in Nietzsche's aesthetic theory.

An aphorism in *Beyond Good and Evil* can show us the way. In
it, Nietzsche questions the "superstition of logicians" which consists
in referring a verb back to a subject (always this faith in grammar!).
Against such a superstition, it must be emphasized that "a thought
comes when 'it' wishes, and not when 'I' wish, so that it is a falsification
of the facts of the case to say that the subject 'I' is the condition of the
predicate 'think.' *It* thinks [*Es denkt*]; but that this 'it' is precisely the

famous old 'ego' is, to put it mildly, only a supposition, an assertion, and assuredly not an 'immediate certainty'" (§ 17). Nietzschean genealogy takes the form, as is its habit, of a "defetishization" of the hypostatization that the illusion of the ego consists in. "One infers here according to the grammatical habit: 'Thinking is an activity; every activity requires an agent; consequently—" (ibid.). The analysis is well known, but here Nietzsche takes it to its conclusion: not only do we need to get rid of the fetishism of the subject (of the sophism that, as Kant had already sensed, consists in taking what is a mere "philology" to be an ontology), we also have to put an end to the idea that there is "something" that thinks. This "something," even if it had another form than that of the Cartesian cogito as retrieved by Hegel's *Phenomenology,* to which Nietzsche alludes here, would still be illusory in putting forth the idea of a substratum *identical* to itself: "After all, one has even gone too far with this 'it thinks'—even the 'it' contains an *interpretation* of the process, and does not belong to the process itself . . . perhaps some day we shall accustom ourselves, including the logicians, to get along without the little 'it' (which is all that is left of the honest little old ego)" (ibid.).

The Nietzschean deconstruction of metaphysical subjectivity cannot in fact be formulated. One might be tempted to replace the formula "I think" with "it thinks in me"—but one would risk ceaselessly confusing the "it" with the "substratum" Nietzsche asks us to get rid of. Besides, it is doubtful that such a deconstruction of subjectivity could be fully carried out without falling into performative contradictions too banal for us to provide the inevitable illustrations here. (What is the subject that declares there is no subject? What does the "we" mean, through which Nietzsche designates, as Hegel also did, the philosopher's position, that is to say his *own* position? What meaning should be assigned to the "in fact"s and "truth to say"s, etc., in the name of which the ideas of factuality and of truth are denounced as "interpretations"? . . .)[30] What matters *here* is to understand that such a philosophical "position" (supposing it can be "held") in the end comes down to saying that neither one of these two terms, objectivity and subjectivity, exists, that there are only interpretations without *interpretans* or *interpretandum,* and that this is what justifies the foremost position art *should* have as the finally adequate expression of the essence of what is, of life or the will to power.

We should better be able to understand now the sense in which it can be stated that Nietzsche's historicism is based on a new form of individualism, on an individualism with neither subject nor systematicity, on a monadology with neither monads nor preestablished harmony. Only evaluations as such—"points of view" or "perspectives"—constitute, in their absolute particularness, forever fugitive moments of individuality, in that each time they happen they represent *specific* and *temporary* expressions of the will to power, or life.

We can therefore put aside the question of the internal coherence of this postmodern individualism—a question whose very relevance would obviously be rejected by an orthodox Nietzscheanism—and ask some questions about its translation into aesthetics. Heidegger, in the first part of his *Nietzsche*, formulates in these terms the problem a radical relativism, concerning the question of the beautiful, seems to meet with: "On the one hand, art is to be the countermovement to nihilism, that is, the establishment of the new supreme values; it is to prepare and ground standards and laws for historical, intellectual existence. On the other hand, art is at the same time to be properly grasped by way of physiology and with its means."[31] But it is clear that "if art is just a matter of physiology, then the essence and reality of art dissolve into nervous states, into processes in the nerve cells. Where in such blind transactions are we to find something that could of itself determine meaning, posit values, and erect standards?" (ibid.).

Heidegger's question can be made more explicit: art is said to be antinihilistic because, unlike science, philosophy, or religion, it presents itself straightforwardly as an *interpretation*, or, in Nietzsche's eyes, as an "honest" expression of the will to power. It thus, in principle, distances itself from the fetishized negations of life that are the Platonic rejection of the sensuous (which therefore withholds all legitimacy from art) and the naïve belief in self proper to herd individualism—with its procession of "democratic" values, foremost among them this "truth" anyone can lay claim to and which claims to be valid for everyone. The "physiological" mode in which Nietzsche envisages aesthetic creation is an expression of this opposition between artistic, perspectivist will, and the will to truth that always shunts aside the sphere of *aisthēsis*. But, in this subversion of Platonic philosophy, doesn't Nietzsche's position itself risk losing all legitimacy, reduced as it is to a pure relativism? For, as Heidegger adds, from the physiological point of view,

there is no establishment of rank or positing of standards. Everything is the way it is, and remains what it is, having its right simply in the fact that it is. Physiology knows no arena in which something could be set up for decision and

181

choice. To deliver art over to physiology seems tantamount to reducing art to the functional level of the gastric juices. Then how could art also ground and determine the genuine and decisive valuation? Art as the countermovement to nihilism and art as the object of physiology—that's like trying to mix fire and water.[32]

Heidegger is right. After the moment of criticism and dissolution of Platonism, new standards have to be established in the end—otherwise relativist individualism falls into flat contradiction. If there are no facts, nothing but interpretations, if these interpretations are themselves but the emanations of a "physiology," then why even discuss Platonism? Why not simply acknowledge that "things are as they are," that Plato's and Nietzsche's viewpoints are "equivalent," at least in the sense that there obviously is no exteriority, no outside of physiology, from which it would be possible to choose between them?

FROM ULTRAINDIVIDUALISM TO HYPERCLASSICISM: THE "GRAND STYLE"

The problem of standards, that is to say, in its most general sense, the problem of truth, returns in and through aesthetics. The paradox contained in such a statement is obvious: Nietzsche never ceased to affirm that "art is *worth more* than truth," (*WP*, § 853), that "we possess *art* lest we *perish of the truth*" (§ 822), etc. How could he, following the classicists, in turn once again make of beauty a sensuous presentation of the true?

As I have suggested, this is only possible through a revolution in the notion of truth. It obviously no longer designates the stable identity of the Ideas in whose name the philosophers claim to "save phenomena," to exhibit their true rationality that is camouflaged for the near-sighted senses. In the terms Heidegger chose so well: truth is no longer the "rectitude of the representation." But it has not for all that ceased to lie in a certain kind of "agreement," that of the "evaluation" with the real.[33] To make the paradox quite explicit, one would have to say that it is because art is false that it is true, and this in at least a twofold sense:

—First of all because, as an interpretation that does not claim to be more than what it is—therefore, because it gives up any claim to an absolute truth—art happens to be in harmony with the perspectival character of existence, with the "truth" that all our judgments are but symptoms, mere evaluations. As Deleuze writes, commenting on one of Nietzsche's famous formulations: "art is the highest power of falsehood, it magnifies the 'world as error,' it sanctifies the lie; the will to deception is turned into a superior ideal . . . Then truth perhaps takes on a new sense. Truth is appearance. Truth means bringing of power into effect, raising to the highest power. In Nietzsche, 'we the artists' = 'we the seekers after knowledge or truth' = 'we the inventors of new possibilities of life.'"[34]

It could hardly be better stated that the classical ideal of an art that would be the expression of truth has not vanished in Nietzsche. On closer inspection, moreover, the definition of truth has not changed all that much, and the Nietzschean "revolution" of Platonism leads us partly back to its starting point: for if art is true, isn't it, despite everything and whatever words may be used, because it is *adequate to reality,* or even much more adequate than the lie that, ever since Plato at least, has habitually been given the name of truth? Deleuze is, in this context, quite right in asserting that the artist is for Nietzsche a seeker after truth; he is in fact par excellence the example of him who is after the "true truth," the only one who does not lie (just as the senses don't lie either)—and that is why, in the final analysis, the "true" philosopher should also become an artist.

—Not only does art thus "have grounds for" presenting itself explicitly as a mere interpretation, as a pure evaluation, but, in playing upon appearances, in producing illusion, it turns out to be truer than any other activity, beginning with intellectual activity. That is the ultimate meaning of the famous fragment which asserts that "the will to appearance, to illusion, to deception, to becoming and change (to objectified deception) here counts as more profound, primeval, 'metaphysical' than the will to truth, to reality, to mere appearance" (*Will to Power,* § 853) because it is at bottom more *adequate* to the multiplicity of life that goes by the name of "will to power." Since, as Nietzsche puts it, "appearance as I understand it is the real and unique reality of things," the one that resists and always will resist "all metamorphosis into an imaginary 'true world,'" we can understand not only that art should be truer than truth, but also *how* philosophy should itself become an aesthetics. All of Nietzsche's interpreters have remarked upon the nonanecdotal, philosophical character of aphoristic writing; many have seen in it, following what seems to be most visibly evident, a "subversion" of the idea of truth, a sort of rebellion against the "systematicity" that is inscribed in even the grammar and syntax of traditional writing. But one can, I think, more strongly argue that it is, rather, a very *classical* concession to the idea of truth.

Of course, at first sight "an aphorism formally regarded presents itself as a *fragment;* it is the form of pluralist thinking" (ibid., p. 31), not in the democratic and "liberal" sense of "pluralist" but in that fragmented writing is supposedly, through its "openness," opposed to the "closure" of the "system," taken to be the final development of the Platonic theory of truth. The aphorism is thus an excellent example of philosophy's *artistic form.* As Deleuze says, "Only the aphorism is capable of saying the meaning; the aphorism is interpretation and the art of interpreting" (ibid.). No doubt. But the subversion is far from being as deep as might be imagined and the aphoristic form is, in many ways, *also* the sign of an astonishing naïveté. In the will to be *adequate* to the "fracture" and the multiplicity of Being as life through the fracturedness and multiplicity of writing, it is, in the end, the old concept of truth as adequacy to the real that is renewed and nearly confirmed, so that Nietzsche's thought, and that of his epigones, seems to suffer from a cruel lack of self-reflection. To use a formula Fichte applied to Spinoza: he thinks well, "but he does not think his own thinking."

It remains for us to understand, in such conditions, the motives that lead Nietzsche to side so vigorously with classicism and against romanticism. There is, as I have just suggested, in the final analysis a profound analogy between classicism and Nietzsche's aesthetics, since in both cases art is assigned the task of expressing truth in a living, sensuous way. But a fundamental difference remains despite the depth of the analogy. In Cartesian aesthetics (defined very broadly, to comprehend Hegelianism), the truth to be presented had been defined as rationality. In Nietzsche, it is "raised to a higher power" in that art presents itself as an exhibition of the true. The goal is no longer that of expressing some sort of Platonico-Cartesian truth, but the "true truth" that difference is, and which permits us to consider his aesthetics to be a "hyperclassicism of difference." How, in that case, to interpret the fact that Nietzsche sees in classicism, and specifically in the French seventeenth century, the most successful incarnation of the artistic summit he calls the "grand style"?

On this point at least his thinking is perfectly lucid, and his definition of "grandeur" is, in all the work of his mature years, flawlessly unambiguous. As is quite well explained in one of *The Will to Power*'s fragments, "The greatness of an artist cannot be measured by the 'beautiful feelings' he arouses" but by the "grand style," that is, in the capacity "to become master of the chaos one is; to compel one's chaos to become form; to become logical, simple, unambiguous, mathematical, *law*—that is the grand ambition here" (§ 842). Only those who make the—absurd but frequent—mistake of seeing in Nietzscheanism some sort of anarchism, or even a theory anticipating the libertarian movements of our century's seventh decade, can be surprised by this text. Nothing could be more misleading; the apology of "mathematical" rigor also has a place in the definition of the multiple forces making up the will to power. The reason is simple to point out: if one admits that "reactive" forces are those which cannot exert themselves without denying other forces, then it must be conceded that the critique of Platonism, however justified, cannot lead to a pure and simple elimination of rationality. Such an eradication would indeed be reactive by definition.

Therefore, if one wants to achieve the greatness that is the sign of a successful expression of the vital forces, one must rank those forces into a hierarchy so that they cease reciprocally mutilating themselves—and in such a hierarchy, reason also will have a place. And a theme that is constant in Nietzsche, moreover, is that the "logical simplicity" characteristic of the classics and classicists is the best approximation to this "grandiose" hierarchical ranking, as this other fragment from *The Will to Power* suggests explicitly: "'becoming more beautiful' is a consequence of *enhanced* strength. Becoming more beautiful as the expression of a victorious will, of increased coordination, of a harmonizing of all the strong desires, of an infallibly perpendicular stress. *Logical and geometrical simplification is a consequence of enhancement of strength*" (§ 800, italics added). Clearly, we are here far from the image of a Nietzsche apologist for a "liberation of mores."

Opposite the grand style stand all forms of activity, aesthetic or not, which, incapable of achieving the self-mastery demanded by the hierarchical ordering of the instincts, give free rein to the surging up and overflowing of the passions; they, that is, make reaction possible, because this overflow is always synonymous with the reciprocal mutilation of forces. This mutilation defines ugliness, which is always "the *decadence of a type,* contradiction and lack of coordination among the inner desires—[ugliness] signifies a decline in organizing strength, in 'will.'"[35] As is well known, it is Platonism that provides the prototype of reaction within the sphere of philosophy. But we have to try to understand exactly how it is symmetrically opposed to the "grand style."

As the *Twilight of the Idols* explains at length, if Socrates invents the "true world," it is, at his profoundest, in order to put an end to the "anarchy of the instincts" that appears when one has left tradition's aristocratic universe behind, and that questioning, interrogation, and doubt have taken the place of authority, command, and of the will that posits values without discussion. Socrates is a "doctor philosopher"; but his "cure" consists in "castration," in the suppression of all the instincts (of the sensible world) in the name of the alleged "truth" (of the intelligible world). But for Nietzsche the solution would have been not the mutilation of vital forces in the name of other forces (the sensible in the name of the intelligible), but their ranking into a hierarchy: in the end, Socrates's sin was lack of mastery.

In art it is, for analogous reasons, romanticism which appears to be the peak of reaction. The passions are there so unchecked they cannot but hinder one another. The archetypal romantic character is unhappy, torn, pale, ill. As one of *The Will to Power*'s fragments significantly suggests, "Whether behind the antithesis classic and romantic there does not lie hidden the antithesis active and reactive" (§ 847). Whereby the Schopenhauerian and Wagnerian conceptions of art as consolation would appear as the aesthetic equivalent of Socratic reaction on the philosophical level. If, that is, classicism is the incarnation of the grand style, since "to be classical, one must possess *all* the strong, seemingly contradictory gifts and desires—but in such a way that they go together beneath one yoke" (§ 848), so that "a quantum of coldness, lucidity, hardness is part of all 'classical' taste: logic above all, happiness in spirituality, 'three unities'" (§ 849). The aesthetics of sentiment that anticipated romanticism must be broken with, "We are enemies of sentimental emotions" (§ 850)—and Nietzsche does so in a way that leaves no doubt about the side he takes in the conflict between classicism and sentimentalism: he invites every artist worthy of the name to cultivate a "hatred for feeling, heart, *esprit,* hatred for the manifold, uncertain, rambling, for intimations" (§ 849), in a word, for everything that Bouhours's and Dubos's aesthetics set at high value.

As we can see, Nietzsche's rehabilitation of the sensible sphere and of aesthetics is not as unambiguous as we might have believed. We can even grant that, coming from Nietzsche's pen, such an invitation to hate the "sensuous," the "multiple," can seem strange. Against Victor Hugo, he rehabilitates Corneille, as being one of those "poets from an aristocratic civilization . . . who made it a point of honor to submit their perhaps even more vigorous senses to a *concept* [Nietzsche's italics], and, on the brutal pretensions of colors, sounds, and forms, to impose the law of a refined and clear intellectuality. In this they follow, it seems to me, in the footsteps of the great Greeks."[36] The triumph of the Greek classics and French neoclassicists thus consists in victoriously fighting against what Nietzsche oddly calls "this sensual rabble," so admired by "modern" (romantic) painters and musicians. The problem is, as he himself points out in another fragment (§ 846), that these terms are ambiguous, and can be taken in various senses. For example, "the desire for destruction, change, becoming" can be "Dionysian," active and anti-Platonist; it can also indicate the *ressentiment* that leads the weak to wish to destroy all (Wagner and Schopenhauer being used as examples here).

We can see that the problem comes down to learning how to articulate the *ultraperspectivist* or *ultraindividualist* critique of Platonism with the *hyperclassicism* that leads Nietzsche, after careful weighing, to find the classics to be quite superior to the romantics, and in a sense, therefore, to find again, in a certain conception of truth, a privilege the work of art possesses over the artist.

NIETZSCHE'S COHERENCE; NEARNESS TO HEIDEGGER

It is difficult to avoid a certain feeling of strangeness after one has read or reread all of the passages in Nietzsche's work he consecrated to art. Depending on whether one considers the texts that evoke the project of a "physiology of art" or those that define the "grand style," one could elaborate two entirely different or even opposite interpretations of his aesthetic theory:

—When he is expressing himself as a "physiologist," Nietzsche often seems to flirt with a materialist relativism that threatens to completely reduce the *work* of art to the psychological or biological reality of the *artist*. And even if we follow Heidegger's interpretation (as in my opinion we should, on this point) according to which Nietzsche's "biologism" is not a form of scientism but an *ontology* (a definition of the Being of beings as equal to life), it still remains true that his aesthetics seem to remain prisoner of the individualistic framework. They continue to conceptualize the work using the subject or, at least, the artist and his "aesthetic" states as starting point, as for instance with the "Dionysiac intoxication" without which there is supposed to be no authentic creation.

—When, on the contrary, Nietzsche looks upon art adopting a

"classicist" attitude, when he invites us to think of the grand style as of a hierarchical ordering of the multiple that implies self-mastery, the "psychologistic" tendency fades away, at which point the subject tends to be eclipsed by the truth of the work.

These two moments—which I have here designated with the expressions "ultraindividualism" and "hyperclassicism"—are, truth to say, indissolubly interconnected in a modality which can be rather simply indicated as we arrive at the end of this analysis. It is indeed enough to perceive the extent to which they both stem from the same source, the extent to which they are both the effect, to the same degree, of the same cause: the subject's "fracture" [la "brisure" du sujet]. Far from opposing, they converge and complete each other.

This is first of all clear as far as ultraindividualism is concerned. It is indeed hardly doubtful that Nietzsche's radical relativism, his perspectivism, issue directly from the genealogical process through which the cogito is deconstructed. If there is no longer any "world," nor "facts in themselves," nor "objectivity," it is certainly because, the subject having been itself opened out onto the infinity of "its" unconscious, it is from now on impossible for it to claim to be stating any kind of absolute truth. As we have seen, it must, on the contrary, resolve itself to consider all its judgments to be symptoms, evaluations, or interpretations strictly *relative* to its specific situation. And the infinity of points thus established (what Nietzsche calls "the new infinity") is not itself ever reducible to the unity of a totality, to a *uni*-verse—which makes for a most profound difference between perspectivism and the monadology.

But if one thinks about it, one realizes that Nietzsche's classicism, inasmuch as it is a classicism *of difference* (an invitation to think of art as the expression of a "reality," no longer of Being, but of Becoming), also finds its origin in the fracture of the subject. It is because the latter is cleft that the world has ceased to be, that objectivity has vanished, that "the real" is a process of change; it is therefore also for the same reason that truth can no longer be defined as identity, as noncontradiction, universal validity, etc., but has become Life, which is to say manifoldness, difference, and temporality.

Interpreted this way, the two moments of Nietzschean aesthetics converge and, all things considered, foreshadow Heidegger's thinking about art rather more than they counter it in advance. For Heidegger, also, the deconstruction of subjectivity leads to making of the art yet to come—to the extent that art, following the Hegelian prophecy he seems near to sharing, is not already dead—a classicism of difference, and of the work an expression of the truth of Being.

A formulation often repeated in "The Origin of the Work of Art" has it that "Art is the setting-into-work of truth" [*das Ins-Werk-Setzen der Wahrheit*]; more precisely, it is "the creative preserving of truth in the work . . . Art lets truth originate. Art, founding preserving, is the spring that leaps to the truth of what is, in the work."[37] Two precautions, in order not to distort the meaning:

—We would be completely mistaken if we did not realize that truth, here, is no longer understood as adequacy to an object, to a being visible in representation. As one of our best philosophers of aesthetics quite correctly points out, for Heidegger, "art is by essence given over to truth. But does that mean that art is supposed to be the 'true' reproduction of the real? That would mean to recreate the traditional conception of truth as adequacy to an object. Instead, the analysis of the work will lead us to a more original definition of truth as unconcealedness"[38]—a term that translates the German *Unverborgenheit* and the Greek *alētheia*.

This is not the place to recall the significance of this theory of truth. Suffice it to say that, in Heidegger's phenomenology, the essential is to be found not in *representation but in the coming into presence of the being, of the existent,* as such, in unconcealedness. What the work of art "shows" is, if we may say so, invisible; what it manifests is that there is "the visible," there is representation, and that this simple fact has nothing banal about it, as the universe of everydayness would have us believe. And yet, in another way, the idea of adequacy has not lost all legitimation. Although truth is no longer the agreement of the judgment with the thing, though it has become unconcealedness, it is nevertheless the case that the notion of adequacy finds a new meaning at a higher level of potency. Authentic art is, then, that which places us "in the presence of" this invisible act that is the coming into presence of beings; it is that which, to borrow a formula Lyotard himself borrows from Kant, "presents that there is the nonpresentable," and which thereby shows itself to be truer, or, if you prefer, more adequate, if not to the "thing itself," then at least to the "matter of thinking"; though it may not be a visible being, an object present in representation, identifiable and stable, but a nothingness, an absence, a *difference,* it is nonetheless this matter that the work of art is about and whose dimensions it must hint at, and it is in this sense that art keeps its classic task of expressing the truth.

—In these circumstances, subjectivity's portion—or, if preferred, the artist's role—tends to be reduced in favor of the work's. When Heidegger makes of art a "setting-into-work of truth," it is to immediately add: "In this proposition an essential ambiguity is hidden, in which truth is at once the subject and the object of the setting (Heidegger, op. cit.). Even though the terms "subject" and "object" are unsuitable since they refer back to a metaphysical conception of truth as the judgment's adequacy to a represented state of things, they do express what they wish to express: that the work is a "founding *preserving*." In other words, everything in it is not invented; its truth does not lie entirely in the artist; it is not, or at least not essentially, the expression of his psychological states, or of his "intoxication" or of his "physiology," as certain of Nietzsche's formulas might lead one to think (but we have just seen how those formulations are less "subjectivist" than they seem). Thence the work's ambiguity, work which is certainly *creation*, and therefore a founding, but a nonsubjective founding, since its essential aspect is the *preserving* of a truth that does not *belong* to the artist, who is neither its master nor its owner.

If one accepts the idea that the notion of subject has already been disassociated from that of the author, "master and possessor of his works," in Nietzsche's thinking, and if one also admits that the will to power that defines the core of all that is, of the Being of beings, is to be thought of more as pure difference and temporality than as the remnant of any kind of conception of subjectivity, one will perhaps agree with the observation that Nietzsche's conception of art is not all that far from Heidegger's.

Whatever the case may be—and this question is, after all, only a "philological" one—it remains true that this new classicism of difference that emerges with Nietzsche and finds mature expression in Heidegger has bequeathed us a difficulty which, as we shall see, runs through the major currents of what is usually called "contemporary" art. I will state it brutally, the nuances will follow in the rest of this enquiry: Can we imagine that an art that would give itself, as main task, that of "saying the difference," of "presenting the fact that there is the nonpresentable," could bring into being works of the same order as those which have punctuated the history of the aesthetics known up until today? To put it more clearly perhaps—since, after all, one could very well not care about the old "metaphysical" conception of the work of art: if art always was the expression of a *world*, as Heidegger joins Hegel in thinking, how then can we conceive that works of art that pretend to say the nonpresentable (what escapes representation, non-being) could ever structure themselves into a *world* as did the—if we may put it this way—"classically classical" works that "only" aimed at the expression of something like "a vision of the world"? I can conceive of the "deconstruction" of the metaphysical tradition occupying a certain, no doubt temporary, place in the history of philosophy since such a deconstruction remains, like it or not, in the conceptual sphere. That an *analogue* of the deconstructive discourse could install itself in art seems to me, improbable, unless this kind of art explicitly adopts its own death as its theme and purpose, as it so often has throughout the twentieth century. But in that case it cannot make the pretence of constituting itself into a *world*.

Paradox: the new classicism that makes of the truth *unconcealed* by the work of art a difference, no longer an identity, will find its vocation in the "avant-gardes" which, from Cézanne to Malevitch and from Mallarmé to René Char, fascinate contemporary philosophy. Nietzsche had announced it prophetically: "Reason, *like Euclidean space,* is but an idiosyncrasy." While thinkers were deconstructing the former, the painters of the avant-garde were not about to shy away from overturning the latter.

SIX

The Decline of the Avant-Gardes: Postmodernity

NEUROSIS AND MODERN ART
That is the title of an announced conference at a waltzer's university at the beach where I spend the month of August. If I knew the
professor who is going to conference [sic], I would invite him to
come see our modern painters from up close. He would decide for
himself if neurosis or pathology has something to do with them.
He would see André Derain, Georges Braque, Maurice de Vla-
minck, Fernand Léger, near-giants, robust with calm and good
sense in what they say, he would see Picabia, sportsman full of
sangfroid, Marcel Duchamp, G. de Chirico, Pierre Roy, Metzinger, Gleizes, Jacques Villon and many others, ornate spirits, gifted
with talent and perhaps afterwards he would ask to change if not
the title of his conference, at least his conclusions.
    —Guillaume Apollinaire
    Chroniques d'art, 1902–1918
    (August 1, 1914)

THE DIALECTIC OF THE END OF THE AVANT-GARDES

WITH THEIR EXHIBITIONS without pictures and their silent
concerts, the dying avant-gardes* have derided art and unwit-

---

*The avant-gardes have been going through a dark phase, not to say an
irreversible crisis, since the end of the seventies. This diagnosis is all the harder
to refute as it most often emanates from the avant-gardes themselves. Some, for
instance Philippe Albéra, director of *Contrechamps* magazine, lucidly agree:
"The ideas of radical rupture, of revolutionary struggle, of the aggressiveness of
the artist who wants to shock the bourgeois and overturn the established order
have virtually disappeared."[1] The same observation is found, barely disguised,

tingly prepared the way for postmodern eclecticism. Through the pretension of shocking or subverting, works of art have become *modest*. Buren's columns at the Palais Royal in Paris do not overwhelm us, they amuse, bringing forth feelings of irritation or approval in reality so fleeting they border on indifference.

Things were entirely different for the first avant-gardes. Still driven by ambitious aesthetic projects, they did not aim at the death of art so much as at its radical renewal. Yet, sometimes decades after their creation, there are works that are still dead letters for the public said to be cultured—not to mention the "larger public," who most often remain in complete ignorance of the contemporary culture that is most esteemed by enlightened amateurs. In this respect, some recent studies show up the impressive economic and sociological marginality of "modern music." (Strangely enough, this term only covers so-called "learned" music, as if the other musical forms (jazz, rock, pop, etc.) were not also contemporary. An effect of the first avant-gardes' elitism.)

Paradigmatic of the crisis, modern music doesn't succeed in reaching a public other than that of professionals or semiprofessionals. Could one blame state institutions, that might wish to hinder a thriving subversive art? Alas! They are the ones that support it and subsidize it, to an amount three times greater than that provided by a market which was, besides, itself dominated until recently in France by public radio and public television. As Maurice Fleuret declares: "For the first time in history, we live without any dominant theory, without references, without landmarks. No major personality emerges out of the young generation. The aesthetic revolution of the last few years is not qualita-

even in the program notes for Paris's IRCAM modern music center: "Having been preceded by a period of radical evolution, the contemporary music of the '70s and '80s seems to be looking for itself," at a time when "certain recent tendencies—bearers of illusions—are exhausting themselves."[2] And Jean Clair, who used to be the director of one of the most important avant-garde reviews, and who organized exhibitions that signalled Paris's renewal within contemporary art, draws up a veritable obituary: "The aesthetics of modernity, insofar as it was an aesthetics of *innovatio,* seems to have exhausted the possibilities of its creation. Within itself, its development during the teens, then its accelerated institutionalization in the '50s exasperated and accelerated its tendencies . . . dealing it a deathblow. The utopia of the *novum* is foreclosed."[3] The very idea of the avant-garde has such bad publicity now that a contemporary musician like Luciano Berio can calmly declare: "He who calls himself avant-garde is a cretin . . . The avant-garde is nothing [*L'avant-garde, c'est du vide*]."[4]

tive but quantitative: the history of recent music boils down to a catalog of works and of names. I have multiplied the credits to creation sixfold without bringing about the blossoming I had hoped for."[5] (A text to be read, of course, as symptom more than as analysis, so obvious is it that the technocratic multiplication of subsidies has little to do with creation.)

Pierre Michel Menger points out in the conclusion to a painstaking sociological investigation: "The function of and the need for a political-ideological justification of avant-gardism have largely lost their importance. Oppositional culture has become official culture; the maelstrom of 'revolutionary' aesthetic innovations is orchestrated by the market and/or largely subsidized by the state; daring, provocation, and the will to rupture have become banal."[6] And young composers don't delude themselves about this, as witness the vivid declaration made by Alain Daniel, author of a remarkable quintet for strings, to a journalist who interviewed him after a day dedicated to him by Radio France-Culture: "People who are always experimenting for the sake of experimenting are god-damned nuisances! You try to show that everything you are about to have played is experimental; it's easy that way, if no one likes it, you can always excuse yourself saying the experiment didn't work out . . . Composers today wear themselves out trying to do something new . . . It is the idea that pleases in contemporary music, in our case, the reaction against what has been done and what is being done, but the music itself? I don't think it pleases."[7]

Some will object, not without reason, that "the serious composer is not—we could almost say by definition—looking for a market share," he is motivated by an inner necessity in comparison with which "the public's approval, quantitatively measured, is not the criterion for aesthetic accomplishment either."[8] We would gladly concede the argument if its aim were to separate the authentic artist from the demagogue. But the logic of the avant-garde goes well beyond this. In the conflict opposing public and artist, the avant-garde holds it to be obvious that the artist, well in advance of the cretinized and manipulated masses, is necessarily right. "Who would not want to reconcile art with society?" the argument continues, "but with what society? To consumer society, art 'of appeasement,' in Malraux's words. Innovative art must show the way, not follow the herd. The marching wing of a merchant society, art does not easily accommodate itself to the market" [*aile marchante dans une société marchande, l'art s'accommode mal du marché*] (ibid.).

Seductive arguments, no doubt, but which in the given instance touch upon a theme a little too dear to the hearts of the larger public, that of the unknown genius, solitary martyr of a soulless world that has been turned over to the domination of technology. Reassuring arguments, even, avant-garde art is doing quite well, in fact it is more alive than ever, and the public's desertion is, so to speak, the surest sign of this. Reassuring because, in the elitist vision that was always that of the avant-gardes, hell is, of course, the others: the culture industry, subject to the imperatives of capitalist (Marx) and technological (Heidegger) profitability; the media—which simultaneously relays and consecrates the eclectic conformism secreted by the economy; and, finally, the "masses" themselves, which refuse—but they must be forgiven, they are manipulated—to be educated, to be initiated to the highest creations of contemporary art.

That questions have to be asked about the dangers of a world dominated by technology, that bourgeois society also lives off the production of a feeble-minded and enfeebling culture, no one can ignore all this. But to go on from there and conclude that this "subculture" and its media relays are suffocating an authentic creation which is supposedly in the best of shapes today, is to take a step one cannot take unless one lacks that minimal tragic sense without which philosophical questioning is, in some fashion, mutilated. In the case of contemporary culture more than in any other, we have to stay away from the idea, which is always too simple, that "the ones at fault are elsewhere." The destiny of this culture is, to a not unimportant extent, linked to that of the avant-gardes, and the avant-gardes, at the exact opposite of what the *pro domo* arguments we have just mentioned suggest, live from the banality of the everyday. Without banality, no avant-garde, *if* the avant-garde is the movement through which a small group, an elite, animated by a *new* project, radically rejects the reigning conformism, received ideas, and the inheritance of tradition. The crisis of the avant-gardes can thus never stem from the oppositions they meet with. On the contrary, it is, perhaps, the exhaustion of such an opposition nowadays, the very absence of conflict between avant-garde artists and a quasi-inexistence public, that truly creates a problem.

Let us try out a hypothesis: and if the avant-gardes are dying out because they have become banal? And what if it were the avant-gardes which, since the beginning of the century, have secretly, and, sometimes against their own intentions, worked towards the abolition of all distinction between "subculture" and "high culture"? Isn't the urinal that Duchamp brought to the museum the symbol of this will to break away

195

from banality that has itself become banal and creative of banality, in that it erases any distinction between work of art and technical object?

We have to look for the origins of the crisis affecting the avant-gardes today within a dialectic internal to them. As Octavio Paz, in his 1972 lectures on the fate of modern poetry, suggests, "Modern art has begun to lose its powers of negation. For years now, its negations have become ritual repetitions; rebellion has become a mere procedure; criticism, rhetoric; transgression, ceremony. Negation has ceased being creative. I am not saying we are living through the end of art. We are living the end of the idea of modern art."[9] Although he keeps his distance from Hegel, who decreed the death of art much more radically, the contradiction Paz uncovers is well and truly a dialectical contradiction in the Hegelian sense; in becoming purely critical, the modernism of the avant-gardes turns against itself. Solely obsessed by the quest for novelty and originality for their own sakes, it slips over into its opposite, the mere empty, dreary repetition of the gesture of innovation for innovation's sake. The break with tradition itself becomes tradition, "tradition of the new" certainly—to appropriate Harold Rosenberg's expression—but tradition all the same and, according to Paz, a tradition that is in our day void of meaning and content.

Paz's reasoning touches on one of the main problems that contemporary "high culture" meets with. The crisis he discerns is all the more serious in that it is an internal one, and not some sort of "reaction" which, from the outside, might seek to put a brake on a blossoming movement. But is it for all that legitimate to indict "modern art" without more information? The formulation is, truth to tell, so vague it nearly loses all meaning, and one can't but be a little surprised to see it taken up so unanimously by the most informed critics and the most subtle philosophers. In what follows, I would prefer referring to the more limited concept of avant-garde. Stravinsky and Ravel are, no doubt, "moderns"; their art would have been unthinkable in the nineteenth century. They are not avant-gardists. The notion merits being dwelt on if we want to understand the nature of the crisis.

The expression "avant-garde" belongs originally to military vocabulary. But it is noteworthy that its first use in a figurative sense (to the extent that it is ever possible to date, with absolute precision, the emergence of a concept)[10] to designate radical movements in the fields of both art and politics, should appear within the scientistic context of a philosophy of history: Saint-Simon's. During the dialogue between the artist and the scholar, found in his *Opinions littéraires, philosophiques et industrielles* (1825),[11] the artist declares to the scholar that artists must "serve as the avant-garde" in the "great enterprise" whose goal is the "establishment of the system of the public weal," "the artists, the men of imagination will begin the march;[12] they shall proclaim the future of the human species; they shall take from the past its golden age and with it enrich the future generations."[13] We will come back to the interpretation of this irreducibly scientistic and progressionist element which, throughout the twentieth century, leaves its mark on avant-gardes, even those that seem most distant from this Enlightenment ideology.

In the realm not of the history of ideas but of real *movements*,* it would appear that, in the French context, the first aesthetic avant-garde worthy of the name was the group known as the "Incohérents."[14] Much talked about between 1882 and 1889 (at which date the movement tired itself out and dissolved), the Incoherent Ones were created from the fusion of various small groups in which habitual Paris cabaret-goers were to be found: "Hydropathes," "Hirsutes," "Zutistes," or "Jemen-foutistes" [Idontgiveadamnists], their main activity consisted in the organization of more or less humorous exhibitions essentially intended to "shock the bourgeois," to symbolically draw the distinction between the Bohemian's and the Philistine's way of life. External signs of recognition thus played a primordial role in the life of the group, as attested by this manifesto, in which the most characteristic elements of an ideology at once elitist and schoolboyish are expressed:

> The Incoherent One is young, he in fact needs suppleness of mind and limb to give himself over to perpetual physical and moral dislocations . . . The Incoherent One therefore has neither rheumatisms nor migraines, he is nervy and robust. He belongs to all the trades that come close to art: a typographer can be incoherent, a zinc worker never . . . The Incoherent One retires through marriage or through developing a rheumatism. (!)

It is, more seriously, during the early years of this century that we observe artists themselves taking up the themes of the ideology of the avant-garde, whose exemplary expression is, no doubt, Kandinsky's essay, *On the Spiritual in Art and in Painting in Particular* (1912). To describe the "spiritual life," Kandinsky has recourse to a metaphor that

---

* As Poggioli remarks, the avant-gardes no longer adopt the form of a school, judged to be too "academic," but rather the more flexible one of "movement" (*Theory of the Avant-Garde*, pp. 12–13).

merits attention, since it contains all the elements necessary for determining the ideal type of the avant-garde:

> A large triangle divided into unequal parts; the smallest and most acute, at the top, being a rather good schematic figure for the spiritual life. The entire triangle moves slowly, barely perceptibly, forward and upward, so that where the highest point is "today"; the next division is "tomorrow," i.e., what is today comprehensible only to the topmost segment of the triangle and to the rest of the triangle is gibberish, becomes tomorrow the sensible and emotional content of the life of the second segment.[15]

The rest of the text draws out the metaphor and deduces its main implications.

The first implication is, without a doubt, *elitism:* "At the apex of the topmost division there stands sometimes only a single man. His joyful vision is like an inner, immeasurable sorrow." His task is to "help the forward movement of the obstinate cartload" of the cretinized populace found at the bottom of the triangle. On the one hand, then, we find the "superior men" who dare challenge the traditions and are therefore fated to solitude; on the other, "the partisans of popular representation," "republicans" and "socialists" buried within mass conformism. "The inhabitants of this large division of the triangle have never managed to solve a problem for themselves and have always been pulled along in the cart of humanity by their self-sacrificing fellow men standing far above them" (pp. 133, 139). The metaphor of the avant-garde thereupon finds again the military accents that had inspired it at its beginnings: the superior men, the artists or scientists of genius "move forward forgetting all prudence, and fall during the conquest of the citadel of the new science as do those soldiers who, sacrificing themselves, perish in the desperate assault of a fortress that will not surrender" (ibid.). The genius is thus alone and the triangle's apex but a point. People "call him deranged" or "a candidate for the madhouse" (p. 134). But this solitude is the surest sign of belonging to an elite, as Schönberg confesses to Kandinsky in a letter on January 24, 1911: "My works are provisionally refused the favor of the masses. They will thereby all the more easily reach the individuals: those truly worthy individuals who alone count for me."[16] This theme is so important for Schönberg that, in 1937, he makes it the center of an essay entitled *How One Becomes a Man Alone,* in which both elitism and the problem of the public (that is, of its absence) are articulated around the notion of individuality. The artist's solitude is the mark of his personality, the sign of his *individualization* as compared to the *shapeless* mass which blindly absorbs the values of the tradition, against which the former rebels.

The second aspect that the triangle metaphor points to could be designated by the term *historicism*. Despite a certain pessimism, that has to do with the triangular structure of a spiritual life that imposes solitude upon the artist, his unwavering belief in progress allows him to bring optimism back within the sphere of history: "Despite [the masses'] blindness the spiritual triangle in fact continues to advance"; it "slowly ascends with an irresistible force." The elite can feel reassured: its solitude is only temporary; sooner or later it will be understood by the mass, to whom it is pathfinder and guide. "Today's pictorial and musical dissonance is nothing but tomorrow's consonance." [17] But, because of this very philosophy of history, the artist has an obligation to break with tradition in order ceaselessly to create the new: "Thus, every period of culture produces its own art, which can never be repeated." Imitation of past and bygone forms of art "resembles the mimicry of the ape," a gesture whose "inner meaning . . . is completely lacking." [18] The avant-garde is tied to the idea of revolution; its mission is to boldly overturn the established order—it being understood that this movement is without end. The artist's originality and individuality are therefore no longer defined only in relation to rules; they are explicitly thought of as a function of a certain placing of art within history.

As a consequence of this elitism and of this historicism, the avant-garde sees itself as the *expression of the Self* or, to use Kandinsky's own expression, the "pure expression of the inner life" of him who, through his originality, finds himself at the same time at the apex of the triangle (elitism) and ahead of his time (historicism), and who therefore alone contributes a veritable *individuality* (the other "individuals," even those just below the apex, already begin to make up a "mass"; they are similar to one another, they have things in common, and they are thus less individualized than the genius). This theme is quite central, it provides the main theoretical justification for the abandonment of "figuration" in painting and tonality in music. If we have to put an end to figurative art, if we have to stop imitating nature, it is so we may be able finally to give full expression to subjectivity, as Kandinsky sums it up in this extremely important formulation: "the total renunciation of accepted beauty, which regards as sacred every means that serves the purpose of self-expression" (ibid., p. 149).

We shall see that the position of the Cubists was, on this point, different. It is nevertheless as a function of this last criterion, and keeping those whom he situates at the triangle's leading point—Picasso and Schoenberg—as a steady point of reference, that Kandinsky sketches out a history of contemporary art in which the three implicit presuppositions (elitism, historicism, individualism) of all avant-garde ideologies come through in most significant fashion. While Debussy, despite certain worthy innovations, still gives way to "the charms of more or less conventional 'beauty,'" Arnold Schoenberg "goes his lonely way unrecognized, even today (1912), by *all but a few enthusiasts*": "Schoenberg's music leads us into a new realm, where musical experiences are no longer acoustic, but purely spiritual. Here begins the 'music of the future.'"

The situation is analogous in painting. Here, it is Picasso who "goes beyond" Cézanne and Manet. Unlike those two, who were, all the same, "in advance" of their time,

the Spaniard Pablo Picasso never succumbs to this (conventional) beauty. Led on always by the need for self-expression, often driven wildly onward, Picasso throws himself from one external means to another. If a chasm lies between them, Picasso makes a wild leap, and there he is, standing on the other side, much to the horror of his compact cohort of followers. They had just thought they had caught up with him; now they must begin the painful descent and start the climb all over again. (Ibid., p. 152)

Avant-gardism's three constitutive moments are here clearly brought together: it is because the artist of genius is gifted with a *personality* that puts him *ahead* of his time—his followers, although they are already, as such, an elite, have something "compact" about them—that he is destined to the solitude reserved for the *elite* of this elite.

AN "INDIVIDUALIST" INTERPRETATION OF THE AVANT-GARDE

If by individualism we understand the modern ideology that holds that, in the name of freedom and of autonomy, the individual must break with the heteronomy of inherited traditions,[19] then it seems that an interpretation of the avant-garde by reference to individualism becomes necessary. Its principle has been put forward by Daniel Bell in his essay on *The Cultural Contradictions of Capitalism*.[20] Taking up certain aspects of the Marxian analysis of bourgeois civil society,* he shows how the emergence of capitalism definitively ruined the notion of tradition and at the same time the holistic social vision that was attached to it: "The fundamental assumption of modernity, the thread that has run through Western civilization since the sixteenth century, is that the social unit of society is not the group, the guild, the tribe, or the city, but the person" (p. 16). And from the moment that this individual thinks of himself as not only a free and autonomous monad, but as the true social atom, he inevitably grants himself the capacity and the right to question any values he has not posited himself, and to modify at will any norms he may institute. Carrying the argument in Bell's direction, we may add that, at the level of political philosophy, this principle has been justified in Rousseau's *Social Contract*: the individuals gathered in assembly give themselves their own laws, they are their own masters and possessors; no one may hinder them from changing these laws at will since it would be "absurd for the will to lay chains upon itself for the future."[21]

At the sociological level, Bell quotes the passage from the *Communist Manifesto* in which Marx describes the revolutionary essence of bourgeois society: "The bourgeoisie cannot exist without constantly revolutionizing the instruments of production, and thereby the relations of production, and with them the whole relations of society . . . All fixed, fast, frozen relations, with their train of ancient and venerable prejudices and opinions, are swept away, all new-formed ones become antiquated before they can ossify." From the beginning, therefore, "bourgeois" individualism had a revolutionary aspect, its temporality was oriented toward the future, and one can see the way in which Bell, a former Marxist, can envision establishing a paradoxical continuity between the bourgeois world and the birth of avant-gardes whose main concern is to break with tradition, to ceaselessly create the new by constantly revolutionizing the world of culture.

A continuity paradoxical indeed, since the spiritual universe of the avant-gardes seems to be the diametrical opposite of the bourgeois way of life. The artist's, the "bohemian's" way of life sees itself as opposed to that of the Philistine and, as Malevich pointed out, the connections between aesthetic and political avant-gardes are sometimes very tight: "Cubism and futurism were the revolutionary forms in art foreshad-

---

*It hardly need be said that, in other matters, Bell keeps his distance from his erstwhile Marxism.

owing the revolution in the political and economic life of 1917."[22] Yet it is this very paradox that Bell places at the heart of his interpretation:

What is striking is that while bourgeois society introduced a radical individualism in economics, and a willingness to tear up all traditional social relations in the process, the bourgeois class feared the radical experimental individualism of modernism in the culture. Conversely, the radical experimentalists in the culture, from Baudelaire to Rimbaud to Alfred Jarry, were willing to explore all dimensions of experience, yet fiercely hated bourgeois life. The history of this sociological puzzle, how this antagonism came about, is still to be written. (Ibid., p. 18)

For Bell, the problem is then one of knowing how to maintain, without contradiction, the idea of an individualist background common to both the bourgeoisie and the avant-gardes (both of them upsetting tradition in the name of individual autonomy) even though the conflict opposing the two forms of life is evident.

Bell's answer presupposes a critique of the dominant paradigms of contemporary sociology, Marxism and functionalism. He argues that, against these paradigms, the *heterogeneity* of the different levels making up capitalist society must be stressed. To this end, we can separate out three spheres: first of all, the *techno-economic structure*, which for the most part can be described in Weberian terms. Governed by a bureaucratic mode of organization, its main principle is efficiency, maximum profitability [*Zweckrationalität* or "instrumental rationality"]. The second sphere is that of the *polity*. Since the emergence of modern individualism—let us say, in the French context, and to limit ourselves to what is most visible, since the 1789 Revolution—it has been increasingly oriented, as Tocqueville's analyses had predicted, by a democratic legitimation whose ultimate grounding is the requirement of equality— formal, at first, then more and more real (p. 12). And finally, there is the *sphere of culture*—and here Bell is referring no longer to Weber or to de Tocqueville, but to Ernst Cassirer (ibid.), whose principle, in the modern world, is self-expression or "self-gratification" (p. xli).

Marxism and functionalism, otherwise completely at odds, have, according to Bell, a shared tendency to represent these three levels as being integrated within a coherent totality (or at least coherent from the interpreter's point of view). One asserts that the superstructures express the infrastructure (with delays, feedback, etc., but they do so all the same); the other presupposes a common value system within a consensus.[23] It is this unitary vision of a social totality that Bell sets out to challenge through the examination of the discordances that appear more and more frequently between the economic, the political, and the cultural spheres. The emergence of these discordances comes in fact relatively late in the history of capitalism (which partly explains the mistakes of the aforecited sociological paradigms). At the beginning, bourgeois society's infrastructure and superstructure were in relative harmony; as Max Weber's analyses show, the ideology of capitalism, for long Puritan and Protestant, managed, until the end of the nineteenth century, to maintain its coherence with the economic sphere. The thirteen "useful virtues" to which Benjamin Franklin claimed to devote thirteen weeks four times a year are the very embodiment of this homogeneity: temperance, silence, order, resolution, frugality, industry, sincerity, justice, moderation, cleanliness, tranquillity, chastity, and humility—qualities whose valorization (if not always their actual exercise) was able to legitimate the entrepreneurial spirit of a nascent capitalism.

But it is clear that this "Protestant ethic" has disappeared today, replaced by a new culture Bell designates as "hedonistic" and "narcissistic." Two stages waymark its development within the context of American history: the nineteen-teens first of all, which witnessed the birth, around a group of "Young Intellectuals" at Harvard, of the demand for a sweeping liberation of mores: "The exuberance of life was summed up in a series of catchwords. One of them was 'New.' There was the New Democracy, the New Nationalism, the New Freedom, the New Poetry, and even the *New Republic* (which was started in 1914). A second was *sex*. Even to use the word openly sent a *frisson* through the readers of the press . . . And a third catchword was *liberation*" (p. 62). This wind of freedom was to lead the United States to discover not only Freud and Bergson—more copies of *Creative Evolution* were sold in two years than in France in the previous fifteen—but also the principal representatives of the aesthetic avant-garde of old Europe.

For this first emancipatory thrust away from the Protestant ethic Bell provides two key reasons: the end of the reign of the "small town" as an effect of demographic growth, and, above all, the birth of a real consumer society in which the development of credit shook up the existence of the masses by ruining the antiquated ascetic ideology of savings and of abstinence: "The cultural transformation of modern society is due, singularly, to the rise of mass consumption, or the diffusion of what were once considered luxuries to the middle and lower classes in society" (p. 65).

203

The second stage was in the 1960s. It did not, for the most part, innovate so much as take up again and democratize the themes already expounded by the "Young Intellectuals" (p. 69). The sixties witnessed the propagation of a *morality of authenticity* whose categorical imperative can be summed up in two words: *Be Yourself*. A simplistic program, of course, but one that passes for a virulent criticism of the bourgeois values and morality of middle-class America [*l'Amérique profonde*]. As a result of this "counter-cultural" period, Bell notes, "traditional morality was replaced by psychology, guilt by anxiety" (p. 72). Psychology, because the problem is no longer one of imposing norms but of understanding the individual personality and furthering its self-realization; anxiety and not guilt, because "not feeling good" is, against the background of a warning "moral law," the mere effect of an intra-psychic conflict. The cultural consequence of this new world-vision: the main themes of the early avant-gardes pass over to everyday existence.

Authenticity in a work of art was defined [in the 1960s] almost exclusively in terms of the quality of immediacy, both the immediacy of the artist's intention and the immediacy of his effect upon the viewer. In the theater, for example, spontaneity was all; the text was virtually eliminated and the reigning form became improvisation—exalting the "natural" over the contrived, sincerity over judgment, spontaneity over reflection. When Judith Malina, the director of the Living Theater, said, "I don't want to be Antigone (on stage), I am and want to be Judith Malina," she aimed to do away with illusion in the theater, as the painters have eliminated it in art. (P. 131)

At the end of this analysis, the opposition between bourgeois and artist looks like the paradoxical effect of a new aspect of individualism: having entered into the era of mass consumption, capitalist society can no longer fit in an ascetic ethic that might restrain this consumption. Therefore the conflict between an economic sphere, still requiring the same efforts and still regulated by the aim of profitability, and a cultural sphere which, though appearing to be a radical critique of the consumer society, in fact cheers it on as never before:

This abandonment of Puritanism and the Protestant ethic . . . emphasizes not only the disjunction between the norms of the culture and the norms of the social structure, but also an extraordinary contradiction within the social structure itself. On the one hand, the business corporation wants an individual to work hard, pursue a career, accept delayed gratification—to be, in the crude sense, an organization man. And yet, in its products and its advertisements, the corporation promotes pleasure, instant joy, relaxing, and letting go. One is to be "straight" by day and a "swinger" by night. This is self-fulfillment and self-realization! (Pp. 71–72)

This interpretation—to which I hardly see how one could remain indifferent so well does it describe one of the profoundest characteristics of contemporary behavior—leads to a paradox: whereas avant-garde art presents itself willingly, not to say complacently, as subversive and antibourgeois, it would in fact be the ultimate expression of a bourgeois society that, in order to satisfy the new consumer demands *it itself* has engendered, has given up the ascetic morality Max Weber described to make room for the hedonistic ideologies of cultural liberation.

I will not come back here to the problems that, at the level of methodology, this type of interpretation brings up.[24] It is clear that, despite the distance it claims to keep from Marxism, it renews the—in my eyes, doubtful—idea that the "superstructures" are but an effect of the "infrastructures" (the ideology of the avant-garde; the effects of the age of credit). And yet, if its conception of individualism undergoes a certain elaboration,[25] it does, it seems to me, rather adequately account for what could be called the "avant-garde *form*" of modernist movements, if their *specific content* is abstracted out. It is indeed obvious that the three moments we saw at work in Kandinsky's text—elitism, historicism, and the cult of self—can be plausibly interpreted within the perspective sketched out by Bell.

It seems to me, moreover, at the level of the content of the different avant-gardes, that we find the limits to Bell's reading of history. Two key difficulties have to be pointed out, both of which seem to require a more complex interpretation of the phenomenon:

1. The first has to do with the fact that, insisting as he does on the continuity linking modernism to classical individualism "since the sixteenth century," Bell underestimates the rupture that the abandonment of perspective and tonality brings into the history of art. In his eyes this rupture is to be classed within the, if we may call it this, "continuity of ruptures" that has characterized the history of democratic/individualist societies since their beginnings. We would thus go over from impressionism to cubism or to abstractionism just as once artists had gone, for instance, from romanticism to impressionism, the only noteworthy difference between the nineteenth and twentieth centuries being, in the end, that in the latter the ruptures become ever more frequent as an effect of a ceaselessly exacerbated individualism. Observing from a not

very distant standpoint, Gilles Lipovetsky has given this continuist vision of art history its full expressive power:

> Modernism is not a first and incomparable rupture: in its rage for destruction and radical innovation, modernism continues, in the cultural order, with a century's delay, the work of modern societies aiming at instituting themselves in the democratic fashion . . . Just as the democratic revolution emancipates society from the forces of the invisible and from their correlate, the hierarchical union, so does artistic modernism liberate art and literature from the cult of tradition, the respect of masters, and the code of imitation.[26]

It is hardly to be doubted that the ideology of rupture with tradition finds its highest expression in the French Revolution, and that, to that extent, we can look for the origins of the "avant-garde forms" therein. But, if we agree that one of the fundamental aspects of the pictorial avant-gardes consists, *as far as content is concerned,* in their abandonment of Euclidean perspective, then the analogy with the French Revolution becomes problematic.* If the movement of art history were to be compared to that of the history of political ideas and realities—an intellectual exercise which, I'm well aware, would not be an exact science—I would say rather that it is the emergence of perspective which, with a few centuries' advance, presages political revolution and coincides, on the level of ideas, with the appearance of the humanism that is expressed in the various social contract theories. That at least is what is suggested by the idea—put forward, for example, in the work of Pierre Francastel—that the valorization of perspective corresponds to a vision of the world dominated by the modern notion of equality, by a metaphysics of subjectivity where man occupies a point of view upon the world from which the latter appears as a material that is manipulable and controllable at will.[27]

It is not, in fact, the individualist interpretation that is here questioned down to its roots, but rather the periodization of the history of the concept of individualism it implies. To formulate the hypothesis which I should like to specify and try out in what follows: though we can make a parallel between the birth of modern individualism and that of classical pictorial perspective, we have to, on the other hand, realize that the rejection of this perspective—like the rejection of musical tonality—has, perhaps, as correlate a new configuration of subjectivity,

---

* It goes without saying that these reservations take nothing away from the interesting and pertinent aspect of Lipovetsky's analyses in other respects.

or, if you prefer, a new era of individualism that cannot be reduced to the features of the first era. On the level of the history of ideas—but also, as we shall see, on that of art history—the parallel between the avant-gardes and the French Revolution leads to a certain underestimation of the rupture brought about, toward the end of the nineteenth century, by the emergence of the new configuration of subjectivity that Nietzsche's philosophy thematizes so well. Where in classical individualism, whose heir and political expression was, simultaneously, the French Revolution, the subject is conceived of on the model of the cogito, of the monad that is closed in upon itself and upon its private interests, the nineteenth century witnesses the appearance of ever more radical critiques of the cogito leading to the elaboration, in Nietzsche above all, of a "fractured subject," of a subject that differs from itself and opens onto an indomitable unconscious.

In liberal theories of the individual, the multifariousness of viewpoints and interests could still be harmoniously "integrated" into a monadology or market theory—"invisible hand" or "ruse of reason." In the perspectivism Nietzsche thematizes but which goes indisputably beyond the framework of philosophy to become the *Stimmung* of the waning nineteenth century, this multifariousness becomes irreducible and irreconcilable. The idea of harmony gives way to that of chaos, and identity to "difference"—and it is this "difference," inherent to a new epoch of subjectivity, that is expressed by philosophy as well as by painting or avant-garde music. From Schönberg to Kandinsky or Malevich, it is this critique of the *cogito* that justifies the avant-garde, if it is true, as Malevich insists, that radically new aesthetic forms cannot be created without having "eliminated from all our arts the petit-bourgeois idea of subject" and "hammered upon consciousness as upon nails one drives into a stone wall."[28]

2. The second difficulty Bell's interpretation encounters stems from the first. The avant-gardes were, in certain aspects—and we shall see the extent to which this observation can be verified right down to the smallest details—characterized by the cult of the self, by the "sacralization," to take up Kandinsky's formulation, of "every means permitting the expression of personality." Yet, as far as the avant-gardes' *content* is concerned, we know, at least since Apollinaire, that two main currents separated themselves out very early in this century. One was that of abstract art, of the "Orphism" which, with Delaunay and Kandinsky, rejects perspective in the name of pure abstraction. The other was cubism, which, despite its rejection of "naturalism," maintains the

strictly speaking classical ideal of an objective or realistic art, one that remains attached to the principles of figuration even when the latter no longer traverses the laws of Euclidean perspective but rather their contrary.

That this distinction, established by Apollinaire in *Les Peintres cubistes* [*The Cubist Painters*],[29] may have been vividly disputed when he undertook to classify each artist as belonging to one or the other camp did not prevent it from becoming generally predominant among painters themselves, as witness one text among many others: this one, dating from 1946, we owe to the great theoretician of cubism Metzinger. From 1912 on, he confesses, "we already envisaged two possibilities: a painting of 'pure effusion' and a 'new realism.' The former is now called abstract or nonfigurative painting, the latter has kept the name cubism.[30] And we may recall how often the surrealists scolded cubism for its concern with realism and objectivism.[31]

If "classicism" is broadly defined as a form of art that defines the beautiful as being an exposition of the true, of the real, then we can state that a classical component is not at all absent from the avant-gardes, not even from cubism, the most remarkable among them. And it would also be misleading to think that abstract art and surrealism set every classical reference to a science of art aside so as to set themselves off from the cubist painters' realism. It would be easy to show how, in Kandinsky himself, color theory tries to adopt the form of a science, or how, in surrealism, automatic writing is legitimated by referring to the "scientific" theory that psychoanalysis is in Breton's eyes. In a word, what the individualist interpretation of the avant-gardes does not account for is this *classicist, realist,* at times even *scientistic* component that counterbalances the subjectivism or narcissism inherent in the avant-garde form. Where individualism's logic disencumbers from the norms of tradition, classicism's logic leads, on the contrary, to laying down constrictive norms. It is this "objectivist" aspect of the avant-gardes—and particularly of cubism—that must be accounted for, to measure more exactly what the individualist interpretation perhaps cannot quite grasp.

THE "FOURTH DIMENSION"

"In the early years of the twentieth century," Pierre Francastel reminds us, "the fashion was all for scientism." The world was "astonished at the constantly renewed applications not so much of science as of technology," which upset the vision of a physical universe that had been thought "stable for several centuries."[32] Such is the context in which the first avant-gardes blossomed; a context that has faded somewhat since scientific progress evokes, nowadays, disquiet rather more than it does astonishment or admiration. We have, thanks to a retrospective illusion, a tendency to forget that the Italian Futurists' fascination with "modern machines"[33] was, all things considered, closer to Jules Verne than to Kafka, or that the first cubist painters could subscribe without reservations to a philosophy that held that "through the modifications of artworks, it was possible to follow the modifications in science step by step," so much did the latter's influence upon the former seem decisive.[34]

Without falling into the trap of a causal vision of the relation between art and science, we do have to agree with Francastel that "cubism's first initiative, towards 1907, was to speculate on the dimensions of space. Influenced by the terms circulating around them, the cubists thought they were carrying out positive scientific work by introducing a fourth dimension in their canvases or in suppressing the third one."[35] As Francastel puts it further on, perhaps without realizing all of the aesthetic and philosophical implications, "For Picasso, the world has a twofold aspect. It is most of all curved and near. He is, plastically, the closest to some of Riemann's and Einstein's geometrical hypotheses" (p. 250).

And yet, strangely, most art historians (with the notable exception of Jean Clair and Linda Dalrymple-Henderson, to whom I shall return) have avoided granting these scientific allusions any importance other than metaphorical. Concerned, and justly so, with avoiding any confusion between painting and the new geometries, between the scientist's mathematical space and the artist's plastic space, they have most often preferred dwelling on the negative aspects of a reference that constantly threatens to furnish fodder for the accusation of "intellectualism" so commonly made against avant-garde art. Allusions to "non-Euclidean" * geometries would, in the end, only have been useful for the painters themselves to legitimate, over against a conservative public used to the naturalism of "perspectival" pictures, the abandonment of a Euclidean space limited to tridimensionality.[36] This was, once again, a legitimate precaution, but one which leads to significantly

---

* We shall see that, in fact, this expression covers quite various mathematical theses.

underestimating the true significance of the recourse to the new geometries. The contemporaries of the first avant-gardes were not misled about this, as witness this passage from *Cubist Painters* that Apollinaire consecrates to modern mathematics:

Up to now, the three dimensions of Euclidean geometry sufficed for the anxieties that the feeling of infinity introduces into the soul of artists . . . But today, the scientists and learned men do not limit themselves to the three dimensions of Euclidean geometry. Painters have, quite naturally and, so to speak, by intuition, been led to take an interest in the possible new measures of extension which, in the language of modern workshops, are jointly and briefly designated by the term of fourth dimension.

This text is all the more noteworthy in that it knowingly and consciously insists upon the importance of this "fourth dimension." Apollinaire knows, better than anyone else, that the aspiration of "geometrism" has already become so banal at the time he is writing his book (in 1912) that it is the origin, no less, of the very term "cubism," which was used at first as an anathema.* And yet he cannot but stress the irreplaceable role the new geometries played, if not in cubism's creation, then at least in the legitimacy accorded the new "intuitive" relation to what he, following the mathematicians' terminology, calls "extension."[37] Painters, in turn, explicitly evoke the need for "going beyond" Euclid's three dimensions and for challenging, thanks to the non-Euclidean geometries, the postulate of the "nondeformity of moving figures."[38] As Metzinger and Gleizes assert, "If one wished to connect space in these painters to some sort of geometry, one would have to make reference to non-Euclidean researchers, and meditate some of Rieman's [*sic*] theorems" (ibid.). The utterance's hypothetical character ("If one wished . . .") should not mislead us. Metzinger and Gleizes were not trying to say—on the contrary—that the new geometries were not pertinent for artists, but only to remind us that artists did not

---

* Forced, so to speak, to take up a pejorative term, but one already consecrated by usage, Metzinger and Gleizes wrote the first pages of their major theoretical work, *Du cubisme* [*On Cubism*, 1912], with the same worry in mind: "The word cubism appears here only to spare the reader any hesitation as to the object of this study, and we hasten to declare that the idea it calls forth, that of volume, cannot by itself define a movement that tends towards the integral fulfillment of painting."

thereby become geometers; that their mathematical knowledge still belonged to the realm of the amateur and remained—as their own misspelling of Riemann's name shows—second-hand.

We know today[39] through what complicated paths painters became acquainted with the new geometries, and we can rather precisely reconstruct the concrete meaning that this famous "fourth dimension" must have had for them. Although the essays of its principal theoretician, Charles Howard Hinton,[40] were not translated, several books on the new geometries were easily accessible to the French public from the first years of this century's first decade. Besides Poincaré's *La Science et l'hypothèse* [*Science and Hypothesis*]—whose influence is as visible in Metzinger and Gleizes's writings as in Duchamp's *Notes sur le grand verre* ["Notes on the *Large Glass*"]—the year 1903 saw the publication of Boucher's *Essai sur l'hyperespace* [*Essay on Hyperspace*] and Jouffret's *Elementary Treatise of Four-Dimensional Geometry*. This last, which has the advantage of providing numerous graphic representations of four-dimensional or "hyperbodies," could certainly attract the interest of artists eager to break with the naturalism of preceding years. Evoking "the universe we dwell in and those we suspect to be beside it," it lets float a promising doubt about the existence of the fourth dimension: "The four-dimensional world exists, no doubt, only in the geometrical sense. But nothing prevents us from assuming its concrete existence also, in which case our world would be part of it."

The foreword sets out to relativize Euclidean geometry's three-dimensional space by reducing it to a mere convention, born out of habit: "This number [three] seems to have no logical necessity, for we can replace it with any other whole number when we wish to formulate any kind of analytical system; it seems thus to be a mere product of experience, not, certainly, of individual experience, but of the accumulated experience that furnishes hereditary ideas" (p. v). If it is, therefore, neither logical truth nor intangible law of perception, how then not to envisage the possibility of a "transformation corresponding to that of the analysis, whose result would be to give our descendents the sensation of seeing themselves, and of conceiving of space, in four dimensions" (p. viii)? For Hinton, quoted by Jouffret,[41] there is not the slightest doubt; the perception of the fourth dimension is well and truly a matter of adaptation; it awaits only the ripening of our mental development: "When the faculty is acquired, or, better: when it is brought to consciousness—for it exists within each of us in imperfect form—

a new horizon opens . . . Our perception is subjected to the condition of being in space; but space is not limited, as we at first believe, to tridimensionality . . .[42]

Jouffret, more prudent than Hinton, no doubt agreed with Poincaré in being convinced tht the fourth dimension would forever remain outside our perception. But he did not for all that cease suggesting that its imperceptible character in no way implied nonexistence:

> The non-perception of bodies external to our space in no way hinders establishing their geometry, that is to say the descriptive and metrical relations they sustain among themselves and with those who, *on the other side,* people the superior extensions. The reader who follows us into these curious regions of thought, into this country that has been called mathematics' fairytale world, will quickly become used to the oddities he finds there, since these oddities are in agreement with the most rigorous logic.[43]

As we will see in a moment, this language comes very near that through which science fiction was to retrieve the fourth dimension from the specialist's domain and bring it to the public's attention. But we first of all have to define this famous fourth dimension—being unable to give it an adequate visual representation.

The difficulty in understanding, or in leading to an understanding of what the fourth dimension could be, has indeed to do with the fact that it lies outside perception. To give an idea of it, we thus have to follow a line of reasoning, actually fairly simple, that Jouffret formulates in these terms: "The geometer conceives of space as being divided into an infinity of *infinitely thin slices* he calls *planes,* these being in turn divided into an infinity of *infinitely thin strips* he calls *straight lines,* and these into an infinity of *infinitely short segments* he calls *points*" (p. viii). One can say then that instead of having three dimensions, as volumes do, planes only have two, lines only one, and points none. Here then is how, beginning with this series's simple elements, we arrive at the idea of the fourth dimension: "Taking the series in reverse, beginning, that is, with the *point,* the geometry that is going to concern us pursues it beyond three-dimensional space. The latter is, for it, only a *slice* (we cannot keep on diversifying words and we therefore gather up the last one left behind by the series we began), an *infinitely thin slice* in the midst of an infinity of other spaces constituting an equal number of similar slices within a four-dimensional extension" (p. ix).

It is an example of reasoning by analogy: just as the point can be thought of as an infinitely thin slice cut out of, so to speak, a line, so the line can in turn be seen as an infinitely thin slice of a plane, and the plane as an infinitely thin slice of volume (for instance, a square is an infinitely thin slice of a cube), so—by *analogy*—nothing prevents us from imagining that a volume, a cube in our example, is itself a slice cut out of a four-dimensional body that will thereafter be called a "hyperbody."

We cannot, as mentioned above, perceive this hyperbody, but nothing hinders us from tracing its figure in *two dimensions*. Let us begin with the straight line. If we shift this line parallel to itself, we obtain a plane and thereby go from the first to the second dimension:

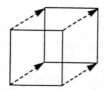

If we now push this square while keeping it parallel to itself, we obtain a cube.[44]

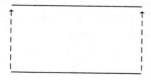

Still by analogy, we can again shift a cube perpendicular to the three dimensions, and obtain a hypercube, meaning a volume in four dimensions.

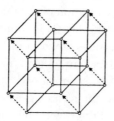

Of course, the representation of the fourth dimension is here given only in two dimensions, and we cannot always intuitively grasp four-dimensionality. But we can say, always by analogy, and taking up the argument in Edwin Abbott's famous fable,[45] mentioned by Poincaré in *Science and Hypothesis,* that we have exactly the same difficulty grasping the fourth dimension as perfectly flat beings, limited to two dimensions, would have in understanding the third.

Not seeking to rely on intuition any longer, we can state therefore that a body of *n* dimensions is always the infinitely thin limit of a body of $n + 1$ dimensions, and that consequently a three-dimensional volume can be looked at as being the slice of a hyperbody, even though this hyperbody escapes our perception. It is in this precise sense that Jouffret could, in one and the same sentence, evoke "the universe we dwell in (in three dimensions) and *those we suspect are next to it* (or beside it)" without our being able to perceive them—nonperception, we repeat, being in no way a mark of nonexistence.

To give the same idea one last formulation, we will add that the hyperbodies can be represented "by projections onto our space, by means of perpendiculars extracted out of various points of the body into this space, much as the bodies of our space can be, through perpendiculars, represented by *projections on a plane* . . . But though, with a projection onto a plane, or, even better, with two projections on two planes, we have no problem constituting a space solid and seeing it with our minds, it is quite impossible to ascend from the projection of a four-dimensional body to the body itself,"[46] so as to have an intuitive representation of it.

We know about the taste the cubist painters developed for geometry: "Art, or that art that has not been accepted, is based on a mathematics," as Metzinger put it.[47] And also: "This science gave me a taste for the arts. It is numbers that permit us to account for sounds and silences, lights and shadows, forms and emptiness. Michelangelo and Bach seem to me to have been divine calculators. I already felt that only mathematics allows for the creation of durable work. Whether it be the result of patient study or of a lightning intuition, only it is capable of bringing our pathetic diversities down to the strict unity of a composition for the mass, or of a fresco or a bust" (p. 20).

We also know those painters possessed a rather exact knowledge of Jouffret's theses, thanks to the lessons given them by a young mathematician, Maurice Princet. Princet was obviously not the "father of cubism" (nor, for that matter, the new geometries' only popularizer), as Vauxcelles jokingly argued in an article of December 1918 that Juan Gris hotly disputed.[48] But it would be inaccurate to deny that his theoretical contribution to the young artists' thinking was unimportant, as witness, among so many others, these two confessions of Metzinger that deserve all our attention: *

> Maurice Princet joined us often. Although quite young, thanks to his knowledge of mathematics he had an important job in an insurance company. But, beyond his profession, it was as an artist that he conceptualized mathematics, as an aesthetician that he evoked *n*-dimensional continuums. He loved to get the artists interested in the new views on space that had been opened up by Schlegel and some others. He succeeded at that. Having listened to him by chance, Henri Matisse was caught one day reading an essay on hyperspace. Oh! It was only a work of popularization! But it at least proved that for the "Great Fauve" the days of the ignorant painter running after the pretty *motif* with his beard to the wind were over.
>
> As for Picasso, the speed of his comprehension astounded the specialist. It was the case that his tradition prepared him better than ours did for problems of structure.[49]

An interesting text, in what it indicates about the change in *Stimmung* when compared to the romantic artist. Though the scientists were becoming aestheticians, the inverse movement, in an atmosphere heavily impregnated with scientism, was no less real: painters had the feeling that a new scientific age legitimized a new artistic age. Metzinger is just as precise as to the content of Princet's teaching:

> It is indeed folly, Maurice Princet declared to me in front of Juan Gris, to want to unite in one sole system of relations color, which is a sensation, and form, which is an organization you have only to accept and which you should try to understand; and, initiating us into non-Euclidean geometries, he incited us to create a painter's geometry. We could not do so in the same way as he. But, from rue Lamarck to rue Ravignan, the pretension of imitating a ball on a vertical plane, or of providing, with a horizontal straight line, the figuration of a vase's circular hole when placed at eye-level, were now considered to be the artifices of an outdated illusionism. Cubism was born. (Pp. 62–63)

Four-dimensional geometries had at least one decisive effect: they legitimated in the minds of painters the critique of traditional perspective as being an "outdated illusion," and they subsequently gave rise to the idea of a reduction of plastic space to bidimensionality. This point is decisive. There was, in the eyes of the painters, no doubt in this re-

---

* See also Duchamp's "Notes on the *Large Glass*." (Duchamp, *Écrits*, op. cit.)

duction that four-dimensional and non-Euclidean geometries could be united. Contrary to a commonly held opinion, Riemann's and Lobachevsky's geometries were not completely inaccessible to the layman who took the trouble of reading the presentation made of them by Poincaré in his *Science and Hypothesis*. Without going into this exposition in detail, we can still grasp how these geometries reinforced the idea of a necessary supersession of perspective.

Until the beginning of the nineteenth century, Euclid's postulate that "only one line parallel to a straight line passes through a point outside this line" was, in fact, less a first principle than a badly demonstrated theorem. The number of mathematicians who tried to fill in this gap by making a direct demonstration was incalculable, until Lobachevsky hit on the idea of trying a demonstration through the absurd: he simply inverted the famous postulate, and set out from the hypothesis that one can lead several parallels through a point outside a given straight line. And, he obtained a new mathematical system, *apparently* irrepresentable, but coherent. Riemann, in his wake, repeated the same procedure, but setting out this time from the inverse hypothesis, that through a point external to a given straight line one can trace no parallels.

Lobachevsky's and Riemann's geometries deduce a series of theorems from these premises that seem to be in perfect contradiction with those of Euclidean geometry. To cite only the two best-known ones: in Lobachevsky's geometry, the sum of angles of a triangle is inferior to 180 degrees, while, for Riemann, it is superior to 180 degrees. Were they dealing—as long as their respective systems were, from a strictly mathematical viewpoint, coherent—with a new space? That, of course, was the question that artists and philosophers would inevitably ask themselves. And if the answer were affirmative—as nearly everyone thought (and as some think even today!)—then what plastic representation could be made of these new spaces in which the angles of a triangle no longer add up to 180 degrees, in which the ends of a line perpendicular to a straight line meet, etc.?

I will not deal here with the question of the real significance of these geometries in the history of the sciences. It is, unfortunately, clear that they have not overturned our perception of space, though they have led to favoring the internal coherence of mathematical systems over the recourse to intuition and to "figures." Here, I am only interested in the ways they could have been understood by artists thanks to a book, Poincaré's, they all knew. A few examples taken from Riemann's geometry should be enough to grasp the main points.

According to Poincaré, this geometry could be presented as the one that would be devised by "infinitely flat" intelligent creatures living on a sphere's surface. It is, first of all, clear that "such beings would attribute but two dimensions to space: a straight line, to them, would be the shortest path from one point on the sphere to another, which is to say the arc of a great circle."[50] Understanding this simple example suffices for us to understand also how, in Riemann's geometry, two lines perpendicular to the same straight line can "meet," and how the angles of a triangle can add up to more than 180 degrees. Let us, as Poincaré invites us to, imagine that for these infinitely flat beings living upon a sphere a straight line is a great circle, comparable to the meridians on a globe of the earth, and we will see that two lines (meridians (a) and (b)), perpendicular to the same line (equator (c)), cross at the North and South poles:

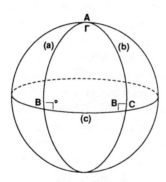

It will also be granted without difficulty that angles α, β, γ, of triangle ABC add up to more than 180 degrees, since α and β already are, by definition, right angles.

Through spherical geometry one can thus, without great difficulty, render visually the at first incomprehensible properties of these theories, that have been perhaps a bit too hastily called "non-Euclidean." But, to repeat, the historical truth is not really what matters most here. What is of interest here is that four-dimensional and non-Euclidean geometries—specially Riemann's—could, in the minds of artists, converge upon one point: in the idea that it was time to put an end to perspective in order to *return to two dimensions*. For, in an easily understandable paradox, the *plastic* effect of four-dimensional geometry was the reduction of the canvas to bidimensionality, within which alone the fourth dimension could be represented *through projection*. Perspective, an art of illusion, is in fact of no use in representing hyperbodies, so that a plastic representation of the fourth dimension can only be effected by considering only the purely mathematical properties of figures that are definitively limited to two dimensions. And, presented in the form Poincaré's model gave it, Riemann's geometry suggested the idea of a curved space, also limited to two dimensions. In short, in a space like that described by Jouffret, at least one thing is certain: that perspective has to be put to an end; in this light, all these geometries could well seem to be, generally speaking, "non-Euclidean."

THE ROLE OF SCIENCE FICTION

It must be added that, though four-dimensional geometry reinforced the idea of a plastic space limited to two dimensions, it also brought in a mysterious element, halfway between aesthetics and science: the "feeling" of there being a hyperspace, peopled with hyperbodies, secretly surrounding our space. It is therefore not surprising that science fiction should have taken hold of the theme to such an extent that it became the main medium of popularization of the new geometries among the avant-garde milieux in the nineteen-teens. It was, in fact, by way of theosophy and science fiction that Charles Howard Hinton's principal theses concerning the fourth dimension reached the public. They were available in French in works such as Leadbeater's *L'Autre Côté de la mort* [*The Other Side of Death*], published in 1910 by the Theosophical Publishing House. One could read therein statements that come rather close to those of a serious mathematician like Jouffret: "In reality, we know only three dimensions in our physical world. Not that only these three dimensions exist, but that only they can be understood by the physical brain. We live, in truth, in a space that possesses a number of dimensions . . . We see only what we are capable of seeing, but there is much more to see." And, going in the same direction, Level's and Noircame's theosophical texts suggested the possibility of gaining access to a four-dimensional world through the development of certain of our mental faculties.[51]

But it was doubtless Gaston de Pawlowski[52] who was to have the greatest influence on modern painters by popularizing, in his essay *Le Voyage au pays de la quatrième dimension* [*The Voyage to the Country of the Fourth Dimension*], Hinton's, Jouffret's, and Poincaré's arguments.

A friend of Jarry's and of Apollinaire's and a doctor by training, but in practice a distinguished humorist, Pawlowski had embarked upon a career as a journalist.[53] In love, like the Futurists, with the "new machines," he was editor of the magazines *Vélo* and *Automobilia* before becoming director of one of the most influential art reviews of the period, *Comoedia*, in which, between 1910 and 1912, he published serially what was to become the *Voyage*. Joining the love of pure fiction to the most recent scientific discoveries, Pawlowski intended to use this book to escape from "bourgeois certainties" the same way the new artists did, by mobilizing the ideas the most opposed to the best-established mental attitudes.[54] Following in Jarry's footsteps, and with reference to the latter's "Commentaire pour servir à la construction pratique de la machine à explorer le temps" [Commentary to be used in the Practical Assembly of the Time Machine][55]—which already mentions the fourth dimension and non-Euclidean geometries—Pawlowski set out to describe after his own fashion the new universe that was thought at the time to be discernible "beyond the one we live in."

Pawlowski's book was a great success from the moment of its publication in 1912. It in essence takes up an argument analogous to the one that had been central to Abbott's novel *Flatland*. Just as, in the latter, a two-dimensional being (a square) against all expectations discovers the existence of a theretofore unsuspected third dimension, in the *Voyage* it is the fourth dimension that is discovered.[56] Pawlowski had fun bringing to light paradoxes such as the "anguishing problem" of the horizontal staircase, which "after an undeniable succession of steps takes you back to the floor you started at":

> These are things one smiles at at first, believing there to be a passing error; the problems become dismaying when one persists in seeking to solve them by following the primitive principles of three-dimensional Euclidean geometry. And, for myself, I confess I felt truly relieved the day I understood that if such staircases could exist, their possibility could only be conceived of within a four-dimensional space, and that only that could be enough to provide a definitive explanation of the problem. And, soon, it was with a strange pleasure, even, that I strolled through some of these old residences, dreamed up once upon a time by transcendental geometry, where the floors mixed itself up [*sic*], where the first floor was not necessarily below the fourth, nor the third above the ground floor.

It was after reading Pawlowski's *Voyage* that Marcel Duchamp thought up the *Large Glass* project,[57] as he states unequivocally in a passage from his interviews with Pierre Cabanne:

I had at that time [Duchamp says] tried to read some things by this Povo-lowski,* who explained measurements, straight lines, curves, etc. All that was running around in my head while I was working, even though I made practically no calculations for the *Large Glass*. Quite simply, I thought of the idea of a projection, of a fourth dimension, invisible since we can't see it with the eyes. Since I found that one could make any kind of object out of the shadow of a thing with three dimensions—like the sun's projection on the earth, making two dimensions—through purely intellectual analogy I thought that the fourth dimension could project an object with three dimensions: in other words, that every three-dimensional object, that we look at so coldly, is the projection of a four-dimensional thing we do not know. It was a sophism, but it was possible. It was on that that I based the *Bride*, in the *Large Glass,* as a projection of an object in four dimensions.[58]

We can recognize here, almost word by word, Jouffret's proposi-tions as popularized by Pawlowski; the interpretation of the *Large Glass* could begin here and continue on into the most apparently insig-nificant details since, as Duchamp put it in a 1955 letter to André Breton: "The *Bride* . . . is a four-dimensional projection (and in the case of the flat glass, a re-projection of these three dimensions onto a two-dimensional surface)."[59] If, finally, we add that the theosophist Pierre Piotr Demianovich Ouspensky, whose *Tertium Organum,* published in St. Petersburg in 1911, fascinated Malevich, drew, like Jouffret, on Hin-ton's works for the core of his reflections on the fourth dimension,[60] we will better realize the theme's importance in the birth of the avant-gardes at the beginning of our century.

THE "FOURTH DIMENSION'S DOUBLE DIMENSION: ULTRAINDIVIDUALISM AND HYPERCLASSICISM

I have already mentioned how, despite certain lacunae, the interpreta-tion of the avant-gardes in terms of individualism has to be taken seri-ously. The reference to a fourth dimension fits in several ways into such an interpretative framework. Even for the most theoretical among the cubist painters, Metzinger,[61] the discovery of a new dimension of space had to be understood as a liberating break with tradition, as a progress for the personal expression of the individual in revolt against the norms

---

*Duchamp is here confusing Pawlowski with a certain Povolowski, who owned an art gallery on the rue Bonaparte in Paris in the 1920s.

admitted by the "schools." Metzinger narrates, in his memoirs, how, very early on, he was to "measure the difference separating art prior to 1900" from what he felt was being born: "I knew that all teaching was over. The era of personal expression was finally beginning. The value of an artist would no longer have anything to do with the finish of his execution, with the analogies his works offer with such and such an archetype. It would have to do—exclusively—with what distinguishes this artist from all the others. The period of the master-teacher was finally through."[62]

One could hardly put better the extent to which the new painters felt that the essential thing was the capacity to express, forgetting all watchwords, the fine edge of individuality through which it is possible to set oneself apart, to arrive at originality, the value above all values within an individualist perspective. That the expression of originality requires a negation of tradition, and especially of the "Euclidean" tradition, was something Metzinger did not fail to bring to mind either: "That Juan Gris disarticulated objects, that Picasso substituted his invented forms for them, that someone else replaced conical perspective with a system based on perpendicular relations: all that proves that cubism was not born from any slogan or watchword, and that it only signaled the will to put an end to a kind of art that should not have survived Pascal's condemnation" (ibid., p. 62). The allusion to Pascal, denouncing the vanity of the type of painting "that attracts admiration by resembling things whose originals we admire not" here becomes perfectly clear: in this critical opinion, Pascal was aiming not at painting in general, but at a particular kind of painting, the trompe-l'oeil,[63] that has no other goal than the perfect imitation of some object or another.

Metzinger, therefore, sees that the tradition that must be broken with is, quite clearly, academic figurative art, which has anyhow been rendered pointless by photography, the contemporary equivalent of trompe-l'oeil.* In an article titled, significantly, "Cubism and Tradition," he goes even farther and perceives that the tradition of art history is already, before the emergence of cubism, a "tradition of the new." A true pioneer, he grasps the essence of the individualist logic at work in this history. Speaking of the avant-garde painters, he writes: "Because

---

* "The excuse of being documentary was becoming ridiculous among painters: photographers and filmmakers could go far beyond anything they did" (*Le Cubisme était né*, p. 58).

they use the simplest, the most complete, the most logical forms, they have been designated as 'cubists.' Because they work at extracting new plastic signifiers out of these forms, they are accused of betraying tradition. How could they betray tradition, an uninterrupted succession of innovations, they who, by innovating, do nothing but perpetuate it?"[64]

Avant-garde painting has often been described, even by its most impassioned defenders, as being "a vast enterprise of demolition, that begins by getting rid of the cardinals, water lilies, and nude ladies of academic painting,"[65] as a "destruction of plastic space" (that is, in essence, Francastel's argument, [Etudes, chap. 3]), the breaking with a tradition—that of treatises on perspective—well-established ever since the schools of the Italian *quattrocento*. And we haven't yet mentioned how perspective was denounced as "repressive," its "demolition" likened to that of a "prison" from which an individuality in rebellion could finally escape. As Jean Paulhan wrote,

> One finds, on every page of treatises on perspective, those model prisons, peopled by cubes, some of which are seen from the side, some from in front, others in three-fourths and two-thirds perspective, and so on. These are the saddest menageries one could imagine . . . This bit of work is called squaring the plan [*mise au carreau*]—an expression that evokes tortures, and it could hardly be more apt. It is indeed a case of making martyrs out of lines, colors, and plane surfaces, until they produce the illusion of depth, some sort of paltry equivalent of infinity. (*Peinture cubiste*, p. 93)

In this analysis, in which the demands and aspirations of revolutionary individualism find expression, we easily discern what the reference to the new geometries could have meant: being, in general, "*non*-Euclidean," they symbolized the break with a history of thousands of years; in the second place, to the extent that Euclidean, three-dimensional space began to seem to be a mere "convention"[66]—in every sense of the word, as mathematical *postulate* and received and passively admitted *habit*—an art that aimed to put an end to traditional perspective could also be thought of as a challenge raised against the certainties that Pawlowski, as we have seen, did not hesitate to qualify as "bourgeois." The geometrical reference, finally, brought in relativism and historicism—the two consummate expressions of the high point of individualism. Didn't the new mathematics demonstrate that what had been considered as the undoubtable truth for thousands of years (tridimensionality) was, in reality, but an illusion, an error connected to a "slow" stage of humanity's scientific and cultural development? As Metzinger and Gleizes confidently declared in the conclusion to *Cubism:*

> To sum up, the cubism that was accused of being a system in fact condemns all systems . . . To the partial liberties conquered by Courbet, Manet, Cézanne, and the Impressionists, cubism substitutes an infinite liberty. Now that objective knowledge is finally held to be a chimera, and that all that the crowd understands as natural form has been proved to be a convention [thanks to the discoveries of the new geometries—L.F.], the painter has no laws other than those governing colored forms . . . There is only one truth, *ours,* when we succeed in imposing it on all. (Pp. 74–75)

This subjectivization of truth, this conception of art as the expression of a distinct and original individuality, was also to have narcissistic consequences. I have already indicated how revolutionary individualism contained the risk of drifting toward narcissistic individualism. Without much problem, we could put together a book consisting exclusively of quotations from artists, giving crude and immodest expression to everything that the ideology of the "tradition of the new" potentially contains in the way of fanatical egotism. It would be an unbroken series going from Marcel Duchamp, beginning a lecture in the United States modestly titled "Apropos Myself" with this touching slide-show commentary, "Blainville is a village in Normandy where I was born and where this picture was painted in 1902, when I was only fifteen years old," to Pierre Boulez, who does not hesitate to publish, as a foreword to *Penser la musique aujourd'hui* [*Thinking about Music Today*], an "auto-interview" no less modestly titled "De Moi à Moi" [*From Myself to Myself*].[67]

It is hard to underestimate this "ultraindividualist" dimension, and I can understand how it could have been argued that this is what the avant-gardes' "modernist" core consisted of. Yet, if we consider the reference to the new geometries in all its significance, we cannot fail to be struck by another dimension, the "objectivist" one I have designated as classicism.

In his 1917 article on "Avant-Garde Painting"[68]—consisting essentially of a detailed elucidation of the meaning the fourth dimension had for modern painters—Gino Severini, one of the master thinkers of Italian Futurism and a great friend of the cubists, already warns against the dangers of an individualistic drift in the tradition of the new: "Today, originality is often confused with singularity, and the illusion is entertained that a more or less apparent originality can alone make up the value of a work of art. I intend by that a brief allusion to this *ultraindividualist* tendency which, remarkably late, emerges today from the ruins of our violent reactions of seven or eight years ago." Convinced that the individual's revolts against tradition should not lead to the narcissistic cult of originality for originality's sake, the veritable avant-garde artist is the one who also knows how to mobilize the resources of scientific objectivity: "If I love trying to support myself with the truths of science, it is because I see in them an excellent means of *control,* and besides, none of us ought to ignore the notions science puts within our reach to intensify our sense of the real" (p. 460). From this a classicist or "realist" interpretation of the avant-gardes that were inspired by the new geometries.

Severini insists upon it: the reference to the fourth dimension does not have an essentially "individualist" significance. In following scientific discoveries, the point is not to seek at any price an originality that breaks off from the Euclidean tradition; if the art of appearances called perspective has to be transcended, it is, above all, to be able to arrive at a "new realism," a realism Severini calls, in allusion to Plato, "ideist," since, in Picasso's famous words, the goal is to paint objects *as we think them,* not *as we see them:* "All of the efforts of avant-garde painters tend toward the expression of this new realism . . . The obsession with penetrating, with conquering the sense of the real by every means, with identifying with life through every fiber of our bodies, has been the basis for our researches and for aesthetics since the beginning of time. We must see in these general causes the origins of our exact geometrical constructions" (p. 452).

It's at this point in Severini's line of argument that the reference to Poincaré becomes all-important. If Euclid must be surpassed, it is not only because tridimensionality is a supposedly bourgeois convention that limits the imagination (it is that *also*), but above all because "the forms that constitute our reconstruction of the object do not live from the imagination or the culture but from the object itself" (p. 451), and the new geometries permit us to capture this object more precisely. Truth to tell, the avant-garde's revolutionary ("subjective") and "realist" ("objective") aspects come together in one and the same struggle against traditional naturalism, denounced as being at the same time oppressive (as concerning the new demand for liberty) and illusory (as concerning the new demand for truth and objectivity):

The [traditional "Euclidean" geometer's] ordinary space is, in general, based upon the unmoveable convention of there being three dimensions; painters of unlimited inspiration have always found this convention too narrow. That is, to the three ordinary dimensions they try to add a fourth . . . People have often tried to insult cubism by applying the epithet "mathematician" to painters like Braque, Picasso, Gris, and Metzinger, whose first plastic analyses constitute, after all, an important contribution to pictorial art. The fact that these researches correspond to certain geometric and mathematical truths, as I will show further on, only create, in the eyes of any impartial person, a supplementary reason for interest and trust in them. (P. 459)

The analogy between the development of the history of art and that of science is not a mere coincidence since, as Severini confesses, "the first cubist and futurist researches are based—relatively, of course, and by intuition [we should not forget that he still had to refute the accusations of 'geometrism'—L.F.]—on the hypotheses elucidated by Poincaré on the fourth dimension and on non-Euclidean geometries" (p. 461). By underlining that the abandonment of perspective does not aim only at freeing the pure expressivity of a personality otherwise hindered by conventions, by declaring that avant-garde art must aim at a deeper figuration than that of traditional perspective, Severini meets up with Princet's teaching: appearances (tridimensionality and the perspective that presupposes a fixed observer) must be overcome in order to attain the true reality, the one that, like the fourth dimension or Platonic ideas, is not visible, but accessible only to the intelligence. As Princet declared to his friends, in the terms one finds again in the cubist painters' main writings: "With the aid of a trapezoid, you represent a table, such as you see it *deformed by perspective*. But what if the whim took hold of you of expressing the ideo-typical table? You would have to straighten it up on the canvas's plane and, from the trapezoid, come back to the *veridical* rectangle. If this table is covered with objects similarly *deformed* by perspective, the same straightening-up movement will have to be operated for every one of them."[69] Here, then, visible perspective becomes "deformed" appearance, and bidimensionality (we have already mentioned that it becomes the plastic consequence of the fourth dimension) becomes the real, that is to say the *intelligible*. Let us, after Princet, listen to Severini, who, in the aforementioned article, defines this new "ideist realism" with great precision:

Italian perspective has been our foundation up to now, but we now know that it does not allow the painter to integrally express visual space . . . Our intoxicating goal of penetrating and giving back reality has taught us to shift this unique viewpoint, because we are at the center of the real and not in front of it; to look with our two moveable eyes and consider in parallel the horizontal and the vertical deformations. These means permit us to give expression to a *hyperspace*, that is, a space as complete as possible. (P. 463)

A strange reversal, but one highly characteristic of the cubist revolution, and invariably found in the period's writings. Contrary to what a naïve naturalism thought, it is not the Euclidian perspective that is true, but rather this fourth dimension and this curved, non-Euclidean space where figures are deformed when shifted. If we believe Gleizes, if "the nineteenth-century geometers (Riemann and Lobachevsky) were right in repudiating the intellectually absolute character of Euclid's postulates," it is because "Euclid is practical, but he isn't 'TRUE'; a science of knowledge cannot be hoped for come out of him [*sic*]";[70] or, as Metzinger insists over against those who denounce the new painting's apparently nonfigurative side, since the *quattrocento* school, since the appearance of treatises on perspective, the academic painters are the ones who find themselves in the wrong: "Exaggerating relief and depth, painters exerted themselves to create an absurd, theatrical space, in which a path's edges meet at one point, preventing you from walking on, in which a vase's circular opening becomes a simple straight line, in which all the imperfections of our visual mechanics are consecrated, and all this with the puerile intention of bringing a supplementary dimension to what, since the time of chaos, counts but two."[71] A remarkable text, in which the interest in a new realism, profounder than that of all past and surpassed forms of figurative art,* converges with it in a

---

* On perspective as a "lie," as the art of deformation and of appearance, cf. Jean Paulhan: "It is also known that brute vision would have us see (as in a photo) the nearer objects much bigger, but the more distant ones much smaller, than a utilitarian vision, rectified at every instant by our mind, shows them to us. In a word, if there is a truth of sight, perspective seems to have no other purpose, through its conventions and ready-made ideas, than to hide this truth. I have—with all the perspectivists—said that, against things, it took the side of their appearance. But that is to say too little. It takes, moreover, against their immediate and sensible appearance the side of their abstract and cold appearance, and treats all objects as if they did not interest us" (*Sur le cubisme*, p. 96). Conclusion: we must therefore, together with the cubist painters, attack "the very lie of trompe-l'œil; the *conventional space* it uses, the glass prison in which it cleverly tries to enclose us—attack that in it that is false in its very essence" (ibid., p. 100; see also pp. 88, 104, 105, etc.).

return to the bidimensionality implied in the plastic interpretation of the new geometries.

We can now better understand in what sense this new classicism counterbalances—at least among the early avant-gardes, those of the very beginning of this century—an undeniable tendency toward "ultraindividualism." For, according to this realism of ideas, the break with tradition aims at more than just freeing the individual, at conquering the new for the sake of the new. Seventeenth-century classicism was also a "realism of ideas," it also claimed to give expression to the essence of things; contemporary painters must try to fulfill its project while leading it, so to speak, beyond itself. What non-Euclidean geometries (in the larger sense, including four-dimensional geometries) demonstrated in their eyes was that what the classicists had held to be the essence of the real and had tried to render through perspective is still only an appearance. In other words, if we may assert that, in their eyes, Euclidean *space* is but an illusion that has to be abandoned for the truth of a *hyperspace,* we can, by analogy, say just as well that *classicism* must in its turn be replaced and furthered by a *hyperclassicism.*

The terminology is not forced. If we follow out Metzinger's line of thought, it could have been agreed upon by cubism's most eminent representatives:

> Cubism, whose influence extends out to its worst adversaries, has not, since 1912, ceased, true to itself, to approach the real by profound paths. If the word *surrealism* had not been appropriated to designate a different movement "I believe," Picasso told me recently, "that it would have defined my painting." . . . Indeed, cubism exceeds the exterior thing the better to envelop it and grasp it. Observing the model is not enough; the painter has to think. He transports it into a simultaneously spiritual and plastic space, about which it is not altogether light-headed to speak of a fourth dimension." (*Du cubisme,* 1946 Afterword, pp. 80–82)

As Boileau would have put it:

> Le Vrai seul est beau, le vrai seul est aimable,
> Il doit regner partout et même dans la fable.

> The True alone is beautiful, it alone is lovable,
> It must govern everywhere and even in the fable.

with the proviso that, at the beginning of the twentieth century, the true is no longer ascribed to the *harmony* in which the classicists saw or thought to see the essence, the "nature" of the real.

Like neoclassicism's purest theoreticians (see chap. 2, above), the avant-garde painters Severini evokes willingly reappropriate the idea that the work of art's capacity to have *universal* value, and not simply value for such and such specific individuals, lies in its scientific objectivity, in its exclusion of the imaginary (of the genius) in favor of the intelligent:

The work of plastic art will not be autonomous and universal unless it maintains its deep attachment to reality; it will be a reality in itself, more alive, more intense and more true than the real objects [since, as with the classicists, it expresses their *essence*—L.F.] that it may represent, that it may reconstruct, as long as the elements that compose it belong neither to the arbitrary, nor to whim, nor imagination, nor to decorative good taste [for] our art does not aspire to represent a *fiction* of reality, but wishes to express this reality as it is. ("Le Peinture d'avant-garde," pp. 454–65)

The interpretation of modernism put forward by Bell, despite its pertinence for the analysis of avant-garde form, is incapable of accounting for the new constraints and new rules that the avant-gardes impose on themselves at the level of content. It will perhaps be objected that that remark applies mainly to cubism. But even if this limitation were to be admitted—and it would have to be proved, the "scientific" component in abstract or surrealist art, though more flexible, is nonetheless quite real—it cannot be denied that in many ways cubism incarnates the ideal type of the avant-garde movement.

It may be more pertinently objected that there is quite a bit of paradox in claiming to discern a "classical" or even "hyperclassical" component in forms of art in which everything, apparently, is opposed to seventeenth-century classicism. In the latter, the goal assigned art was to represent the essence of a nature that was, since Descartes, held to be *rationally* and *harmoniously* established. In the eyes of the classicists, to "imitate nature" was to imitate whatever nature had that was identical, eternal, and stable, beyond the apparent diversity of its sensuous manifestations. When Molière pretends to "paint after nature" and make "public mirrors" out of his comedies, it is because he intends to unveil the essence of man through the presentation of archetypes—the miser, the misanthrope, etc.—that unify the specific diversity of individuals. Therefore this definition of beauty, found in treatises on the Beautiful from Leibniz to Crousaz: "Unity in plurality is nothing other than harmony, and it is from the fact that a thing agrees with this other thing and not with any other that emerges the beauty that awakes love."[72]

Isn't avant-garde art the very contrary of this classicism that aims at identity and harmony? Doesn't it go after "distortion, dispersion, difference, and exteriority to every form," rather than "the rule, the synthesis, the beautiful totality, the thing lost or recovered, the fulfillment of unifying eros"?[73]

In the first letter he wrote to one who was to become his friend, but who here is still addressed with deference as "Professor Schoenberg," Kandinsky insists with all his energy, "Precisely, I believe that we cannot today find our harmony through 'geometrical' paths, but, on the contrary, through the most absolute anti-geometry, anti-logic. This is the way of 'dissonances in art'—in painting as in music" (*Correspondence*, p. 154). However imprecise,[74] the parallel Kandinsky establishes between pictorial and musical "dissonances" is so significant it will be taken up again by the most authorized theoreticians, notably by Pierre Boulez, in an article significantly entitled "Parallels" (*Contrechamps*, no. 2 [1984], p. 154), "I would readily place the emancipation of tonality in parallel with the emancipation of the object or of the subject." And in the same vein, Adorno wrote, "Modern painting's turn away from the representation of objects (*Gegenständlichkeit*) points to the same rupture there as atonality is in music . . . what was valid before this break, the constitution of musical contexts through tonality, is irremediably lost."[75]

Dissonance, atonality, illogicality, rupture, difference: those are the key words preferred by the painters and musicians of the first avant-gardes in their theoretical writings. What is new in the reality cubism wishes to represent, according to Gleizes, is that in it that is shocking compared to a traditional, "logical, classical, Euclidean" image of the world.[76] And Metzinger adds that modern painters, "conscious of the miracle that takes place when the canvas evokes space, as soon as the line threatens to take on a descriptive, decorative importance, they break it up."[77]

If we were to pursue this parallel between new painting and new music we would see how the latter aims at putting an end to all the reference points and all the factors of identity that make up the tonal system, so as to open the way for a music of *pure difference* that in its most radical principle excludes any "pole of attraction," thus bringing forth in the listener the feeling of a "nonidentifiable" music that is almost impossible to reproduce mentally, the way one hums the "melodies" of the "classical" repertoire. René Leibowitz, who, through his teaching, initiated a group of young French composers—Boulez, Philip-

pot, Martinet, Rigg . . . to the principles of Schoenbergian dodeca-
phony, points this out with a certain vehemence in his *Introduction à la
musique de douze sons* [*Introduction to Twelve-Tone Music*]: "Consciously or through bad faith, most contemporary musicians remain the
slaves of what I would call a certain *musical psychologism. Without
even speaking of those who wallow in an odious hedonism,* it is a fact
that what hinders certain so-called "advanced" composers from taking
the decisive step toward the new musical language is their, I would say,
atavistic fear of writing 'something not beautiful.'"[78]

The point is then to break with all the "classical" representations
of the idea of the beautiful, understood as the *harmonious* synthesis of
a multiplicity of sounds. "It is enough," Leibowitz adds, "to listen to
the music or to read Schoenberg's theoretical work to realize that such
considerations no longer have any place in musical art. The *Treatise on
Harmony* [Schoenberg's major work] is full of passages in which the
author rebels against the tendency to qualify such and such an aggregate as 'beautiful' and such other as 'ugly,' appreciations that issue out
of a false and confused 'psychologism'" (ibid.).

The very idea of beauty is without meaning. It cannot therefore
provide any kind of principle of orientation for the artist, nor can the
"odious" idea of aesthetic pleasure. Thus tonality, with the reconciliation, the supersession [*Aufhebung*] of dissonances that it always allows,
still thinks difference against a background of identity; it is with a certain perceptiveness that Leibowitz remarks how "Schoenberg's attitude
participates in the radical movement of contemporary thought, and resembles Husserl's phenomenology" (ibid.).

On their side, phenomenologists won't fail to see this either, and
will look upon "modern art" as an attempt at going past the classical
visions of the beautiful, of the harmonious synthesis, with the aim of
negatively presenting the nonpresentable, whether it be designated as
the "Invisible" (Merleau-Ponty) or as "Difference" (Heidegger). "I
would call modern," writes Jean-François Lyotard, "the art that dedicates its little technique, as Diderot used to say, to presenting the fact
that there is the nonpresentable. Make us see there is something one can
conceive and neither see nor bring to seeing: that is what is at stake in
modern painting."[79] The "pictorial avant-gardes" thus aim at "allud-
ing to the nonpresentable through visible presentations" (ibid., p. 28).
Once again, to that extent, isn't the avant-garde the very opposite of
classicism?

I accept the objection and, as I have said, were the expression not so vague, I would readily adopt the definition Lyotard proposes here of "modern art." Besides, isn't the fourth dimension the very symbol of this invisible thing whose idea has been *negatively* presented, or attempted, through two-dimensional projections? Isn't it the analogue for the hidden facets of the cube the phenomenologists also use as a metaphor for Being or Difference?

And yet, *how can we not see that the essential aspect of classicism remains, that the project of "rendering the real," of gaining access to it, albeit by indirect methods, subsists?* Moreover—and this is the reason I spoke of hyperclassicism—did not the avant-gardes claim, with the new realism they were setting into motion, to be more realistic than the classicists were, therefore, in a way, more classicist than the latter were themselves? Commenting on Malevitch's famous black square, Andrei Nakov remarks in his Introduction to the painter's *Writings* that "the notion of free plane constitutes one of the cornerstones of his conception of a new logic." And the latter, he adds, is incomprehensible if not brought into relation with the fourth dimension: "The purely conceptual relation of *our* logic to another—superior—one is symbolically illustrated by the choice of bidimensional projections of a reality whose existence we only partially perceive. These *surfaces* only represent the 'façade' of a four-dimensional object, the way a bidimensional figure represents the only projection into another dimension of a three-dimensional geometric body" (p. 87). Isn't this a concrete way of illustrating what I have here called hyperclassicism, meaning a classicism of difference and no longer of identity or, to speak as Lyotard does, a classicism that seeks to "present that there is the nonpresentable"? As with the classicists, doesn't avant-garde art continue to be guided by the project of imitating a real that has meanwhile ceased to be defined as *order*, but which nonetheless remains the artist's "objective"?

Indeed, we can't forget that one of the principal motives for the abandonment of Euclidean space for the one indicated by the new geometries lies in the idea that the habitual space, in Gleizes's formulation, "is not true" but only "comfortable." As Jean Paulhan puts it, "I can see traditional space's advantage: it lets us live in a simple world, where events take place in proper order . . . There is only one problem, and that is that it does not *resemble*. It does not in the least resemble, I won't even say nocturnal space, but our everyday space, with all its differences and all its chaos" (*Sur le cubisme*, p. 104).

We have therefore to distinguish, at the heart of the early avant-gardes, between two divergent, not to say contradictory moments: the

will, on the one hand—elitist, historicist, and "ultraindividualistic"—
to break with tradition to create the radically new; but, on the other,
the no less remarkable project of leading classical aesthetics to their
logical end, of taking them to their limits in the name of a new realism
that, however much it may be oriented to the expression of what reality—whether internal or external does not matter much—may contain that is chaotic and "different," remains all the same bound to the
intelligence more than to the imaginary and, to that extent, accepts new
constraints and new rules.

It is this duality that has led me to judge the interpretative frameworks that refer back to individualism to be too narrow. And yet it is
the duality that we have to try and understand if we wish to glimpse the
nature of the specifically contemporary phenomenon the avant-gardes
constitute. One of Apollinaire's texts puts forward a hypothesis:

> Greek art had of beauty a purely human conception. It took man to be the
> measure of perfection. The art of the new painters takes the infinite universe as
> its ideal, and it is to this ideal that we owe a new measurement of perfection
> permitting the painter to give the object the proportions befitting the degree of
> plasticity he wishes to give to it. Nietzsche had intuited the possibility of such
> an art . . . Using Dionysus as mouthpiece, Nietzsche passes judgment on Greek
> art. (*Les Peintres cubistes*, p. 52)

The Greek art Nietzsche criticized in the name of the Dionysiac is
the art of consciousness, of identity, of order, of the visible, and the
Dionysiac symbolizes chaos, fracture, difference, and intoxication. We
may recall how, in one of the *Gay Science*'s most celebrated paragraphs,
Nietzsche defined the "new infinite" to which Apollinaire perhaps
alluded:

> the human intellect cannot avoid seeing itself in its own perspectives, and only
> in these. We cannot look around our own corner . . . But I should think that
> today we are at least far from the ridiculous immodesty that would be involved
> in decreeing from our corner that perspectives are permitted only from this
> corner. Rather has the world become "infinite" for us all over again, inasmuch
> as we cannot reject the possibility that it may *include infinite interpretations*.
> Once more we are seized by a great shudder.[80]

The sense of Nietzsche's discovery is clear: it works toward liberating thought from the illusion inherent to the unique point of view, to
the idea that there is supposed to be an *absolute truth*. This "moment"
of Nietzsche's thinking thematizes the possibility of what I have here

designated as the avant-gardes' "ultraindividualism," that is to say their absolute freedom with respect to norms, with respect to the habitual, traditional definitions of truth. That is indeed the significance of the "new infinite": perspectivism, the infinite multiplicity of viewpoints that cannot, as in Leibniz's definition of harmonious beauty, be reduced to the identity of a unique point of view.

Perspectivism therefore signals the end of the classical perspective. But the project of attaining the real cannot thereby be abandoned, even if the real is life, with its radical multiplicity of forces and points of view. Whether as such it can be reduced to unity is one thing; that we should give up trying to seize it is another, and Nietzsche, in a formula that foreshadows cubism, exhorts us to see the world "with the greatest possible number of eyes."

Apollinaire suggests, through the juxtaposition he makes between the avant-gardes and Nietzsche's philosophy, that the "new painters'" project is inseparable from a certain conception of human subjectivity. What Nietzsche formulates in his philosophy and what the artists spontaneously invent or reinvent, is the idea that the subject can no longer be reduced to consciousness, that it is a fractured subject and that the era of the "cogito," of the "I think"'s closed in upon themselves under the hegemony of consciousness, is over. Schönberg writes to Kandinsky: "Every search that tends to produce a traditional effect is more or less marked by the intervention of consciousness. But art belongs to the unconscious."[81] It is this conception of the unconscious that is formulated by Nietzsche, before anyone else perhaps, in his critique of philosophies of the cogito. This conception introduces into the history of subjectivity (or of individualism, if we wish to keep the term) a rupture comparable to that represented by atonality or the rejection of Euclidean perspective. It is this conception that should be considered in parallel with the emergence, symbolized by the fourth dimension, of a new representation of the real as a real that is also fractured and chaotic.

Much was at stake here and remains so today, for each of the basic facets of modern aesthetics carries an obvious danger with it. On the one hand, ultraindividualism risks foundering in a dialectical contradiction in which it wears itself out in the empty repetition of the gesture of rupture and creation of the new. Literally obsessed by historicist consciousness, by the imperative of originality when faced with a history of art, the artist ceases to be a "genius," a free and unconscious creator. Confronted with the demand for originality, he must integrate into his work a reflection on tradition which risks leading him to the privileging of consciousness over the unconscious, mastery over the genius's freedom; his work becomes a meta-work, his aesthetic reflection a meta-reflection. Since imitation or repetition tend to become the sin against taste par excellence, in fact the only one that is unanimously so regarded, the artist, who believed himself to be finally free from rules and constraints see himself subjected to the constraint of constraints, the one imposed by his own historical consciousness. In our day, postmodernism is timidly attempting to abolish this new prison. In this it is not at all the comeback of historicity (contrary to what Felix Torres argues in the book he dedicates to postmodernism) but, on the contrary, the naïve attempt to break free of it by proclaiming the right to reestablish links with the past. I very much doubt that this could be a "solution." It is at best a symptom of the impasse ultraindividualism leads to.

And, on the other hand, hyperclassicism carries the risks of any classicism within itself. When it declines, realism, even of a new kind, even if it is a realism of "Difference," also becomes academic. Art is given the "mission" of embodying a vision of the world, a conception of the real, and, here again, paradoxically, it falls under the hegemony of consciousness and of intelligence.

This opposition between "subjectivist" and "objectivist" tendencies is not new.[82] It stands in fact at the origin of aesthetics as a philosophical discipline, and we were able to discern its premises in the conflict opposing rationalist aesthetics and aesthetics of sentiment during the Age of Reason. It is from this very opposition that postmodernism is trying to liberate itself today.

Nietzsche, who was perhaps modernity's true prophet, announced it in one of the most beautiful pages of *Morgenröte* [*The Dawn*]: from now on, authentic grandeur would not be satisfied with the mere display of power, with the visible and objective manifestation of its drives. For those who can see it, it lies in the individual more than in his productions, "in the spectacle of that strength which employs genius *not for works* but for *itself as a work;* that is, for its own constraint, for the purification of its imagination, for the imposition of order and choice upon the influx of tasks and impressions" (§ 548, Colli-Montinari ed.). The "grand style"—Foucault understood this so well he consecrated his last writings to the subject—is nothing other than the "care of the self": a care that is not to be confused with mere "egoism," but which is not connected either (at least not in unmediated fashion) to the libertarian-anarchist project of liberation from institutionalized forms of "repression"; which implies, on the contrary, a most rigorous discipline in effort, for the purpose of shaping one's existence the way an artist would a sculpture.

In the contemporary universe, characterized by the "withdrawal from the world" whose history is reflected in that of aesthetics, the tension between the work of art's subjective and objective moments tends to fade away to the benefit of the subjective. After the era of the avant-gardes comes that of "postmodernity." The expression is, of course, far from having been unanimously adopted, and its uses are so various that at times they are diametrically opposed. But, to the extent that the semantic problem is not without importance, its assumptions can here be usefully reviewed.

THE THREE MEANINGS OF "POSTMODERN"

The term first seems to appear in the sixties, used by certain American literary critics to designate fictional works that aim to break with—the model here being William Burroughs—the first modernism, and in particular with Joyce. This is the sense in which the expression is employed in Ihab Hassan's book *The Dismemberment of Orpheus: Toward a Postmodern Literature* (1971). But it has to be perceived that this new rupture sees itself as an extension, not a questioning, of avant-gardism. As the British critic Charles Jencks—who truly popularized the notion—points out, among these sophisticated theoreticians postmodernism is still applied to the search for novelty for novelty's sake, ending up in fact in "ultramodernism."[83] But this is, according to Jencks, the preoccupation that must be left behind. For him, as for the architects he gathers under the banner of the postmodern—Graves, Venturi, Rossi, Ungers, Bofill, Hollein and a few others—the point is to put an end to the tyranny of innovation at any price, of finally granting oneself the right to reestablish the links with the past. The conflict of interpretations is, as we can see, such as to call for clarification.

1. The Postmodern as Summit of Modernism

If by "modernism" we understand, following Anglo-American usage, the twentieth-century's avant-gardes or what we ordinarily call "modern art," the postmodern appears to be, on first approach, an exacerbation of the modern. Why then, in such circumstances, speak of "post-" rather than "ultra-" modernism?

To understand, we have to recall that modernity, for most contemporary philosophers, designates what Heidegger called "humanism," that is, essentially the rationalism stemming from Descartes, and notably, of course, the philosophy of the Enlightenment and its technico-scientific fallout. Understood this way, modernity is not to be confused with "modernism." The latter in many ways seeks to break off from the illusions—in particular those of a clear and distinct cogito and of a "euclidean" order—that have weighed so heavily on the "metaphysics of subjectivity" and through them on the history of art. The postmodern would then have to be understood as the indication of a break with the Enlightenment, with the idea of Progress that holds that scientific discoveries and, more generally, the rationalization of the world ipso facto represent a liberation for humanity. According to this first definition, Nietzsche, Heidegger, or Freud, since they lay down a challenge to the "philosophies of consciousness," are postmoderns just as much as Malevitch, Picasso, Kandinsky, Schoenberg, Berg, or Stockhausen. Simply put, when it opposes the project of modernity, in the meaning the Enlightenment gave it, the postmodern joins the "modern," understood as the avant-gardes' "modernism."

This is, most notably, the meaning one finds—with an explicit reference to "modern art" and to the "avant-gardes"—in the texts Jean-François Lyotard devoted to the analysis of the concept. As it did for Adorno, the deconstruction of the *Aufklärung*'s philosophical universe expresses itself in the most radical contemporary works, the ones that, according to Lyotard, deserve to be called "postmodern" because of their will to break with the primacy of rationality and of representation (Heidegger would have said, "presence"). The goal now is "to allude to the nonpresentable through visible presentations," to "show [*faire voir*] that there is some thing one can conceive of but neither see nor cause to see [*faire voir*]."[84] The postmodern consequently turns out to be a part of the modern, in the sense the word takes in "modern art." It designates the *philosophical* rejection of representation, of which the rejection of tonality and of figuration are supposed to provide aesthetic translations. In Lyotard's vocabulary, "I would call modern the art that applies its 'bit of technique,' as Diderot used to say, to presenting the fact that there is the nonpresentable" or, in other, just as easily identifiable domains, to "show" that there is something invisible in the visible, absence within presence, Being beyond beings, difference hidden by identity, etc.—which is why Lyotard can conclude that the postmodern "is surely a part of the modern," in that "everything that has been perceived, even if only yesterday . . . must be suspected." This suspicious attitude is in turn expressed in the indefinite succession of ruptures and innovations that have marked the history of the avant-gardes: "What kind of space did Cézanne set out to attack? The Impressionists'. And Picasso and Braque: what kind of object? Cézanne's. What presupposition did Duchamp break with in 1912? That a painting has to be made, even if it is a cubist one. And Buren questions another presupposition, that he thinks remained intact in Duchamp's work: that the work needs a site, a place for its presentation. Astounding acceleration; the generations rush forward" (pp. 29–30).

We have seen that this "acceleration" that fascinates Lyotard is not in fact very astounding, implicit as it is in the best known and most observed dynamic logic of democratic societies, which ceaselessly tend toward innovation and the erosion of traditions. But that is not important here. On the semantic level—the only one that interests me for the moment—we may note that modern and postmodern are clearly installed by Lyotard within one and the same genre which he (inadvertently?) calls "avant-gardist history," supposedly the incontestable site (we shall see that it isn't that simple, far from it) of subversion of modernity in the sense of *Aufklärung*. The difference between this history's two constitutive moments—the modern and the postmodern—is infinitesimal or downright inessential. In the project of presenting the nonpresentable, of demonstrating the invisible, we can either stress the attempt's failure (since it has, by definition, a paradoxical aspect) or on the contrary the innovative power of the faculties it calls into play (the model for this analysis then being found in Kant's theory of the sublime). The modern would then comprise "melancholy," and the postmodern, "*novatio*" [innovation].

Lyotard explains: "You will understand what I mean through the cartoon-like distribution of a few names on the playing field of avant-gardist history: on the side of *melancholy*, the German expressionists; on the novatio side, Braque and Picasso. On the first Malevitch, on the second Lissitzky; on one de Chirico, on the other Duchamp" (ibid.)—whereby we see that moderns and postmoderns are equally "antimodern" in their common opposition to the "Cartesian," enlightened, and rationalist heritage; they each indicate a way to translate the desire or necessity to not naïvely install oneself within representation. Postmodernism can even be said to be even more "modern," even more "deconstructive" than "modern art." It is its quintessence, which is why the "post" does not here have any chronological meaning: "The postmodern is that which in the modern alleges the nonpresentable within

SIX

presentation itself, that which refuses the consolation of proper forms" (ibid.) and thus resolutely, "joyously," takes over the concern with innovation that was constitutive of the avant-gardes.

We can no doubt begin to glimpse what ambiguities may be nourished by the notion of postmodernity:

—On the strictly terminological level, it will have antinomic meanings according to whether the "modern" it refers back to (and it must refer back to it if it is to be its "post-") indicates Enlightenment rationalism or its avant-gardist deconstructions.

—More to the point, perhaps, another problem, strangely ignored by Lyotard, has to do with the fact that the Enlightenment and its radical critique within the philosophic or aesthetic avant-garde are far from being diametrically opposed. The emergence of nonfiguration and of atonality are doubtlessly fractures in the history of art that one can, if one wishes, call "postmodern." A continuationist history is here certainly untenable. It nevertheless remains the case that, as we have seen, the avant-gardes in many respects also carry on the revolutionary project of innovation (of the tabula rasa), that they willingly nourish themselves on scientific or philosophical theories, and that they thereby join fully in the enlightening and rationalist modernity they may otherwise claim to divorce from.

This fundamental ambiguity must be kept in mind to understand the second meaning of postmodern, the only one, truth to tell, that has gone well beyond the small circle of professionals of philosophy to become a "cultural unit of communication."

2. The Postmodern as "Return" to Tradition: Against Modernism

The tyranny of innovation has played itself out and, from about the middle of the 1970s, we are witness to a vast movement, especially in architecture, of reaction against the ultramodernism of the 1950s, itself heir to the modernism of the twenties. The movement now goes, as in the title of one of Tom Wolfe's books, *From Bauhaus to Our House.* Humor is more at hand than the messianism of the avant-gardes, as we see in the way Charles Jencks writes up their obituary: "Modern architecture died in St. Louis, Missouri, on July 15, 1972, at 3:32 P.M. (or thereabouts), when the infamous Pruitt-Igoe scheme, or rather several of its slab blocks, were given the coup-de-grâce by dynamite . . . Boom! Boom! Boom!" (*The Language of Postmodern Architecture*, p. 9). Need it be recalled that "Pruitt-Igoe," built in the Bauhaus low-cost-housing-style, and winner of a 1951 prize awarded by the International Modern

Architecture Congress, was one of this architecture's most impressive symbols, "like the Berlin Wall and the collapse of the high-rise block Ronan Point, in England, in 1968"? (ibid., p. 9).

In its second meaning, postmodern thus designates the result of the dialectical contradiction affecting the very principle of the will, ceaselessly reactivated to produce the new for the sake of the new. Confronted with the new academicism such a constraint has engendered, architects, in Jenck's analysis, "began again to run the gamut of the repertoire in order to try and communicate with the public: metaphor, ornament, polychromy, convention," but also their right to renew aesthetic traditions that might be distant from the architectural creator, whether in terms of cultural space or of temporality (the return to the past, for example, of Ancient Greece or of medieval villages, as in "revivalism," or, on the contrary, the presence of the new in an old neighborhood, as in Paris's Beaubourg/Centre Pompidou).

Defined this way, postmodernity has, indeed, rapidly reached all the other artistic domains. Much of contemporary painting has rediscovered the pleasures of figuration, and "high" music, though it most often remains atonal, has explicitly broken with the serial imperialism of the 1950s. We therefore have to speak of a work's postmodernity in a sense entirely opposed to the first meaning. But we have to go further: it is not only isolated aesthetic creations which could be called postmodern, as others are classic or modern, but rather the present historical period as a whole. For the most characteristic trait of the culture we bathe in today is without a doubt its eclecticism. In principle, everything can cohabit within it, or, if one prefers putting it in a way that conforms even more to the spirit of the times, nothing in the culture is a priori illegitimate. Every style, every historical period benefits from the "right to difference"—including, in the Italian Transavant-garde, avant-gardist productions themselves. Nothing is ruled out, neither a collaboration between Pierre Boulez and Frank Zappa nor matching blue jeans with a tuxedo jacket. Aggrippine, Claire Bretecher's comic-strip teenager, studies for her French high school finals while leafing through a comic book titled *Heidegger in the Congo*.

3. Postmodernity as Supersession of Modernism

Though the second meaning of postmodernity seems to be a paradoxical but logical consequence of the first—avant-gardism's dialectical self-destruction giving rise to its "determinate negation"—we can allow ourselves to envision a going-beyond of modernism that does not take the Hegelian form of an *Aufhebung*. To this we have been invited, for some years now, by the various philosophical undertakings which, in Germany as in France, are trying to elaborate anew, after the avant-gardist deconstructions of rationality and subjectivity, a renewed, more differentiated and nuanced, conception of reason and of the subject. Along these lines, I think I can subscribe to the postmodern project such as it is described by Albrecht Wellmer, a thinker close to Habermas:

> Against rationalism as a whole, we have to object that we cannot expect from it either final justifications or definitive solutions. But that does not mean that we have to say goodbye to democratic universalism, nor that we have to give up on the Marxian project of an autonomous society, nor give up on reason. It means, rather, that Enlightenment universalism, and the ideas of individual and collective self-determination, and of reason and history, have to be thought through again. In the attempt to do *that* I see an authentic "postmodern" impulse towards an autosupersession of reason.[85]

It is, it seems to me, from an analogous perspective that the present contribution to the history of modern subjectivity has been conceived: as the necessary positive addendum (since one cannot be contented forever with "neither-nor") to the critique of the philosophical avant-gardism of the 1960s as it was carried out in *La Pensée 68*.

In what follows, I will leave aside postmodernity's first and third meanings and concentrate on the second, which alone, in reality, occupies a visible place in contemporary culture, proportionate to the importance of the social phenomenon it points to. It seems clear that the eclecticism Jencks describes raises decisive questions within the perspective of a history of aesthetics understood as a history of modern culture (i.e., "subjective" or individualist culture). It forces us in particular to face up to the intimidating problem not so much of decline per se as of the significance and meaning of this theme today. It is indeed difficult to see how our historical consciousness, which has not stopped growing in the last two centuries, to the point that it now, in the guise of historicism, bathes in its light every aspect of contemporary culture, could accommodate itself to the idea that we could now do without the new. It is doubtful under such circumstances that we could explicitly give up innovation without the threat of a real or supposed "decadence" finding expression in such a way that it would delegitimize the postmodern *Stimmung*, which would then be suspected of being, at best, empty of meaning and creative energy and, at worst, reactionary. After the end of utopias and the great narratives, are we today witnessing that of great works of art? That is the interrogation we cannot avoid today, like it or not.

The theme, far from being new, is as old as modernity. It comes back periodically, following a logic inherent to the very functioning of a democratic universe that ceaselessly secretes its own antidotes. What is different today is that the idea of a decline of the liberal worldview is put forward ever more insistently by authors who are, in other respects, at the very opposite of traditional counterrevolutionary right-wing ideas. I would like to comment on one of these "left" critiques of liberalism, namely, the one Cornelius Castoriadis has developed in the texts he has consecrated to aesthetics and to the state of contemporary culture, the better to make out the reasons for the diagnosis that has it that we are witnessing, at the end of the twentieth century, the exhaustion of Western culture.

THE END OF INNOVATION: DECLINE OF THE WEST?

Castoriadis's position deserves our interest. Among those who hold the modern world in contempt he is no doubt one of the most radical, yet his attachment to the values he calls democratic is no more to be doubted than his rejection of the ideological pathos that weighs on the work of a Spengler or, on another level, of a Heidegger.

His works evince a certain vehemence against the "platitudes," "ineptitude," "futility," "intellectual dishonesty," etc., characteristic of the contemporary period, as we can observe on reading the very first pages of the preface to *Carrefours du labyrinthe II* [*Crossroads in the Labyrinth*, vol. 2]. This is how Castoriadis describes our times: "Comic epoch—excremental perhaps? No, excrements fertilize the soil, the epoch's products pollute and sterilize it—of prostitution? No, why insult those women; epoch that disarms every epithet . . ." In the artistic realm, every creation worthy of the name supposedly disappeared around 1930: what was "done over half a century ago" by Schönberg, Webern, and Berg; Kandinsky, Mondrian, and Picasso; Proust, Kafka, and Joyce; Reinhardt, Meyerhold, or Piscator. Since then, "they pretend to make revolutions by copying and making bad pastiches—thanks also to the ignorance of a hypercivilized and neo-illiterate public—of the last great moments of Western culture." The conclusion is, in a word, obvious: "Contemporary culture is, as a first approximation, a zilch [nulle]."[86]

This at least has the merit of being said, and written, without beating around the bush. To drive the point home, Castoriadis asks us to make two mental experiments, after whose conclusion the nullity of culture today could not possibly be doubted any more.

The first would consist in asking "the most notorious, the most celebrated of contemporary creators this question, eye-to-eye: Do you sincerely consider yourself to be at the same mountain height as Bach, Mozart, or Wagner, as Jan Van Eyck, Velazquez, Rembrandt, or Picasso, as Brunelleschi, Michelangelo, or Frank Lloyd Wright, as Shakespeare, Rimbaud, Kafka, or Rilke?" From how many contemporaries would a positive response *not* make us smile? (Ibid.)

Second experiment: Whereas the ruins of the Acropolis, when they were destroyed by the Persians, were used to level out the ground so as to build the foundations of the Parthenon and the new temples, "if Notre Dame Cathedral were destroyed by a bomb," can we imagine "for a moment that the French would do something other than piously gather up the debris, try to restore it, or leave the ruins as they are?" (Ibid., p. 45.)

Indeed, a hard question, and one that leads to another: that concerning the status of culture in a democratic society (I use the term here, in its Tocquevillian sense, and not in the "self-management" [*autogestionnaire*] sense given it by Castoriadis). Is it through sheer optical illusion, out of lack of "historical distance," that we hesitate to put contemporary works at the same level as those of other centuries?—a phenomenon that is all the more strange in that it is not necessarily tied to the purely subjective pleasure usually called "taste" ("pop" music is much like what wordgames were for Freud: the honest person has to learn to give it up, even if with regrets). Or is there in fact something wrong with our culture, a loss of individual creative power within the liberal universe—and, under these circumstances, how are we to interpret it?

As we have probably already guessed, Castoriadis's answer consists in choosing with assurance the second of these two alternatives. In this "bureaucratic society," that outlived itself until the 1930s to then become manifestly absurd, what has to be challenged is the very status of our relation to values. Now that they have been finally unmasked, liberal "values" (we will see in a moment why quotation marks have to be used) are, at best, nonexistent. The activity of individuals in this society is essentially oriented toward "the antagonistic maximization of consumption, power, status, and prestige (the only objects of social investment pertinent today)." They are, on the one hand (and at least on this point Castoriadis's analysis follows Heidegger's), handed over to a social functioning that is itself "subjected to the imaginary signification of the unlimited expansion of 'rational' mastery (technology, science, production, organizations as ends in themselves)." And, to satisfy the demands put upon them in this "world of technology," they must constantly withdraw into the narrowness of a private sphere, about which it is little enough to say that it is disenchanted. The technical pseudo-mastery, "at the same time vaine, empty, and intrinsically contradictory . . . can only constrain human beings to put themselves at its service through the deployment, cultivation, and socially efficient utilisation of essentially 'egoistic' motivations, in a mode of socialization in which cooperation and community are only considered and only exist from an instrumental and utilitarian point of view" (p. 36).

It is thus clear that the supposed "liberal values" in fact lead to the collapse of every value, and that capitalist society is the very example of one that "believes in nothing [and] does not truly value anything unconditionally," since mastery over the natural world refers back to nothing but itself (Heidegger called it "will to will"). How could there, in these conditions, be a truly innovative creation? Indeed, the work of art—meaning here the great work—"maintains a strange relation with the values of society, it doubts and questions them"; in more trivial terms, it is subversive, "its intensity and its grandeur are inseparable from a commotion, a vacillation that can only come about if and only if meaning is well established, if values are solidly founded and are lived as such" (ibid.). But it is this very solidity that is always being ruined by the liberal universe, to the extent that it gives way to a cynical relativism that gives every indication, according to Castoriadis, of being what shapes the mentality of what represents itself to itself as today's cultural elite. The dramatization of absurdity and of the tragic aspect of existence in *Hamlet* and *Oedipus the King* could and did legitimately jolt, perhaps elevate their publics; how could this same absurdity, so dear nonetheless to contemporary theater, still shake anything up now that "there is no pole of nonabsurdity against which it could, by opposition, strongly reveal itself as absurdity"? (Ibid.)

Under such circumstances the forms characteristic of great art, whether popular or not, disappear. The essential relation between work and public vanishes first of all, just as towards the end of the nineteenth century the distinction emerges between the philistine's and the artist's lives, with its inevitable correlate: the "avant-garde" public. Thereafter it is genres which wear themselves out so manifestly one can legitimately ask "whether the form 'novel,' the form 'painting,' the form 'play,' are not outliving themselves. Finally, the work, understood as a "durable object, destined in principle to a temporally indefinite existence, individualizable, imputable, at least in principle, to an author, a milieu, a precise date" disappears in turn, replaced by "products" which share with the period's other products the trait of being destined not to last, not to have any certain author, and not to be "particularizable" any longer (we can, for example, bring to mind "chance" music).

It must be stressed that, despite appearances, Castoriadis is not at all interested in taking up again the too familiar theme of "the decline of the West." Not that the slogan, which has impregnated the "antimodern" deconstructions of liberalism from Spengler to Heidegger, is entirely false in its critical aspects; but, according to Castoriadis, it tends to "mask the potentialities of a new world that the decomposition of the 'West' posits and liberates." In other words, the collapse of liberal culture is not history's last word, a history that would have no other choice but to link up again with an origin lost in the world of tradition. On the contrary, it is the forerunner of the possible renewal of an authentic democratic culture: "What is dying today, what is, in any case, being profoundly challenged, is 'Western' culture: capitalist culture, the culture of capitalist society . . . What is being born—with difficulty, fragmentarily, and with contradictions—for the last two centuries and more, is the project of a new society, the project of social and individual autonomy" (ibid., p. 34).

We may wonder whether this encouraging forecast does not have more to do with wishfull thinking than with a real observation. Besides, Castoriadis himself points out that no one can predict the future and determine, a priori, "what the values of a new society will be, or create them in its stead." It is, rather, a matter of wagering that an autonomous society where autonomous individuals (the one cannot work without the other) could set up their own ways of life in common would open up a space that would render possible a reinvestment in collective values, therefore a renewal of the creative powers of individuals.

Well, why not? We can, and we should, always grant the benefit of the doubt, as a matter of principle. But if we want, as Castoriadis urges, to "look at what *is* with 'sober senses' and chase away illusions," then we have to admit that, starting out with the selfsame premises of the analysis we have just briefly outlined, another hypothesis—that, rushing things a bit, we can call "pessimistic"—seems to become much more obvious. If the crisis of contemporary culture consists essentially in the fact that in a liberal society the undergirding of values wears away to such an extent that all contestation (and the work of art is primarily contestation) becomes impossible because of the lack of a foil, how then not to conclude that it is well and truly a return to tradition, if it were possible, that could save us—rather than a democratization of the world, about which it is hard to see how it would not accelerate the movement of erosion already brought about by capitalism? A crucial point, especially if we add that it is on this point that Castoriadis differs from the neotraditionalist theories of the "decline of the West."

With a bit of reflection we can see that the whole problem comes down to knowing whether, from tradition's point of view, liberalism and democracy are or are not, at bottom, "the same thing": the same demand for autonomy that democracy, truth to tell, would only exacerbate, rendering the idea of a "firm foundation of values" even more problematic. Directly instituted by men, these values would perhaps be subjectively "stronger" (admitting for the moment that this project makes any sense); but, objectively, they would, by definition, fluctuate even more (because they would be subject to men's and women's immediate will) and be even less assured than they are in a representative system. The erosion of common traditions and values perhaps does not come, as Castoriadis believes, from some sort of disaffection from politics that is connected to liberalism, but from a demand for autonomy that could hardly, as far as we can see, be the remedy for a crisis of culture it itself has so powerfully contributed to bringing about. From this perspective (which could be elaborated on setting out from Marx as well as from de Tocqueville), what is characteristic of contemporary culture is less its "zilchness" than—precisely because it moves toward autonomy—its absence of reference to a shared world, its *Weltlosigkeit*.

SEVEN

The Problem of Ethics in an Age of Aesthetics

THE IDEOLOGIES OF DECLINE are a bad translation of an exact observation: we no longer live in an a priori common world. That does not mean, as is usually believed, that there are no longer any social bonds, nor that atomization and the age of the masses are the inevitable future for modern societies. It is simply the case that cohesion must from now on lie in interindividuality (to avoid saying intersubjectivity), and not in the transcendence provided by a cosmic reality that would be humanity's shared lot. We can now perhaps better understand, at the end of this history of aesthetics, why democratic culture, whose every part is oriented towards the withdrawal from this shared world, has a tendency to structure itself around three aspects: in the artistic realm, the work can no longer be anything other than an extension of the artist himself. To the extent that there still is a world, it can only be a microcosm engendered by the mini-demiurge called the genius. Objectivity continues to rule in the scientific realm, of course. The surest indication of this is the constraint over minds it still exerts there. But it has to be pointed out that objectivity is conceived of only in relation to the theoretical constructs produced by a subject. Where there is no subjectivity, there is no objectivity either, following a line of argument well developed by Heidegger and also, mutatis mutandis, by most contemporary epistemologists. "Nothing is given, everything is constructed," as Gaston Bachelard used to say.

History, finally, finishes the job of providing the individual with the knowledge lacking which he could never achieve autonomy, since he would remain forever a prisoner of the past. For the slow work of emancipation from traditions to be fulfilled, the past has to become *our* past. Only at the price of such an appropriation can it cease to appear as a determination, in essence hostile to the democratic demand for liberty.

The world is no longer our shared lot. This proposition is also an indication of the liquidation of the principles that were once the basis for ethics, without our yet being able to assess the full consequences of this. The ancient world considered justice as an art destined to bring about, in the city or the individual, the *order* within which each element finds the place and proportion due to it—a vision of the world whose trace has been conserved for philosophical language in the German word for justice, *Ur-teil:* originary share. It is along these lines that, for instance, Plato's *Gorgias* invites us to meditate on the analogy connecting the various disciplines that aim at establishing or restoring order. Gymnastics is thus to the body what legislation is to the soul, they both tend toward creating the harmony that results from a just proportion of parts, from a successful hierarchization of, in the one case, organs or muscles, and in the other, the three components of the human soul: intelligence, courage, and appetite (or of the three classes, artisans, warriors, and magistrates, that correspond to them in the structure of the city).

One can also compare medicine and justice: each one has for mission the restoration of what has been perturbed or shattered within its own sphere. The purpose is, in each case, to assign to every element the just share due to it within the microcosm and the macrocosm. How could such a sharing still be possible when, after the world's withdrawal, there is nothing substantial to share? That is, it seems to me, the question we are faced with in the ethical sphere when trying to take into account the paradox that modernity, by abandoning reference to a world, leads to associating the collapse of traditions to the ever-growing emergence of new existential questions.

The status of ethics, and especially of the *limits* that we have a right, at times perhaps a duty, to put on individual freedom, has never been as problematic as it is today. It is indeed hard to see how to set the rules for this very touchy game absent all objective reference, and this at the very time when progress in science and technology, we could also say, in the power of man over man, is raising more questions than ever before. Confronted with the withdrawal of the world, the temptation to restore lost traditions becomes strong, and the nostalgia for the past that is the most frequent companion of the ideologies of decline seems to be the obligatory concomitant to the anguish created by the disappearance of well-established reference points. In this respect, a historical approach to ethics appears necessary prior to any reflection that seeks to comprehend current events. It alone can permit us to understand the seductive aspect of the project to reactivate lost traditions—but also its absurd and dangerous aspects. It will be the subject of another book, but it is important here at least to glimpse what is at stake, in order to grasp in what way the history of subjectivity, reviewed, as I have tried to do here, using aesthetics as a starting point, converges with practical concerns.

THE THREE AGES OF ETHICS: EXCELLENCE, MERIT, AND AUTHENTICITY

The opposition between ancient and modern is habitually dealt with as if it overlapped perfectly with that between hierarchy and equality. From Alexis de Tocqueville to Louis Dumont or Leo Strauss, analyses stemming from quite different intellectual perspectives converge upon this observation: the universe of the Greeks, closed, hierarchical, and finalized, does as a matter of fact seem at every point contrary to the one that seems evident to us after Galileo's and Newton's discoveries and, especially, after the upheavals occasioned by the French Revolution and the explicit appearance of an egalitarian ideology. Such a presentation of the case is, no doubt, generally exact. But it does not for all that hinder certain confusions. The point is often made against it, as if it were a serious counterargument, that there are examples of equality in the world of antiquity and, even more obviously, of inequality in the modern world. A misunderstanding is at work here, one that must be cleared up prior to any correct understanding of that which most profoundly differentiates the moral vision of the ancients from that of the moderns—let us say, to respectively evoke their two most brilliant philosophical thematizations, the *Nicomachean Ethics* from the *Critique of Practical Reason*.

The misunderstanding can, in a first approximation, be easily cleared away. To truly understand the notion of formal equality it is enough to realize that it does not claim to exclude differences in talent or fortune, but only discriminations before the law *that might be written into the law* (which is why its most memorable symbol in the tradition of the French Revolution is the abolition of aristocratic privileges on the night of August 4, 1789). One can perfectly well consider our democratic universe to be even more inegalitarian than was that of antiquity—that differences in wealth, especially, are even more pronounced than was ever before the case in human history. It nevertheless remains the case that these inequalities are *juridically* mercurial, that they are not *by nature* assigned to certain individuals, and that therefore the project of a struggle against "real" inequalities can and should be accomodated without difficulty into the ideological frameworks issuing out of the great Revolution.

1. Aristocratic Excellence

The notion of *natural* hierarchy remains, on the other hand, so alien to modern conceptions of justice that its exact meaning within the Greeks' moral vision does not, for us have the immediacy of obviousness. Let us consider for a moment what is perhaps its most famous example: Aristotle's justification of *natural* slavery in the first book of the *Politics*. Many commentators, especially Peripatetic ones, today take the stance of considering these texts to be secondary ones; Aristotle's position is supposedly only the tribute any philosopher, even the greatest ones, has to pay to the ideologies and customs of his time. Not only is this attitude contrary to the elementary rules of philological honesty, it also, above all, misses or masks the essential, the fact that, far from being a concession to the spirit of the age, the justification of natural slavery obtains its full meaning only within antiquity's hierarchical vision of the universe. There is nothing accidental about it, and, in his *Metaphysics*, Aristotle does not hesitate to give this justification cosmological weight when he compares the universe to a big family where the stars correspond to free men whose actions are inflexibly *ordered*, and sublunary beings to slaves and domestic animals. It is instructive to observe how the most eminent interpreters have tried to get around the inevitably troubled feeling we moderns experience when we have to reconcile the idea that Aristotle was, incontestably, one of the greatest thinkers in the history of humanity, and the fact that he nonetheless attempts to elaborate a complicated argument in order to defend an institution that to us spontaneously appears as unjustifiable and so outmoded that it would be boring even to discuss it.

Yet discuss it is precisely what Jacques Brunschwig has tried to do in his article in the *Cahiers philosophiques* (Sept. 1979). He thinks the texts in the *Politics* are perfectly clear if we recall that "there are species in which a distinction is already marked, immediately at birth, between those of its members who are intended for being ruled and those who are intended to rule." Aristotle defines "natural" slaves (those who have not been reduced to that state through the hazards of war) thusly: "We may thus conclude that all men who differ from others as much as the body differs from the soul, or an animal from a man (and this is the case with all whose function is bodily service, and who produce their best when they supply such service)—all such are by nature slaves, and it is better for them . . . to be ruled by a master" (1254 b). In the hierarchy of beings they are halfway between man and animal: "Herein he differs from animals, which do not apprehend reason, but simply obey their instincts. But the use which is made of the slave diverges but little from the use made of tame animals; both he and they supply their owner with bodily help in meeting his daily requirements" (1254 b; Ernest Barker trans.).

Brunschwig's concern is, here, a pedagogical one: how to make young people beginning the study of philosophy understand that they ought to withhold their first reflex—rejection—and suspend judgment, to give themselves time for reflection. For these texts, this is the wager, are more complex than they seem; they can in no way be reduced to an "ideological" justification of the then status quo.

This is Brunschwig's main argument, one that leads us to the heart of the Greek conception of hierarchy and, thereby, of excellence. It is that the "state of things" (the empirically observed reality of slavery) is misleading. Aristotle, in fact, makes a point of this: nature can "imprint freedom and servitude even into bodily habits," so that, for instance, we observe "robust bodies made for carrying loads," while others, "slimmer and more ornamented, seem good only for the political life." But *nature can also mislead us,* since "the opposite often happens: beastly men have the outer form of freedom, while others, not having the appearances, have only a free soul." The same thing applies to the inheritance of virtue and nobility: it is far from being always guaranteed. In these circumstances—continues Brunschwig's reasoning—"there may be, by nature, free men and slaves, but what good can that do us, if we are incapable of knowing which are which, and if we have no right to suppose that their real situation corresponds to their natural one." One cannot therefore hold that Aristotelianism is an ideology of legitimation of the established order since, on the contrary, by stressing that facts do not coincide with law (with nature), Aristotle cannot but instill doubt into the minds of the slave owners.

I will not discuss here the validity of Brunschwig's remarks. I in fact have some reasons to fear that his defense might turn against itself and, despite its intentions, end up suggesting the conclusion that is necessary to finally harmonize fact and law, so that the social order's hierarchy would not be vulnerable to the least criticism, with everyone de facto occupying the position assigned him by nature. It is, on the other hand, essential to point out that his analysis illustrates perfectly well the abyss separating the Greek conception of hierarchy from that current in modern societies. That fact and law may not come together in slavery's empirical reality is one thing. That does not prevent there being, *by nature*, slaves and free men, and the ideal to have been that the former should obey and the latter command. In other words: modern hierarchies are a priori empty. In principle, if not in fact, any individual has the *right* to occupy any position in the social and political hierarchy; no one is excluded or elected because of some supposed nature. In the universe of antiquity, on the contrary, hierarchies are, in principle, "filled," and it is only de facto that they can be, so to speak, "improperly filled."

Fact and law thus take up inverse positions in the two universes, and it is beginning from that circumstance that we should reflect on the notions of equality and difference. Even if it were convincingly demonstrated that the world of the ancients was in fact more egalitarian than that of the moderns (Hannah Arendt suggests somewhere that, all things considered, the situation of the slave is better than that of stateless persons today, and French political scientist Michel Villey has not hesitated to take up the same argument again on the subject of the modern working class), it would remain true that the inequalities in place there were *ascribed to the nature of individuals,* and were, as such, *insuperable.* One can never raise oneself above one's nature, and each person's definition constitutes, so to speak, the prison from which one cannot escape. Inversely, when modern democratic societies are criticized for the "formalism" of the equality they proclaim, with the aim behind the critique being the edification of a real equality of opportunities; what is in fact taking place is that the logic of modern equality is being pursued: it is because human beings are equal by right that the fact of it must some day end up rejoining what is, from now on, an ideal.

It is because it is based on a specific natural cosmology, on the reference to an order of the world, to a cosmos, that the moral vision of the Ancient Greeks culminates in the concept of *excellence.* To go straight to the essential point, we may define this latter quality as perfection, meaning the bringing into reality, for each being, of that which constitutes its nature and thereby indicates its function. That is why the *Nichomachean Ethics* could not but begin with a reflection on man's *finality,* as distinct from that of other beings: "For just as a flute-player, a sculptor, or any artist, and, in general, for all things that have a function or activity, the good and the 'well' is thought to reside in the function, so would it seem to be for man, if he has a function. Have the

251

carpenter, then, and the tanner certain functions or activities, and has man none? Is he born without a function?"[1]

Here it is, therefore, nature which establishes the ends of man and thus provides a direction to his ethics. That does not mean that, in the execution of his proper task, man does not meet with difficulties, that he does not need to exert his will and his capacity for reasoning. Ethics is like any other activity in this, like, for example, learning to play a musical instrument; to become excellent at it, one needs to exercise, but one needs above all talent. Even though it does not exclude a certain use of the will, only a *natural* gift can indicate the path to be followed and permit us to overcome the obstacles we encounter (which is how Aristotle's texts on "deliberation" must be read, and not as some sort of forerunners of a modern "free will" theory).

This is also why virtue, the "proper measure" or "intermediateness" or "mean," can still coincide with excellence. If the aim is to perfectly realize our natural destination, then virtue can only be located in a median position; courage keeps its distance from cowardice and from temerity, so that the proper measure has nothing to do here with some sort of boringly moderate "centrist" position. From an ontological point of view (Aristotle writes "in respect of its substance"), virtue certainly is an intermediateness: the being that perfectly realizes its nature or essence is equidistant from extremes which, being at the limit of their definition, lead to monstrosity. "Hence in respect of its substance and the definition which states its essence virtue is a mean, with regard to what is best and right an extreme" (ibid., 1107 a 5).

We can better measure the extent to which such an ethics can seem strange, from the standpoint of modern conceptions, when we keep in mind the fact that it permits speaking of the "virtue" or "excellence" of a horse or of an eye:

> We may remark, then, that every virtue or excellence both brings into good condition the thing of which it is the excellence and makes the work of that thing be done well; e.g., the excellence of the eye makes both the eye and its work good; for it is by the excellence of the eye that we see well. Similarly the excellence of the horse makes a horse both good in itself and good at running and at carrying its rider and at awaiting the attack of the enemy. (1106 a 15)

The virtuous being is the one that functions well and even excellently, according to its own nature and function. In such a vision of ethics the problem of limits receives an "objective" solution: we must track them down within the order of things, in the reality of the world, just as the physiologist, through understanding the end purposes of organs and members, also perceives the limits within which they can exert their activity. The problem, for us moderns, is that such a reading of the cosmos has become impossible, quite simply, because of the lack of a cosmos we can scrutinize and a nature we can decipher.

2. Democratic Merit

I will not dwell here on the causes of this disappearance stemming from the passage "from the closed world to the infinite universe" that has been so well described by Alexander Koyré. And I have elsewhere analysed what such a revolution meant in the juridical sphere.[2] From the point of view of a history of subjectivity, it is the emergence, with Rousseau, of a new representation of man that has modified the presuppositions of the problem of ethics from top to bottom: from the moment the human being is defined by its "perfectibility," by its freedom, defined as the capacity to tear oneself away from any *natural* or *historical* determination,[3] antiquity's "functionalism." The idea of a natural teleology loses all meaning if man is the only being that is, by essence, lacking in specific function. If he is "nothingness," as was already suggested by Fichte in the wake of Rousseau, if he possesses no "nature" in which some sort of "mission" could be deciphered, then virtuous activity can no longer be thought of in terms of end purposes and the problem of limits becomes problematic once again. Absent all "objective" reference to a cosmos, to a natural order that transcends and encompasses individuals, it is indeed hard to see what could put a limit to their infinite freedom. That, anyhow, is the challenge that must be taken up by the morality of the moderns.

It means that we have to, in morality as in other domains, "ground transcendence on immanence"; seek, within the subject itself, and no longer in an external order, the means—the "reasons"—for a limitation that must from now on be thought of as *autolimitation, as autonomy.* The question of what is proper to man—of the definition of the human subject—turns out to be inseparable from that of the ends of man, and of the limits within which he must try to maintain his actions. It will be more easily understood, under such circumstances, that, where the ethics of the ancients began from a reflection on man's natural *finality,* that of the moderns begins with a theory of "good will," of the free and autonomous will.

Such a starting point leads in two directions, both of them radically counter to the morality of antiquity. From a *subjective* point of view, the problem is one of knowing which attitudes of the mind are worthy of being considered virtuous; along the way we come upon the problem of *disinterested* action, one that is contrary to man's sensuous *nature*. From an *objective* point of view, it becomes necessary to determine which, among all the ends a free will can set out to meet, are properly speaking "moral"; we are then confronted with the problem of universality as the new form of the common good or of the "general interest." We need to review both aspects briefly to see how they are diametrically opposed to Aristotelianism.

Subjectively—considering the *intentions* that can motivate any kind of activity—"good will" is defined as "disinterested" will. For reasons Kant analyzes methodically in his *Groundings of the Metaphysics of Morals,* there is among the moderns a consensus in considering that only disinterested action can be truly held to be moral. That is the meaning of the famous distinction Kant establishes between "legality" and "morality." I can always act in conformity to a law (the prohibition on theft, in the example given in the *Groundings*) *out of interest*—in this case, out of the fear of being arrested and put in prison—but one could of course come up with other examples where the interest would be "positive" and would reside in the hope of reward and not in the fear of punishment. From the point of view that concerns us here, it is clear that both motivations are equivalent, since they are both "self-interested." My action is, in such circumstances, no doubt legal (*gesetzmäßig:* literally, "in conformity with the law"), but everyone will agree that it does not for all that have anything virtuous about it. We associate, without even thinking about it, the idea of virtue to that of effort, and merit, for us, supposes in some way the will's struggle against its own interests, against egoism. As far as its motivations are concerned, moral action, therefore, has to be carried out because of sheer respect for the law.

We can thus better understand that only good will can be called, strictly speaking, moral. Talents, which are *natural* gifts, have in themselves no *ethical* value. Intelligence, force, beauty, even courage, can be put at the service of not only our egoistic interests but also of crime (of illegality). We can assess here the extent to which we are now at the opposite extreme from the idea of excellence. Virtue, far from residing in the perfection of natural gifts, in the fulfillment of a function in conformity with man's specific nature, becomes among the moderns a struggle against the naturalness that is in us, the capacity to *resist* the inclinations of our egoist nature.

The extraordinary power of Kantian ethics stems from the fact that none of us is quite capable of thinking in different terms. I have never yet met, among those who call themselves anti-Kantians (be they Spinozists, materialists, phenomenologists, or partisans of an ethics in the ancient style), a modern who could completely do without the concept of merit (except in words, and even there). If it is thrown out the door of philosophy, it returns through the window of everyday life and of the innocuous value judgments it continuously forces us to make when we are outside the control of a system of concepts. And, like it or not, the notion of merit only makes sense within a modern perspective. If we reflect on it, we will see that it always presupposes the idea of liberty defined as the power to resist the nature within us, *therefore as the capacity to act disinterestedly.* It has in practice become impossible for us to, for example, consider that the fact of being tall, strong, good-looking, skillful in bodily or even in intellectual activities is, properly speaking, a virtue—and this whatever may be the extraordinary power of seduction such qualities can sometimes exert on us, or whatever real admiration they may call forth. For seduction, for us moderns, no longer has anything to do with ethics, but with aesthetics.

From a subjective point of view, the morality of merit is thus a morality of *duty.* Since the goal is no longer, as it was for the ancients, to fulfill one's nature but, most often, to oppose it, rules almost always have to take the form of an imperative. Moral demands take the form of a "You must . . ." or an "It must be so, that . . ." But we still need to spell out in detail what the ends that thus impose themselves on us consist in objectively in what concerns their precise content. This is the second aspect of the modern reflection on ethics. It is not enough simply to be capable of disinterest, of detachment from one's egoistic nature, one must also be able to indicate the direction this separation from oneself should take. If virtuous action is subjectively disinterested, what then is its objective?

It is common knowledge that the term has a double meaning—an ambiguity around which plays the contemporary notion of "objective reason," whose origins go back to Kantianism. The objective is the *goal,* but it is also that which is not subjective, *that which is valid not merely for me but also for the others.* The *common* good is therefore objective in a double sense—this is what the Kantian doctrine of imperatives expresses in its own fashion through its three levels: skill, prudence, and morality. In going from one degree to another, we raise ourselves along both the scale of ends and that of objectivity. The imperatives of skill, indeed, reflect upon nothing other than means. They are still purely technical or instrumental. They say only: "If you wish to achieve an end *X*, do *Y*," without in the least concerning themselves with knowing whether this end should or should not be pursued, whether or not it goes beyond the sphere of my strictly egoistic interests. Skill, for Kant, corresponds to Epicure's morality or to utilitarianism: the "objectives" it permits us to attain remain, if we may put it so, entirely *subjective* and *particular*.

With prudence—a translation of Aristotle's *phronêsis*—we move up one level in the scale of objectivity. The ends the prudent person pursues are common to humanity, not specific to such and such an isolated individual, the way the ends pursued by skill can be. The typical example here is the health everyone—with the exception of attempted suicides—cannot but wish for himself, at least to the extent that the human being is also an animal whose body must be taken care of. Prudence arrives at the level of *the general* or, as it is so well said, of "common sense." But it is not yet at the level of the rigorous universality characteristic of moral ends. The proof of this is that, when morality demands it, one has to be "imprudent." Freely consented to sacrifice cannot be excluded from modern ethics.

With the ends of morality we therefore reach the level of veritable objectivity. Here, the goals of our actions impose themselves on us in the aspect of a universal law, absolutely valid for all. But since this law, being a law of reason, is *our* law, since there is thus *autonomy* (which does not happen in the case of a religious vision of ethics), we can say that transcendence is here grounded in immanence. It is, so to speak, within ourselves that we have to find the reasons—in fact, Reason—to forget our personal interest. Merit is linked to this internal tension between the particularity of egoistic desires and the universality of the law, whose triumph is consecrated by virtue.

The two moments of modern ethics—disinterested intention and universality of chosen ends—are reconciled in the definition of man as perfectibility or nothingness. They both find their ultimate origin in this philosophical anthropology: liberty is above all the capacity to act outside the determination of our "natural," that is to say particular, interests. By distancing ourselves from the particular, we raise ourselves toward the universal, and therefore toward taking the other person into account.

If excellence is in essence aristocratic, merit on the other hand is of democratic inspiration. Since it is ascribed to a domain other than that of innate talent, no one can be said to be a priori wanting of it. It "merely" requires good will. In the eyes of the moderns, the slave Aristotle would have called "natural" can be virtuous, just as much as, if not more than its master. And, in one of the most celebrated examples in Kantian ethics, even the child is enlightened enough to know where evil is—something that, for obvious reasons, we formally ruled out in Aristotle's morality.

3. Contemporary Authenticity

Effort, merit, duty, imperatives, respect, law, virtue—the terms modern ethics are formulated in are eloquent; they express well the extent to which the realization of the moral ideal is a difficult, is a *constraining* matter for the subject who wishes to abide by it. The hierarchical cosmos ancient virtue referred to has disappeared, and the substantial world has retreated. The thinking of the moderns has, for all that, remained attached to the idea of the law's transcendence when compared to the desires of the individual, and practical reason, though it is, after a fashion, "in ourselves," through its universality and its transcendental status, remains external to empirical man. The idea of auto-nomy no doubt presumes that the law is *my law*, but the distance separating *autos* from *nomos*, self from norm, is not thereby canceled. Ethics does not converge with psychology, nor with the sociology of morals that leads certain of our contemporaries to consider every norm as being the historical product stemming from the conditions of a specific society.

There have been, for a number of years, any number of indications that we are witnessing a mutation linked to the momentous rise of democratic individualism. Both in the United States and France, several excellent studies have shown how hedonistic and narcissistic ideologies have, especially since the 1960s, taken hold of traditional moral questions. If we were to draw up identification cards for them, the key word would no longer be excellence, and even less merit, but, without a doubt, *authenticity*. Without having to repeat those analyses here, we can very briefly review the double tendency characteristic of contemporary individualism on the ethical plane.

The main thing, first of all, is no longer to come up against imperative external norms, but to arrive at the expression of one's personality, at the development and opening up of the self. Let us bring to mind Daniel Bell's admirably concise and exact formulation: "traditional morality was replaced by psychology, guilt by anxiety." When the notion of transcendence vanishes, when, as a consequence, one faces oneself all alone, existential conflict and despondency can no longer be interpreted in any other way than as "psychic conflicts": the victory of therapy over religion is assured.

On the other hand, the ethics of authenticity compensates the narcissism of the command to "be yourself" with an increase in tolerance and respect for the Other. "Otherness" has become the one sure value today, the inevitable and undebatable watchword. It is, in this respect, significant that the declarative discourse of human rights—at the beginning, we mustn't forget, the most accomplished expression of the "geometrical" universalism of the French revolutionaries—has today become synonymous with "the right to difference." The French Revolution did, of course, emancipate the Jews, and it fought against slavery. But we need to keep in mind that it did this in the name of *principles* and by virtue of an *assimilationist* ideology, not at all out of respect for a *plurality of cultures,* the very idea of which no doubt never even came close to entering into any Jacobin head.

I will not come back here to the dead ends the ethics of authenticity often (though not always) leads into—especially in the shape of cultural relativism or of the "differentialist" antiracism whose traps we are now beginning to see.[4] As a sort of conclusion, I should merely like to bring to our attention a great difficulty that this ethics involves us all with, like it or not.

Whether it was right or wrong in doing so (I believe it was right), what I have here designated as the ethics of the moderns had not abandoned the project of finding a solution to the problem of *limits.* Though they are no longer located in a transcendent cosmos, but within the subject's reason, the latter are nonetheless constraining, on a moral as well as a juridical level. The principles of *autolimitation,* which hold that my freedom ends there where the other person's freedom begins, and of universality of the law provide, whatever neotraditionalist Heideggerians or Thomists (not to mention fundamentalists) may think, general indications that can—at least that's the wager made by the moderns—become specific in every concrete case through the organization of the public discussions that are indispensible to the elaboration of just compromises. The problem with the ethics of the contemporaries and with the consecration of the authentic as such is that reference to the very idea of limit seems to fade away, delegitimized as it is by the imperious demands made by individual self-cultivation and by the right to difference. When it is "forbidden to forbid," dogmatism becomes the supreme sin, and tends to be confused with the very thing the moderns

THE PROBLEM OF ETHICS

held to be the truth of *reason*. Hatred of rationalism blossoms upon the ethics of authenticity, and criticism of the former, until recently the prerogative of contemporary philosophy, now finds echoes even in the scientists' universe—witness the success of various essays on epistemology that happily trample on reason.

That is, at bottom, the argument we wanted to put forward in *La Pensée 68* when, making a distinction between "autonomy" and "independence," Renaut and I wrote that "the subject perishes with the rise of the individual." We wished to stress the narrow and paradoxical correlation uniting the deconstructions of reason, and therefore of modern subjectivity, to the liberal universe, where the full flowering of individualism calls for the invention and dissemination of relativist ideologies holding that there are no facts, only interpretations.

It would, however, be mistaken to go to extremes and transform the opposition between modern subject and contemporary individual into a real antinomy, to believe that the golden age of the Enlightenment is vanishing with the inexorable decline the West is supposedly fated toward ever since the "era of emptiness" began. The history of aesthetics teaches us—and I believe the lesson is also valid for ethics—that the withdrawal of a shared world is not synonymous with decadence. It opens new horizons we would do better to investigate before giving in to the facile attitude that neoconservatism has become. Nothing says that these horizons are idyllic, but nothing proves either that they are ineluctably leading us to new forms of totalitarianism. Indignation is not called for, not, at least, before the comprehension of our moment comes to justify it if need be—a task that is not being carried out by anyone, as far as I can see.

That the advance of science and technology, especially in everything having to do with biological life, raises the question of limits in a new and urgent manner is undeniable. That individualist ideology does not really predispose us to bring clear and decisive answers to it, and that irresolution leaves the door open to the harsh laws of the market, is more than probable. That this situation is the expression of a radical evil, the mere glimpse of which should incite us to suspend our critical judgment, to leave behind judicial humanism and replace it with a return to traditional forms of thought is, on the other hand, extremely doubtful, and this for two reasons we need to clarify.

It is, first of all, not certain that there is a perfect continuity between humanism and individualism, and that therefore it would be valid to transform a condemnation of individualism into one of humanism. On the aesthetic as on the ethical levels, it is crucial to distinguish as carefully as possible between the modern and the contemporary. Unless we aim to radicalize Heidegger's reading of history, we have to admit that, from Kant to Nietzsche, ruptures are at least as important as continuities.

Second and above all, we should guard ourselves from immediately putting a value judgment on the distinction between the autonomy of the subject and the independence of the individual. The latter, even when he is not aiming at the moral autonomy we attribute to the subject, is not for all that reduced to merely consumerist activities. Between the animality of the life cycle and the virtuous action through which we claim autonomy, there is an entire sphere of intermediate activities, for which aesthetics provides the model, and which allow the individual to make use of forms of expression with fruitful possibilities. We would be concealing nothing less than the sphere of culture if we were to neglect this observation, and we are therefore in no way restricted to a binary choice of life: for or against a transcendent law, for or against immanence within life, etc. What is unprecedented in the contemporary period is the fact that the three ages of ethics, though they would seem to be antithetical, do not in fact cancel each other out—the requirement of authenticity does not imply a total and definitive withdrawal of the principles of excellence or merit. On the contrary, we are witnessing today, if I am not mistaken, a return of the principle of excellence within the democratic universe, while the meritocratic principle has never really ceased to be at work. Authenticity, in fact, tends more and more to be valued only when it is accompanied by either the courage of virtue or the power of seduction, when, therefore, it is the authenticity of an inner richness whose manifestation calls forth agreement or admiration for another. Expressivity for expressivity's sake no longer interests anybody, and the discourse against the society of the spectacle is becoming the dominant ideology even as it pretends to be more subversive than ever—following in that the most outmoded fashions among the intelligentsia.

To say that the individual is neither exclusively autonomy (modern morality) nor exclusively consumeristic independence (contemporary authenticity), is to evoke one of the profoundest significations of the notion of individuality. We should not forget that the individual is, before anything else, the indivisible being, the atom that, being unique, is distinct from all the others. No one is going to be distinct, to stand out, through the mere assertion of his independence and his selfness [*ipséité*]. Following a line of argument whose model is provided by the *Phenomenology of Spirit,* in the dialectic of sense-certainty, the exacerbation of bare particularity reverts into its opposite and falls into the banality of the abstract universal. We are all individuals, we are all "me"s in the here and now; this "particularity" is not what differentiates us from each other. Nor is it our capacity to consume nature's or society's products. In the spectrum of reflection inaugurated by the *Critique of Judgment* and taken up by German romanticism, true individuality cannot reside in anything other than a synthesis of a concrete particularity with the universal. For the individual to be an individual, he has to be rich with a discrete, specific *content* that is all the same *generalizable.* At that price, and only at that price, can the requirement of authenticity be kept up. Individuality then resembles the *ideal* in which Hegelian aesthetics saw the pinnacle of art. Comprehended this way, individuality cannot at all be reduced to the anything-goes of consumerism, to the arbitrary freedom that consists in doing "whatever I feel like."

Illuminated by the history of aesthetics, ethical reflection today can no longer do without this triple dimension of excellence, merit, and authenticity. Each requirement traces the outline of a general theory of limitations, one we shall have to resolve ourselves to think through outside the framework of any cosmology, if we wish to meet the challenge put forth by the withdrawal of a shared world without giving in to the mirage of a lost tradition.

NOTES

(Any unattributed translations in the text are by Robert de Loaiza)

ONE

1. Karl Borinski, *Balthasar Gracian und die Hofliteratur in Deutschland* (Berlin, 1984).

2. Cf. A. Bäumler, *Das Irrationalitätsproblem in der Ästhetik und Logik des 18 Jahrhunderts bis zur "Kritik der Urteilskraft"* (Halle, 1923), p. 19, no. 3.

3. Alexis de Tocqueville, *La Démocratie en Amérique*, vol. 2, chap. 1.

TWO

1. K. Heinrich von Stein, *Die Entstehung der neueren Ästhetik* (Stuttgart, 1886).

2. Charles Batteux, *Les Beaux-Arts réduits à un même princips* (1746), p. 13.

3. N. Boileau, *Art poétique*, chap. 1.

4. Boileau, *Twelfth Satire*, "On the Ambiguous."

5. Bouhours, *Des manières*, p. 432 (of the 1743 edition).

6. Cf. also pp. 435–36.

7. Ernst Cassirer, *The Philosophy of the Enlightenment*, trans. Fritz C. A. Koelln and James C. Pettegrove (Princeton: Princeton University Press, 1951), p. 297.

8. J.-B. Dubos, *Réflexions critiques sur la poésie et la peinture* (1719), part 1, § 4. (All texts are from the 1770 edition.)

9. Batteux, *Les Beaux-Arts*, p. 102.

10. Dubos, *Réflexions critiques*, p. 341.

11. Cf. Bäumler, *Das Irrationalitätsproblem*, pp. 25–26.

12. Dubos, *Réflexions critiques*, pp. 53ff., where this point is correctly analyzed.

13. Immanuel Kant: *Kritik der Urteilskraft* [*Critique of Judgment*] (Suhrkamp Taschenbuch Verlag: hrsg. Wilhelm Weischedel; 1974), § 56, p. 279.

14. Kant, *Kritik der Urteilskraft*, § 57, Remark 2.

15. See especially, David Hume, "Of the Standard of Taste," in Hume, *Es-*

says: Moral, Political, and Literary, ed. T. H. Green and T. H. Grose (London: Longmans, Green, and Co., 1875), vol. 1.

16. Hume, "An Enquiry Concerning the Principles of Morals," in *Essays,* ed. Green and Grose, vol. 2, p. 174.

17. Hume, "Of the Standard of Taste," *Essays,* vol. 1, p. 266.

18. Cassirer, *Philosophy,* p. 305.

19. David Hume, "The Sceptic," in *Essays,* vol. 1, p. 217.

20. Hume, "Of the Standard of Taste," p. 268.

21. Dubos, *Réflexions critiques,* vol. 2, § 34.

22. Hume, "Of the Standard of Taste," p. 268.

23. Dubos, *Réflexions critiques,* pp. 369–70.

24. Hume, "Standard," p. 270.

25. David Hume, *Four Dissertations* (London, printed for A. Millar, in the Strand, 1757), pp. v, vi.

26. Gottfried Wilhelm von Leibniz, *New Essays Concerning Human Understanding,* book 4, chap. 2, § 14.

27. Cf. for example, Christian Wolff, *Psychologia empirica,* § 545. On the notion of perfection, see ibid., *Ontologia,* § 503.

28. G. W. Leibniz, *Von der Weisheit: Deutsche Schriften,* ed. Guhrauer, vol. 1, p. 420.

29. Moses Mendelssohn, *Gesammelte Schriften,* vol. 1, p. 114.

30. On these modifications, cf. Bäumler, *Das Irrationalitätsproblem,* pp. 192ff.

31. A. G. Baumgarten, *Meditationes philosophicae de nonnullis ad poema pertinentibus,* §§ 15 and following.

32. Ibid., § 9. Cf. also § 5.

33. On the same theme, cf. §§ 555, 560, and 563 of the *Aesthetics.*

34. Cf. §§ 14, 15, 561, and 562.

35. Cf. also § 565.

THREE

1. Immanuel Kant, *Kritik der reinen Vernunft* [*Critique of Pure Reason*], 2d ed., Akademieausgabe, vol. 3, pp. 399–400. (The full title of the German edition used is *Kant: Werke in sechs Bänden,* hrsg. Wilhelm Weischedel [Frankfurt: Insel Verlag, 1964].—TRANS.

2. Martin Heidegger, "What is Metaphysics?" In *Basic Writings,* ed. David Farrell Krell (London: Routledge and Kegan Paul, 1977), p. 100.

3. Kant, *Kritik der reinen Vernunft,* p. 452.

4. On the link between the idea of reflection and the critique of metaphysics it presupposes, see Luc Ferry, *Political Philosophy,* vol. 2, *The System of*

Philosophies of History, trans. Franklin Philip (Chicago: University of Chicago Press, 1992).

5. Kant, *Kritik der Urteilskraft,* ed. Wilhelm Weischedel (Frankfurt: Suhrkamp Taschenbuch, 1974), Introduction, § IV.

6. I use again here an analysis already outlined in my *Political Philosophy,* vol. 2.

7. Cf. Christian Wolff, *Psychologia empirica,* §§ 257–58.

8. Cf. Bäumler, *Das Irrationalitätsproblem,* pp. 203ff.

9. Kant, *Kritik der Urteilskraft,* § 40.

10. Ibid. See also Kant's *Reflections,* no. 626, in Kant's *Gesammelte Schriften,* hrsg. von der Königlichen Preußischen Akademie der Wissenschaften (Berlin: Druck und Verlag von Georg Reimer, 1913), vol. 15 (handschriftliche Nachlaß. vol. 2, 1st half: Anthropologie), pp. 271–72.

11. Ibid., p. 342 (Reflection 782).

12. Jean-François Lyotard and Jacob Rogosinski, *L'Autre Journal,* December 1985, p. 34.

13. Kant, *Kritik der Urteilskraft,* § 22.

14. Lyotard and Rogosinski, op. cit.

15. Martin Heidegger, *Kant and the Problem of Metaphysics,* trans. James S. Churchill (Bloomington: Indiana University Press, 1962 [1929]), p. 165.

16. Ernst Cassirer, "Abhandlung über *Kant und das Problem der Metaphysik:* Bemerkungen zu Martin Heideggers Kant-Interpretation," in *Kant-Studien,* Philosophische Zeitschrift, vol. 36 (1931), pp. 15–16.

17. It was the principal project of *Political Philosophy,* vol. 2. Cf. also "La Dimension éthique chez Heidegger," in *Nachdenken über Heidegger* (Gerstenberg Verlag, 1980); and *La Pensée 68: Essai sur l'antihumanisme contemporain* [*French Philosophy in the Sixties:* An Essay on Contemporary Anti-Humanism] (Gallimard, 1985), last chapter.

FOUR

1. Georg Wilhelm Friedrich Hegel, *Einleitung in die Geschichte der Philosophie* [Introduction to the History of Philosophy], hrsg. J. Hoffmeister (Hamburg: Felix Meiner Verlag, 1959), p. 94.

2. Hegel: *Vorlesungen über die Ästhetik,* in *Hegel: Theorie Werkausgabe* (Suhrkamp Verlag, 1970), vol. 1 (of the *Ästhetik*), p. 21. [At this point, Prof. Ferry discusses the French translation of the *Lectures on Aesthetics,* which he judges so defective he has seen fit to make his own translations from the German. I have judged the most recent English translation, by T. M. Knox (Oxford University Press, 1975), to be satisfactory, and have used it with minor modifications. The parentheses after the quotations indicate the volume number in the *Werkausgabe*'s edition of the *Lectures,* the page number, and, after the slash, the page number in English: e.g., 1:100/70.—TRANS.]

FIVE

1. Gilles Deleuze, *Nietzsche and Philosophy,* trans. Hugh Tomlinson (New York: Columbia University Press, 1983 [1962]), p. 8.

2. Friedrich Nietzsche: *Die Geburt der Tragödie,* in Nietzsche, *Kritische Studienausgabe,* hrsg. Giorgio Colli and Mazzino Montinari (Munich and Berlin: DTV/de Gruyter, 1967 and 1988), Band 1, p. 111.

3. Nietzsche, *The Will to Power,* § 422. [Prof. Ferry refers to the Karl Schlechta edition (1956) of Nietzsche's works, which uses a different arrangement of Nietzsche's "left-behind" writings of the 1880s from the one made by Elisabeth Förster-Nietzsche and published as *Der Wille zur Macht* (1908). For the convenience of the English-speaking reader, I have gone back to the earlier version, the one adopted by Walter Kaufmann and R. J. Hollingdale in their translation of *The Will to Power* (New York: Vintage Books, 1968), except where a fragment cited has not been reproduced there.—TRANS.]

4. Nietzsche, *Unzeitgemässe Betrachtungen,* vol. 2, § 8; Karl Schlechta ed., vol. 1, p. 95.

5. Nietzsche, "Aus dem Nachlass der Achtzigerjahre," in *Werke,* ed. Karl Schlechta (Munich: Carl Hanser Verlag, 1966), vol. 3, p. 677.

6. Nietzsche, "History in the Service and Disservice of Life," trans. Gary Brown, in *Unmodern Observations,* ed. William Arrowsmith (New Haven and London: Yale University Press, 1990), p. 127.

7. Nietzsche, F. *Twilight of the Idols,* "The Problem of Socrates," § 5, in *The Portable Nietzsche,* trans. and ed. Walter Kaufmann (New York: The Viking Press, 1954), p. 475 (trans. mod.).

8. Martin Heidegger, *Nietzsche,* in Heidegger, *Gesamtausgabe;* vol. 43: *Nietzsche: Der Wille zur Macht als Kunst* (Frankfurt am Main: Klosterman GmbH, 1985), p. 87.

9. Heidegger, "Overcoming Metaphysics," in *The End of Philosophy,* trans. Joan Stambaugh (New York: Harper and Row, 1973), p. 95.

10. Heidegger, *Nietzsche,* vol. 1, p. 551 (German ed.).

11. *Beyond Good and Evil,* trans. W. Kaufmann (New York: Vintage Books, [1886], 1966), § 268.

12. Friedrich Nietzsche, *The Gay Science,* trans. Walter Kaufmann (New York: Vintage Books, 1974 [1882–87]), sect. 354.

13. *The Will to Power* (hereafter, *WP*), § 786.

14. Nietzsche, *The Twilight of the Idols,* in the *Viking Portable Nietzsche,* ed. Walter Kaufmann (Harmondsworth and New York: Penguin, 1968), p. 534.

15. *Werke,* Schlechta ed., vol. 3, p. 689.

16. Cf. Nietzsche, *Posthumous Works,* Kroener ed., vol. 10, p. 277, in *Nietzsche Gesamtausgabe* (Leipzig: A. Kröner, 1910–1922 [völlig neu gestaltete ausgabe]).

17. *Werke,* vol. 3, p. 585.

18. *WP*, § 997.

19. *Posthumous Works*, Kroener ed., vol. 11, pt. 2, § 504.

20. *WP*, § 485.

21. *Posthumous Works*, Kroener ed., vol. 14, pt. 2, § 63.

22. *WP*, § 556.

23. L. Strauss, "The Three Waves of Modernity," in *Political Philosophy: Six Essays by Leo Strauss* (Indianapolis: Bobbs-Merrill, 1975).

24. See Luc Ferry and Alain Renaut, 68–86, *Itinéraires de l'individu* (Gallimard, 1987), chap. 3.

25. Michel Foucault, "Nietzsche, Genealogy, History," in *Nietzsche*, Colloque de Royaumont (Paris: Editions de Minuit, 1964).

26. Nietzsche, *Beyond Good and Evil*, § 289 (Kaufmann trans.).

27. *WP*, § 804.

28. See, for instance, Heidegger: *Nietzsche*, vol. 1.

29. *Beyond Good and Evil*, § 21.

30. On these difficulties, see Ferry and Renaut, 68–86, *Itinéraires de l'individu*.

31. Heidegger, *Nietzsche*, vol. 1, "Der Rausch als ästhetischer Zustand," p. 110 (D. F. Krell translation, p. 92).

32. Ibid. (Krell trans., p. 93).

33. Cf. Heidegger, *Nietzsche* (Krell trans., p. 93).

34. Deleuze, *Nietzsche and Philosophy*, pp. 102–3.

35. Ibid., Schlecta ed., vol. 3, p. 755.

36. *Posthumous Works*, Kroener ed., vol. 14, pt. 1, § 370.

37. Martin Heidegger, "The Origin of the Work of Art," in: *Poetry, Language, Thought*, trans. and ed. Albert Hofstadter (New York: Harper and Row, 1971), p. 77.

38. J. Lacoste, *La Philosophie de l'art* (Paris: Presses Universitaires de France, 1985).

SIX

1. *Contrechamps*, no. 3, Sept. 1984, "Avant-garde et tradition."

2. IRCAM, Programme 1987, editorial.

3. Jean Clair, *Considérations sur l'état des beaux-arts: Critique de la modernité* (Gallimard, 1983), pp. 115–16.

4. *Libération*, Nov. 1983.

5. *Le Point*, April 21, 1986.

6. P. M. Menger, "L'Elitisme musical," *Esprit*, March 1985, pp. 5ff.

7. *Restons simples*, no. 2, January 1986.

8. J.-C. Risset, "Le compositeur et ses machines," *Esprit*, March 1985, p. 71.

9. Octavio Paz, *Point de convergence: Du romantisme à l'avant-garde* (Gallimard, 1974), p. 190.

10. See Donald D. Egbert, "The Idea of 'Avant-Garde' in Art and Politics," *The American Historical Review* (Dec. 1967), p. 343. On the concept's history, the books by Renato Poggioli, *The Theory of the Avant-Garde* (Cambridge: Harvard University Press, 1968 [Italian original, Il Mulino, 1962]), and Peter Burger, *Theorie der Avant-Garde* (Suhrkamp, 1974), do not contribute anything noteworthy.

11. Claude Henri de Rouvroy, comte de Saint-Simon, *Opinions littéraires, philosophiques, et industrielles* (Paris, 1825), p. 331. (This text was in fact written by Olinde Rodrigues and cosigned by Saint-Simon and Léon Halévy).

12. See also *Lettres de Henri de Saint-Simon à messieurs les jurés.* (Paris: Coméard, 1820), A., VI. p. 422: "New meditations have proved to me that the order of march for things should be: the artists at the head, then the scholars and scientists, and the industrialists only after these first two classes."

13. Saint Simon, *Opinions littéraires*, p. 137.

14. On this strange movement, more amusing than truly innovative, see the *Encyclopédie des farces et attrapes et mystifications* (Paris: Jean-Jacques Pauvert, 1964), as well as Daniel Grojnowski's article in the *Actes de la recherche en sciences sociales* (1975) from which I borrowed some of the following remarks.

15. Vasili Kandinsky, *On the Spiritual in Art and Painting in Particular* (1912). In Kandinsky, *Complete Writings on Art,* vol. 1 (1901–1921), ed. and trans. Kenneth C. Lindsay and Peter Vergo (Boston: G. K. Hall and Co., 1982), p. 133.

16. "Correspondance Kandinski-Schönberg," *Contrechamps*, no. 2, April 1984.

17. Kandinsky to Schoenberg, Jan. 18, 1911.

18. Kandinsky, *On the Spiritual,* pp. 127–28.

19. For a more elaborate analysis of this concept, see Ferry and Renaut, *68–86, Itinéraires de l'individu* (Gallimard, 1987).

20. Daniel Bell, *The Cultural Contradictions of Capitalism* (New York: Basic Books, 1976).

21. Jean-Jacques Rousseau, *Du contrat social,* book 2, chap. 1.

22. Text commented on by Bell in *Cultural Contradictions,* p. 18, n. 17.

23. Ibid., p. 11, n. 10; cf. also pp. 36ff.

24. See Luc Ferry and Alain Renaut, *La Pensée 68* [*French Philosophy in the Sixties*].

25. Cf. Gilles Lipovetsky, *L'Ere du vide* [*The Era of Emptiness*], (Paris: Gallimard, 1983), who introduces a Tocquevillian perspective into the analysis of modernism.

26. *Le Débat,* no. 21, 1982, p. 48.

27. See Pierre Francastel, *Etudes de sociologie de l'art* (Denoël, 1970), pp. 156, 178, 183, etc.

28. K. S. Malevich, *Ecrits* (Éditions Gérard Lebovici, 1986), pp. 185–86.

29. See Guillaume Apollinaire, *Les Peintres cubistes* (Hermann, 1965), pp. 25ff.

30. J. Metzinger (with A. Gleizes), *Du cubisme* (Éditions Présence, 1980 [Afterword from 1946]), p. 79.

31. See J. Lacoste's excellent book, *L'Idée du beau* (Bordas, 1986), pp. 146ff.

32. Francastel, *Etudes*, p. 55.

33. Gino Severini, *La Peinture d'avant-garde* (Mercure de France, 1917), ser. 1, vol. 6.

34. A. Gleizes, *Art et religion, art et science, art et production* (Éditions Présence, 1970), p. 55.

35. Francastel, *Etudes*, p. 247.

36. Cf., among others, Jean Paulhan: "Euclidean space is an extension that could be entirely filled by juxtaposed, equal-sized cubes, without any row having a last cube . . . But it is well known that the notion of Euclidean space is, in our day, rather badly treated by mathematicians" (*Sur le cubisme* [Denoël, 1970], p. 103). Later on in this same text, the "it is well known" seems to be an elegant denial.

37. In his *Traité élémentaire de géometrie à quatre dimensions* [*Elementary Treatise of Four-Dimensional Geometry*] (1903), with which Apollinaire was acquainted, the mathematician E. Jouffret carefully distinguishes "space," characterized by an *n* number of dimensions (three for Euclid), from "extension," which, in four-dimensional geometry opens up to dimensional infinity: "We shall call EXTENSION the ensemble formed by this infinite number of spaces and which contains them, as each space contains an infinite number of planes, each one of these in turn containing an infinity of straight lines, and each of the latter containing an infinity of points. Nothing hinders us from considering extension as being itself inserted into a five-dimensional field, and so on indefinitely" (p. IX).

38. Metzinger and Gleizes, *Du cubisme*, p. 49.

39. Thanks to the remarkable work of Linda Dalrymple-Henderson in the United States and Jean Clair in France. For the former, see *The Fourth Dimension and Non-Euclidian Geometry in Modern Art* (Princeton University Press, 1975); for J. Clair, "L'Échiquier, les modernes et la quatrième dimension," *La Revue d'art*, no. 39 (June 1978), and *Marcel Duchamp ou le Grand Fictif* (Galilée, 1975). These are the most enlightening works I've read on the subject and what follows owes a lot to them.

40. See especially C. H. Hinton, *A New Era of Thought* (London, 1888).

41. To be honest, Jouffret does not share Hinton's point of view, and agrees rather with Poincaré, who holds that the fourth dimension will forever remain imperceptible. See *Revue générale des sciences* (1891), p. 774; and also "L'Espace et la géométrie," *Revue de métaphysique et de morale* (1895), pp. 631ff.

42. Hinton, *New Era* (quoted in English by Jouffret, *Traité*, Foreword).

43. Jouffret, *Traité*, p. XVII.

44. Cf. Jean Clair, "L'échiquier, les modernes, et la quatrième dimension."

45. Edwin Abbott, *Flatland, a Romance of Many Dimensions, by a Square* (New York: Dover Publications, [1884] 1952).

46. Jouffret, *Traité*, p. XIV.

47. J. Metzinger, *Le Cubisme était né* (Éditions Présence, 1972), p. 23.

48. The article appeared on December 29, 1918, in the *Carnet de la semaine*. See L. Dalrymple-Henderson, *Fourth Dimension*, p. 72.

49. Metzinger, *Le Cubisme était né*, pp. 43–44.

50. H. Poincaré, *La Science et l'hypothèse*, p. 65.

51. Level, "L'Esprit et l'espace: La quatrième dimension," *Le Théosophe*, March 16, 1911; Noircame, *Quatrième Dimension* (Paris: Editions Théosophiques, 1912).

52. See Jean Clair, *Marcel Duchamp ou le Grand Fictif*, chap. 2, as well as L. Dalrymple-Henderson, *Fourth Dimension, passim*.

53. On Pawlowski, see Dalrymple-Henderson, *Fourth Dimension*, pp. 51ff.

54. See the Preface to the 1923 edition of the *Voyage*.

55. Alfred Jarry, "Commentaire pour servir à la construction pratique de la machine à explorer le temps," which appeared in February 1899 in the *Mercure de France* review, as an appendix to the French publication of H. G. Wells's *The Time Machine*. A sign of fiction's increasing interest in the new geometries, one could read in its introduction: "It is no more difficult to conceive of a machine to explore time than it is of one to explore space, whether one considers time as space's fourth dimension, or as a site essentially different because of its content . . . Time is usually defined as the site of events, as space is the site of bodies. Or, with greater simplicity, succession, whereas space—be it three-dimensional Euclidean space; four-dimensional space, implied by the intersection of several three-dimensional spaces; Riemann's spaces, in which spheres can be turned inside out, circles being geodesic lines on spheres of equal radius; Lobachevsky's spaces, in which a plane cannot be inverted; or any space other than Euclidean, recognizable in that one cannot, as in the latter, build two similar figures there—is simultaneity."

56. See Gaston de Pawlowski, *Le Voyage au pays de la quatrième dimension*, p. 30.

57. See Clair, *Marcel Duchamp ou le grand fictif*.

58. Marcel Duchamp, *Ingénieur du temps perdu*, Interviews with Pierre Cabane (Belfond, 1967), pp. 66–67.

59. See the brilliant pages Jean Clair devotes to this letter: "All of the *Large Glass*'s problematic is, one may say, one of point of view, of perspective. The figure is transformed according to the observer's position—a position in relation to an observed object, but also to the reference system this observer uses according to whether he lives in a two-, three-, or *n*-dimensional world. It thus all comes down to a problem of projection, projection of a three-dimensional object on a plane, of a four-dimensional entity on a volume, etc.,

these projections themselves altering depending on the angle one is considering them from" (*Duchamp*, p. 47 [cf. pp. 43ff.]). This interpretation of the *Large Glass* not only renders a work intelligible that is certainly not so on first approach; it is also the only one, to my knowledge, concordant with Duchamp's own declarations and fully compatible with the preoccupations of his age, as numerous, very explicit, passages of Duchamp's *A l'infinitif* [*In the Infinitive*] confirm (*Duchamp du signe: Ecrits* [Paris: Flammarion, 1975], pp. 105ff).

60. See Dalrymple-Henderson, *Fourth Dimension*, chap. 5, "Transcending the Present: The Fourth Dimension in the Philosophy of Ouspensky and in Russian Futurism and Suprematism."

61. The way Duchamp judged Metzinger is telling: "In 1911, two distinct groups of painters gave shape to the new theory of cubism, then going through an incubation period. Picasso and Braque on one side; Metzinger, Gleizes, and Léger on the other. Metzinger was then cubism's most imaginative theoretician, and he must be largely credited with the ever increasing interest the public gave this new form of expression. Through his articles and his book, *Du cubisme* [*On Cubism*], written with Gleizes, he was able to give a substantial exposé of the new painters' main intentions, and contributed to the clarification of the truly obscure results obtained up to then" (*Duchamp du signe*, p. 208). We note that this opinion had already been expressed by A. Salmon in a Sept. 30, 1911 article in *Paris-Journal*: "More intellectual than Braque, Jean Metzinger gathers up the confused, diffuse elements of cubism. He outlines, if not a doctrine, at least a theory; so that though, truly, cubism comes from Picasso, Jean Metzinger is, all the same, justified in calling himself its head."

62. Metzinger, *Le Cubisme était né: Souvenirs*, p. 60.

63. See Jean Paulhan, *La Peinture cubiste*, pp. 83–84.

64. J. Metzinger, "Cubism and Tradition," *Paris-Journal*, August 16, 1911.

65. Paulhan, *Peinture cubiste*, p. 53.

66. Poincaré, *La Science et l'hypothèse*, p. 66.

67. Cf. *Duchamp du signe*, p. 217.

68. *Mercure de France*, Ser. 1, vol. 6, 1917.

69. Cited by Jean Clair in "L'échiquier, la quatrième dimension et les modernes," n. 3.

70. Gleizes, *Art et religion*.

71. Metzinger, *Le cubisme était né*, p. 62.

72. G. W. Leibniz, "Von der Weisheit," in *Deutsche Schriften*, ed. Guhrauer, vol. 1, p. 442.

73. Jean-François Lyotard, *Des dispositifs pulsionnels* (1973), pp. 8–9.

74. C. Dahlhoun, "La construction du disharmonique," *Contrechamps*, no. 2, pp. 137ff.

75. Theodor Adorno, *Philosophy of Modern Music* [*Philosophie der neuen Musik*], *Gesammelte Schriften* (Frankfurt/Main: 1975), Bd. 12, pp. 16–17.

76. Gleizes, *Art et religion*, p. 105.

77. J. Metzinger, "Cubisme et tradition," *Paris-Journal*, August 16, 1911.

78. René Leibowitz, *Introduction à la musique de douze sons* (L'Arche, 1949), pp. 13–14.

79. Jean-François Lyotard: *Le Postmoderne expliqué aux enfants* (Galilée, 1986), p. 27.

80. Nietzsche, *The Gay Science*, Kaufmann trans., § 374, "Our New Infinite."

81. "Correspondance Kandinski-Schönberg," Schoenberg letter of Jan. 24, 1911, *Contrechamps*, no. 2, p. 13.

82. Lacoste, *L'Idée du beau*, p. 5.

83. "I used the term to mean the opposite of all this" (i.e., of a return to the past). Charles Jencks, *The Language of Postmodern Architecture* (London: Academy Editions, 4th ed. 1984 [1977]), p. 6.

84. Lyotard, *Postmoderne expliqué*, pp. 27–28. On Adorno, see the excellent article by Albrecht Wellmer, "Dialectique de la modernité et de la post-modernité," *Cahiers de philosophie*, no. 5, Spring 1988.

85. Wellmer, "Dialectique de la modernité," p. 159.

86. Cornelius Castoriadis, *"Transformation sociale et création culturelle,"* in *Capitalisme Moderne et Révolution* (Paris: U.G.E., 1979), p. 37.

SEVEN

1. Aristotle, *Nichomachean Ethics*, 1097 b 26; trans. W. D. Ross, in *Introduction to Aristotle* (Chicago and London: University of Chicago Press, 1973).

2. Luc Ferry, *Political Philosophy*, vol. 1, *Rights: The New Quarrel between the Ancients and the Moderns* (Chicago and London: University of Chicago Press, 1990).

3. Cf. Ferry and Renaut, *Heidegger and Modernity* (Chicago: University of Chicago Press, 1990), last chapter.

4. On this subject, it pays to come back repeatedly to Pierre-André Taquieff's outstanding book on racism, *La Force du préjugé: Essai sur le racisme et ses doubles* [*The Force of Prejudice: Essay on Racism and Its Double*] (La Découverte, 1987).

INDEX